A Skeptic's Guide to Belief

A Skeptic's Guide to Belief

KEN CRISPIN

RESOURCE *Publications* · Eugene, Oregon

A SKEPTIC'S GUIDE TO BELIEF

Copyright © 2019 Ken Crispin. All rights reserved. Except for brief quotations in critical publications or reviews, no part of this book may be reproduced in any manner without prior written permission from the publisher. Write: Permissions, Wipf and Stock Publishers, 199 W. 8th Ave., Suite 3, Eugene, OR 97401.

Resource Publications
An Imprint of Wipf and Stock Publishers
199 W. 8th Ave., Suite 3
Eugene, OR 97401

www.wipfandstock.com

PAPERBACK ISBN: 978-1-5326-7851-6
HARDCOVER ISBN: 978-1-5326-7852-3
EBOOK ISBN: 978-1-5326-7853-0

Manufactured in the U.S.A.   04/02/19

To my brother, Peter Crispin,
a scientist whose commitment to truth has never wavered.

Contents

Acknowledgements | ix
Introduction | xi

1 Skepticism and The Quest for Truth | 1
  A RICH LEGACY OF DOUBT?
  IS REASON ENOUGH?
  IS CERTAINTY THE ONLY REASONABLE GOAL?
  SHEEP IN SKEPTICS' CLOTHING?
  SO WHAT IS EVIDENCE?
  CAN ONE REALLY APPROACH RELIGION SKEPTICALLY?

2 Peering through The Fog | 17
  HOW RATIONAL ARE WE?
  CAN WE SHAKE OFF OUR PRESUPPOSITIONS?
  CAN WE REALLY PUT ASIDE OUR EMOTIONS?
  DO SCIENTISTS DWELL ON A MORE OBJECTIVE PLANE?
  CAN MATERIALISM BE A SACRED COW?
  CAN SCIENCE ANSWER RELIGIOUS QUESTIONS?

3 Fundamentalism and Other Distractions | 40
  RELIGIOUS FUNDAMENTALISM—A REASON FREE ZONE?
  A RESPONSE—EQUAL AND OPPOSITE VEHEMENCE?
  ARE ATHEISTS REALLY SUPERIOR BEINGS?
  A BURDEN OF PROOF?
  WHO NEEDS EVIDENCE?
  THE NEED FOR RATIONAL ASSESSMENT

4 The Case for Atheism | 54
  A CURIOUS CLAIM ABOUT PROBABILITY
  A PLEA FOR CONSCIOUSNESS RAISING
  THE NEED FOR AN 'ABRACADABRA!' MOMENT OF CREATION
  IRREDUCIBLE COMPLEXITY
  GAPS
  FINE TUNING AND ANTHROPIC PRINCIPLES
  HOW MANY UNIVERSES CAN DANCE ON THE HEAD OF A PIN?

KINDLY EXPLAIN THE EXISTENCE OF GOD.
THE FIRST CAUSE AND SIMPLICITY
SUFFERING
SO HAVE YOU SEEN THE LIGHT YET?

5 The Classic Arguments for God | 86
INNATE KNOWLEDGE
ARGUMENTS FROM IMAGINATION AND REASON
MORALITY AND CONSCIENCE
THE FIRST CAUSE
SIGNS OF DESIGN
OTHER ARGUMENTS

6 Are We Just Meat? | 112
LIFE
CONSCIOUSNESS
FREE WILL

7 What of Our Experiences? | 137
SPIRITUAL EXPERIENCES—MORE THAN SENSORY PERCEPTIONS?
CONVERSION EXPERIENCES
OTHER ENCOUNTERS WITH THE NUMINOUS
IS ANY OF THIS REAL?
NEUROTHEOLOGY, GOD HELMETS AND THE QUEST FOR THE UNHOLY GRAIL
ARE PRAYERS REALLY ANSWERED?
A PERSONAL PERSPECTIVE

8 Does The Fat Lady Sing at Funerals? | 161
THE PHENOMENON OF NEAR DEATH EXPERIENCES
THE MAN WHO LOST HIS TEETH
THE WOMAN WHO SAW A SHOE
THE MUSICIAN WHO HEARD A PERFECT 'D'
THE NEUROSURGEON WHOSE OWN BRAIN SHUT DOWN
HOW CAN THIS BE?
OTHER POSSIBILITIES

9 A Way Forward? | 186

Bibliography | 193

Acknowledgements

I acknowledge with thanks the assistance and support graciously provided by my wife, Rev Dr Pamela Crispin, my son, Timothy Crispin, my brother, Peter Crispin, Rev Dr David Oliphant, Rev Professor Richard Campbell AM, and Rev Professor James Haire AC.

All Scripture quotations, unless otherwise indicated, are taken from the Holy Bible, New International Version®, NIV®. Copyright ©1973, 1978, 1984, 2011 by Biblica, Inc.™ Used by permission of Zondervan. All rights reserved worldwide. www.zondervan.com The "NIV" and "New International Version" are trademarks registered in the United States Patent and Trademark Office by Biblica, Inc.

Introduction

In theory at least, skeptics question the claims of others, consider the available evidence for themselves and make their own decisions. They should not need to be guided like sheep who have to be shooed back to a warm barn lest the night become too cold. And it is skeptics for whom I have written. If you are unwilling to think through things for yourself and are anxious to find a guru who can resolve all of your doubts and set your feet upon some sure path to enlightenment, then this is not the book for you. Whilst I make no secret of my own beliefs, I have no wish to tell you what to believe.

What I hope to do is encourage a rational approach to some of the great questions of life, by raising issues, asking questions and suggesting facts or lines of argument you might wish to to consider. From time to time I will offer opinions, some ventured tentatively and others with more confidence, but it is for you to determine how relevant any of these thoughts may be when you are wrestling with your own views. If you think I am wrong about some point, then ignore what I have said. But be a skeptic. Continue to ask, 'why should I accept that?' Imagine the alternatives, probe the contrary arguments and ask whether they are more plausible. I ask only that you do your best to put aside any existing prejudices, try to maintain an open mind and consider the relevant issues as objectively as you can.

Not everyone sees the need for such an approach. In fact, the world seems to be full of delightfully naive people. Some, like Sebastian Flyte in Evelyn Waugh's novel *Brideshead Revisited*,[1] seem to believe things simply because they are lovely. They apparently see no need to question whether the gods, fairies, sprites or other supernatural beings that live in their imagination, if not their gardens, actually exist. It is enough that they are beautiful. I have no wish to sneer at their innocence; it can be strangely touching in a cynical world. And our most fundamental beliefs are not merely intellectual abstractions; they bring comfort and hope to many who struggle with grief,

---

1. Waugh, Evelyn, *Brideshead Revisited*, 109.

fear and other destructive emotions that are sadly endemic to our human condition. Those who attempt to tear down the emotional props of others may assume moral responsibilities not always recognized.

Yet there is something ineffably sad about the plight of people living out their lives in reliance upon beliefs they dare not question. Perhaps that is why many of us come to a point at which we feel compelled to confront our doubts and pursue the truth, no matter what the implications. That can require courage, resolution and perseverance. But can we ever really know the truth? Can we even find a promising path through the scientific, philosophical, experiential and theological thickets that surround the great questions of life? Can we really bring ourselves to evaluate the competing claims that emerge from them and honestly weigh the available evidence? And if we somehow managed to do all that, would we at last know the truth and be set free? Would we be forced to embrace a long feared despair? Or would we find ourselves still staring impotently at an enigmatic universe?

This is a book that may disturb many people. It is intended to challenge, not to comfort. It asks some of the questions humanity has always asked. Is there a god? Do we really have free will? Do spiritual experiences really occur? Is death the end? But it does so from a skeptical viewpoint, raising issues, but insisting that readers form their own judgments. Whilst some may shrug their shoulders and assume that this is what they always do, few people ever really bring an unflinching logic to issues of this kind. That is understandable. It can be emotionally challenging to expose long held beliefs to the glare of reasoned analysis and accept the possibility that they may be rationally unsustainable.

Some people actually make a virtue of their refusal to question their beliefs. They may cavil at any suggestion of willful blindness, but they baulk at looking too closely at anything they fear might raise unsettling doubts. Some even rationalize this as faith. Others seem immune to even that level of insecurity; their confidence in their beliefs is so great that they apparently see no reason to consider whether there are adequate grounds for them. Even people who see themselves as hard headed realists sometimes seem absolutely committed to propositions without any obvious rational basis. That may also be understandable. We inherit our beliefs as well as our genes from our parents and these may be strengthened by traditions and practices inextricably linked with our culture. Of course, some jettison earlier beliefs and embrace new ideas, usually in their youth when idealism and hormones seem to run rampant together, but such changes often reflect little more than the opinions of influential peers, perceptions of the intellectual stance de jour, or the blandishments of some religious or secular celebrity.

Not all who cling to unquestioned beliefs are stupid or naive; many are intelligent people who approach other aspects of their lives in an entirely rational manner. But beliefs about the fundamental issues of life are often treated differently. In fact, many people seem to form a mental capsule, like the intellectual equivalent of a diving bell, so their cherished beliefs can be maintained in an enclosed and protective environment, hermetically sealed from the wider and perhaps threatening sea of knowledge and reality. Such capsules are usually formed subconsciously and they are entrenched as time passes. The walls may lack the steel plate of diving bells, but they are forged from powerful emotional factors, such as loyalty, duty and fear, and may be equally impenetrable.

It is often assumed that only religious adherents sequester their beliefs in such a manner, but this is also true of atheists, whose self perceptions as champions of reason and objectivity sometimes seem dependent upon remarkably superficial reasoning. One need only read the outrage so vividly expressed in Christopher Hitchens' book, *God is not Great*,[2] to appreciate the extent to which a rejection of religious belief may be buttressed by emotion. Even those who pride themselves on an unrelenting skepticism often seem surprisingly reluctant to question their more cherished convictions. Whether we recognize it or not, we all have a great deal invested in beliefs that have shaped our lives and continue to influence our sense of purpose, emotional security and even our self image.

Some dismiss religious convictions as comforting fantasies, legacies perhaps of pre-scientific ages in which people sought to explain things beyond their intellectual grasp by superstitions now sustained only by our naivety and human weaknesses. Not all who reject religion do so unsympathetically. Karl Marx famously suggested that "religion is the sigh of the oppressed creature, the heart of a heartless world, and the soul of soulless conditions. It is the opium of the people."[3] Of course, opium is a potent analgesic and he was not the last to suggest that people cling to religious beliefs only because they provide an anodyne for the pain of living in a world that offers few certainties but the inevitability of death.

But are Christians, Muslims, Hindus, Jews and others who believe in a god or gods all naive, ignorant or too frightened to face the truth? Are there really no rational grounds for their beliefs? Are we humans merely the latest and perhaps most sophisticated products of mindless processes triggered by an apocalyptic explosion at the beginning of time? Has science finally

---

2. Hitchens, *God is not Great*.
3. Marx, *Introduction to A Contribution to the Critique of Hegel's Philosophy of Right*, 3.

swept away any possibility of the supernatural and shown that we live in a purely physical universe? Have the most soaring feats of intellect, artistic expression and compassion all been revealed as nothing but artifacts of the meaty substances that evolved between our ears? Have the mysteries of life now been reduced to a series of practical questions that will soon be solved by new high priests wearing laboratory coats rather than clerical robes? Are atheists the only realists? Is the intellectual contest a lopsided affair in which religiously motivated Luddites seek to hold back the tide of knowledge now being taken at the flood by scientists and others willing to face the truth? Or is atheism itself based upon flimsy grounds? And when both sides have fired their best argumentative shots and the rhetorical smoke has been allowed to drift away, will agnosticism be revealed as the only rationally defensible position?

Of course, many people who believe in God will not only assume they know all the answers, but will also insist that these are merely threshold questions and that one must go on to consider the claims of their particular religion. Some may demand recognition of what they see as simple, fundamental truths, whilst others may raise issues that would plunge one into arcane worlds of theological complexity. Such issues may be of real significance, but they fall outside the scope of this book. Even the most devout enter their churches, temples, mosques or synagogues via thresholds and the issues I wish to discuss are threshold questions; questions of fundamental importance to anyone who may be drawn by a perhaps indefinable feeling that there must be more to life than the physical world alone, yet fear being seduced into abandoning their intellectual integrity. It is not my intention to chart a path into any religious tradition; only to review relevant evidence and point to considerations that may help people to chart their own course. It is for you to consider the issues and decide whether to cross any particular thresholds and embrace any of the beliefs and practices that may lie beyond them.

But how can such profound and seemingly imponderable issues be approached? And, more importantly, how are you willing to approach them? What does the concept of a skeptical approach mean to you? For some people it means the peremptory rejection of all that remains outside their experience or perhaps all that is unfashionable to believe. Hence, anything that may be described as religious or superstitious is ipso facto excluded. Such an approach is not really skeptical; it merely reflects faith in certain presuppositions. People who adopt such a stunted version of skepticism may be on the other side of the theological fence, but their dogmatism can be as intellectually limiting as that of the most committed fundamentalist. Skepticism actually has a rich history and the first chapter in this book explores some of the concepts that have been advanced over the centuries. It asks, in effect, whether the attitudes you have adopted are really skeptical. Are they helping you to sift the wheat from the chaff or merely to shy away from an open-minded examination of the issues?

Of course, as any realist will recognize, we are not biological computers whose judgements are the unalloyed products of pure reason, but flesh and blood people whose perceptions and reasoning capacities are influenced by the emotional legacies of our experiences. Hence, this is followed by a chapter dealing with the effects of emotion, presupposition and even subconscious bias. The importance of such factors is not always recognized, but they affect the judgments we make in every aspect of our lives and they have a profound impact on the manner in which we approach questions about the existence of God and other issues about which we may feel deeply. That is why debates about such issues tend to become so heated. People on both sides of any religious divide should surely agree that calm and rational approaches are more likely to prove enlightening, but human emotions are intractable. Those with strong views often defend them with vehemence and this often means that discussion of competing arguments gives way to little more than an exchange of epithets.

But those who speak with obvious conviction may also be be persuasive, if only because their apparent confidence lends credence to the views they express. This is well understood by the marketing industry. When did you last meet a diffident salesperson? We may recognize that advertising often involves emotional manipulation, but that does not seem to make us wholly immune from the effects. What of more serious issues? Can we really approach the more profound questions of life with the rational objectivity we might imagine? Can we make adequate allowance for the maelstrom of emotional crosswinds that may buffet our perceptions and make truth an elusive target? And are we really willing to pursue truth no matter what the emotional cost? Many people find the prospect of questioning the grounds of their beliefs daunting. It can require real courage to take an unflinching look at the fundamental questions that confront us in our common humanity. It is one thing to speak about a quest for truth; it may be another to be willing to confront whatever you might find.

Anyone who sets out on such a journey will inevitably be confronted by the strident claims of the more extreme religious fundamentalists. Every religion has variants of them, each seemingly convinced that God agrees with them and is displeased with those who refuse to acknowledge that they are right. Their dogma is usually based upon simplistic interpretations of scriptural texts, garnished with tradition and spiced with a fervor that excludes rational debate.

Perhaps ironically, some of the more strident atheists share these attributes. Yes, I understand that this suggestion may shock those convinced that the renunciation of religious belief inevitably cleanses one of all unreasonableness and leads to everlasting objectivity. Unfortunately, the evidence for such irreligious sanctification is actually quite thin on the ground. Atheistic dogma, sometimes held with a depth of conviction that would do credit to an Old Testament prophet, is often defended by empty rhetoric involving little more than expressions of bitterness towards those outside the fold, a melange of cliches, vague allusions to science and arguments based upon confused concepts.

Of course, not all religious adherents are unreasoning fundamentalists, not all atheists are driven by cynicism and emotion, and even the most ill informed and irrational people can sometimes prove to be right. But can one really hope to gain rational insights from people whose vehemence often seems intended to drown out any still small voice of doubt? Skeptics conscientiously seeking the truth may wish to consider even the most dogmatic claims but, having done so, they may find themselves unconvinced and inclined to move on. So the discussion will move from concepts of skepticism to the influence of presuppositions and emotion, competing articles of faith, arguments for atheism, arguments for the existence of God, insights from human life and spiritual experience and even the possibility of existence beyond physical death.

I should first define a couple of terms. People who describe themselves as 'atheists' vary not only in the strength of their conviction but in their understanding of the word. Some who embrace this description have no belief in the existence of God, but may not wholly discount the possibility of his existence. Others might suggest that such people are really agnostics. Perhaps surprisingly, Richard Dawkins has accepted this description, though he has also explained that he is "6.9 out of 7" sure there is no god.[4] Others are more dogmatic. So far as they are concerned, the issue is closed; there simply cannot be a god. Some defend this position with a fervor that, in other circumstances, might leave a pulpit thumping evangelist breathless with admiration. For present purposes I have used the term "atheist" to refer to those who insist that there is no god and have treated those who simply lack any affirmative belief as "agnostics." Purists may protest that this does not reflect the etymology of these words, but it is well supported by common

---

4. "Richard Dawkins: '6.9 out of seven' sure that God does not exist," *The Telegraph* (UK) 23 Feb 2012.

usage[5] and agnostics often define their own position in contradistinction to the conception of atheism I have adopted.[6]

I should also make it clear that the issues have been approached from the perspective of a skeptic starting with a clean slate and prepared to question any proposition that does not seem to be adequately supported by the available evidence. This may concern some people who are convinced that the Bible or some other holy book provides all the evidence one needs, but perceptions about the authority of scriptures are obviously dependent upon belief in the existence of the God said to have inspired them and that is an issue that will be examined by reference to the factual evidence. The same skeptical approach will be taken to the arguments advanced by Dawkins and other prominent atheists, some of which, I suggest, are not only unconvincing but also lacking in logical cogency. Those who fear that such heresies might cause their blood pressure to rise to dangerous levels should either give this book away or spend some time meditating on the need for open minded objectivity before proceeding further. But, since both atheists and religious believers claim to be committed to the path of truth, let us see where it leads.

---

5. The Cambridge Dictionary of Philosophy states that: "A widely used sense denotes merely not believing in God and is consistent with agnosticism. A stricter sense denotes a belief that there is no God; this use has become the standard one." The Oxford English Reference Dictionary (2nd ed) defines 'atheism' as "the theory or belief that God does not exist. The Stanford Encyclopedia of Philosophy similarly defines "atheism" as "the negation of theism, the denial of the existence of God." The same distinction is drawn in Russell, "What Is an Agnostic?" 577.

6. For example, in explaining why he was an agnostic, Carl Sagan said that an atheist is "someone who is certain that God does not exist, someone who has compelling evidence against the existence of God." Head, *Conversations with Carl Sagan*, 70.

1

Skepticism and The Quest for Truth

What does it really mean to be a skeptic? The term is often used to describe people who disbelieve things they see as superstitious or unscientific, like astrology, 'New Age' theories and some forms of alternative medicine. Perhaps ironically, it is also applied to those, like 'climate change deniers', who are seen to unreasonably reject the truth. Of course, much depends upon the attitude of those using the term; a person seen as a doyen of reason and common sense by some, may be derided as a "doubting Thomas" by others. But in common parlance, skeptics are simply people with a propensity to doubt or question unsubstantiated claims.

There have probably been people who raised skeptical eyebrows ever since our fledgling languages first enabled our forebears to express dubious ideas in coherent forms, but not everyone warms to those who challenge deeply held beliefs or entrenched practices. In some societies dissent, and even overt expressions of doubt, have been brutally repressed and, sadly, there are still many places in the world in which people are publicly executed for perceived crimes such as apostasy. Demands for proof or even reasoned debate do not always impress mobs carrying rocks.

Despite the promise of the enlightenment, the public face of skepticism has sometimes intruded into public discourse only to be forced to retreat and re-emerge in more tolerant times. And even in our modern western democracies, which profess to respect freedom of speech, skeptics can be seen as irritants, if not troublemakers, bent on displaying their intellectual superiority and unfairly suggesting that others are stupid or dishonest. There may be times when tact, if not the instinct for self-preservation, suggests it may be unwise to question the beliefs of others, but naivety is not one of the cardinal virtues and skepticism is not one of the cardinal sins.

It can be difficult not to wince when innocent souls gullibly embrace the sales pitch of people peddling contemporary equivalents of snake oil or claiming some special revelation apparently denied lesser mortals. And it is not only the dull-witted who succumb. Highly intelligent people sometimes reveal a startling naivety in relation to particular issues. Even some who embrace the term 'skeptic' as a self-awarded badge of honor seem curiously unwilling to extend their skepticism beyond a narrow range of targets they obviously regard as conceptual sitting ducks. A surprising number seem to believe that the essence of skepticism is to be found only in a rejection of anything with religious or spiritual connotations, and seem surprisingly willing to accept other things without question.

Of course, true skeptics should be willing to question anything, perhaps even their own conception of skepticism. So what does skepticism mean to you? Is it merely a reluctance to believe? Should one doubt everything? Is skepticism a blind alley leading nowhere? Or can it be an aid to finding the truth?

A RICH LEGACY OF DOUBT?

Historically, skepticism seems to have emerged as a philosophical doctrine challenging the very assumption that knowledge is attainable. Socrates (470–399 BC) encapsulated this concept with the succinct confession, "all I know is that I know nothing,"[1] but skepticism really came into prominence during the teaching of Pyrrho (360–270 BC) and the later years of the academy founded by Plato. Pyrrho thought that neither our senses nor our opinions enable us to distinguish between truths and falsehoods and it is impossible to ever know the truth.[2] He found a silver lining in this cloud of ignorance, maintaining that it could free us from anxiety.[3] Why worry about things that may not be true? Diogenes tells us that Pyrrho so mistrusted his senses that he ignored obvious dangers and would have fallen off cliffs, been run over by carts or savaged by dogs had friends not followed him to keep him from harm. Such anecdotes may have been apocryphal,[4]

---

1. Attributed to Socrates by Plato,*The Republic*, 354c.

2. Gifford, E. H., translator, Aristocles *apud* Eusebius, *Praeparatio evangelica* 14.18. See also Long and Sedley, *The Hellenistic Philosophers*, 5–7. It has been argued that Pyrrho may have been expressing a metaphysical concept that things are essentially indefinite or indeterminable rather than the proposition that we are unable to determine their nature and should suspend judgment on them. Bett,"Pyrrho," paragraph 4.

3. Bett, Pyrrho," 3.

4. It has been suggested that the anecdotal evidence cited by Diogenes is suspect. *Internet Encyclopedia of Philosophy*, part 3a. "Pyrrho and Timon."

though Pyrrho did enjoy a privileged status after accompanying Alexander the Great on his expedition to India and would have had a loyal following. It would be interesting to know whether lesser mortals prone to ignoring obvious hazards remained equally serene during their accident-prone and perhaps short lives.

The so-called father of western skepticism was Michel de Montaigne (1533–1592), who said that trying to know reality was like trying to clutch water.[5] Whilst socially conservative, he was keen to share ideas with others, and pontificated about the relationship between men and women, "a thing not to be spoken of without blushing", and love in marriage, which he seemed to think should not be expected.[6] Later, perhaps speaking for many of us, he ruefully exclaimed, "What do I know?"[7] Of course, this echoed what Socrates had said nearly two thousand years earlier, but Montaigne managed to avoid any potentially damning allegations and was not made to drink hemlock, even by a disappointed wife. He had a pragmatic streak, maintaining that one could suspend judgment on any theories not based on experience, comply with the rules and customs of society and remain in the religion into which one was born, whilst accepting only those principles that God had chosen to reveal.[8] Yet, sadly, he failed to find the tranquility promised by Pyrrho's approach. On his 38th birthday, "long weary of the servitude of the court and of public employments, while still entire, (he) retired to the bosom of the learned virgins, where in calm and freedom from all cares he will spend what little remains of his life, now more than half run out."[9] It was obviously tough being a skeptic in those days.

The coy Montaigne was followed by René Descartes (1596 – 1650), who rejected established learning and even his own experiences and sensations, all of which he thought were inherently unreliable. He insisted that reason alone was the path to certainty. He began by questioning everything but his own existence, which he accepted on the basis of his famous affirmation *"cogito ergo sum"*—I think therefore I am. (This must have made life hell for his maid, Helena, though he gave her existence sufficient credence for her to bear him a child, even if he remained dubious about such unverified hypotheses as dirty dishes, garbage etc.)

---

5. *The Cambridge Dictionary of Philosophy*, 581.
6. Montaigne, *Essays of Montaigne*, book 3, 5 "Upon Some Verses of Virgil."
7. Montaigne, *The Complete Essays*, book II, 23, "Apology for Raimond Sebond."
8. *The Cambridge Dictionary of Philosophy*, 581
9. Quoted by Regosin, "Montaigne and His Readers," 249.

Despite suggestions that even this seemingly modest argument for his own existence was logically invalid[10] and some quibbles about its meaning,[11] it did suggest a skeptical attitude to life, the universe and everything. This may have been a prudent approach for a man who claimed to have been inspired by visions. In one dream he saw a fragment of an ode by the Roman poet, Ausonius: "*Quod vitae sectabor iter?*"—What path of life shall I follow?[12] That is a profoundly important question we all must face, even if our sleep is not interrupted by dead poets wanting to interrogate us in Latin. For present purposes it might be reframed as "what road should a skeptic take to explore the great questions of life?"

Descartes responded by developing some fundamental principles of methodological skepticism. Yet, ironically, this led him down an intellectual blind alley. He insisted that only things that are "certain and indubitable" provide an adequate basis for knowledge,[13] and he vigorously advanced this proposition in a public confrontation with a contemporary, Dr Chandoux, who had propounded a scientific approach based upon probabilities.[14] There was no adjudicator to declare who won the debate, but Descartes is said to have given a "dazzling public refutation" of Chandoux's arguments. The hapless doctor went on to personally confront one of the few certainties commonly recognized: death. He was executed for counterfeiting.[15] But, whilst Descartes' rhetorical skills may have prevailed and he was freed from any fear of a rematch, cracks soon appeared in the logical edifice he sought to create. The pursuit of certainty led him to discount human perceptions and experience.[16] Convinced that his own thinking provided the only reliable guide, though fearful that even he could be deceived, he chose to rely upon what he saw as clear and distinct ideas. He dismissed existing theories of physics, astronomy, medicine and other sciences dealing with complex

---

10. Russell, *An Outline of Philosophy*, 171–172; *History of Western Philosophy*, 567. See also Russell, *An Outline of Philosophy; and,* Egner, *The Basic Writings of Bertrand Russell 1903–1959*, 557–565.

11. See, for example, Fumitaka Suzuki, "The Cogito Proposition, 73–80.

12. Davis, *Descartes' Dream*, 3.

13. Descartes, *Meditations on the First Philosophy*, Meditation I at 1–6, 1–9 (the phrase is used twice) & 1–21.

14. For a brief account of this confrontation see Sarkar, *Descates' Cogito Saved from the Great Shipwreck*, 1.

15. Sarkar, *Descates' Cogito Saved from the Great Shipwreck*, 1.

16. For a succinct account of the dispute between rationalism and empiricism see Markie, "Rationalism vs. Empiricism."

structures and tried to redefine natural phenomena in terms of arithmetic and geometry, which he accepted as necessarily true.[17]

Yet, by a somewhat tortuous process of reasoning, he claimed to have proven the existence of God, which he believed was as self-evident as the most basic mathematical truth.[18] He also deduced that the soul was seated in the pineal gland of the brain. Perhaps most disturbingly, he became convinced that his beliefs could only have come from God and that God could not have deceived him.[19] The last person I met who made assertions of that kind was a man explaining why he felt he should kill members of his family. He had told his alarmed psychiatrist that the voice he kept hearing could only be that of God. He was devoted to his wife and children, but convinced that the word of God must be obeyed. "Isn't that what Abraham did when told to sacrifice Isaac on an altar in the wilderness?" he asked.

Fortunately, Descartes seems to have been relatively harmless, though there is a recent theory that he may himself have been murdered by a priest who gave him a communion wafer laced with arsenic. Descartes was appointed as Queen Christina's tutor and Jacques Viogué, a Catholic missionary working in Stockholm, is said to have feared that the prospect of her conversion to Catholicism would be jeopardized by Descartes' skepticism about Catholic theology.[20] His contemporaries may have thought he had died from pneumonia but, as Salmon Rushdie was to discover more than three centuries later, skepticism is not always a safe choice.

Most of us now embrace skepticism, not as a philosophical theory, but as a questioning attitude towards propositions that might not be true. We ask, in effect, "why should we believe that?" We consider the available evidence and weigh the competing arguments. Of course, this is not always easy to do.

IS REASON ENOUGH?

Reason is a wonderful, if underused, human capacity, but it must be applied within a factual context. It is not an adequate substitute for investigation. History is littered with examples of intelligent people making rational deductions that proved to be entirely wrong. It would be nice to think that this has occurred only because people have been too naive and trusting but

17. Descartes, *Meditations on the First Philosophy,* Second meditation.
18. For an account of this argument see Nolan, Lawrence, "Descartes' Ontological Argument."
19. Descartes, *Meditations on the First Philosophy,* Third meditation.
20. Davies, Lizzy, "Descartes was 'poisoned' by Catholic priest."

suspicion and cynicism have also been misplaced. In 1799 when the first specimen of a platypus arrived at the British Museum in London, naturalists thought they may have been victims of a hoax and suggested that Chinese sailors may have stitched together a hybrid body. A surgeon, Robert Knox, later said that scientists had felt inclined to class the specimen with "eastern mermaids and other works of art."[21] He was not the only well qualified expert to find seemingly rational conclusions demolished by further evidence. When the discovery of X-rays was announced at the end of 1895, the eminent scientist, Lord Kelvin, regarded it as a hoax.[22] Later generations of scientists have been startled by discoveries in the new field of quantum mechanics that seem to defy common sense, and new observations constantly challenge prevailing theories. No matter how brilliant one's reasoning power may be, deductions about what may lie on the other side of the hill are often no substitute for walking round to have a look.

David Hume (1711–76) rejected Descartes' view that reason offered the only sure path to truth and insisted that philosophy could not go beyond experience. He stressed the imperfections and narrow limits of human understanding[23] and suggested that our perceptions fall into two categories: "impressions" which consist of sensations or reflections, and "ideas" which consist of mental states that are dependent on impressions. He thought that impressions could not provide sure grounds for belief because their ultimate causes are inexplicable by human reason. However, he recognized that our lives and actions are dependent upon fundamental notions we derive from our perceptions, such as space and time, causal connections, existence and mind, and he conceded that some inferences about their truth or falsity could be drawn from their "coherence."[24] Pyrrho might have thought that such pragmatism polluted the purity of skeptical theory, but even skeptics have to confront the practical challenges of their lives, not just complain that everything is unverifiable.

I will not strain your patience by continuing to leap from one long dead skeptic to another as if their graves were stepping stones to a safe intellectual shore. As any budding philosopher will have realized, I have shamelessly skated over the theories of those already mentioned and I intend to compound this approach by completely ignoring the work of countless others. This is not a philosophical tome, merely a guide for skeptics, and I am

---

21. Moyal, Ann, *Platypus*. See also Ritvo, *The Platypus and the Mermaid*.

22. For an account of this and other misconceptions by this famous scientist see Thompson, *Life of William Thomson: Baron Kelvin of Largs*.

23. *The Cambridge Dictionary of Philosophy*, 2nd ed at 399.

24. Hume, *A Treatise of Human Nature*, Book 1.

seeking only to highlight some of the more extreme forms of skepticism and the cognitive dead ends to which they have led.

Truth is an elusive quarry and neither reason nor experience can provide a wholly infallible guide to capturing it. One need only reflect upon our forebears' understanding of matter. Throughout almost all of human history men and women picked up rocks, whether to throw at each other, build primitive shelters or chock the tires of chariots, and assumed that they were not only heavy but solid. Later generations built forts and castles secure in that assumption. Yet as early as the sixth century BC Indian philosophers suggested that all matter was constructed from tiny particles.[25] A Greek philosopher, Democritus, who came to the same view about a century later, called these tiny particles "atoms." Unfortunately, the idea didn't catch on. Public imagination was instead captured by the theory that the world was made from the "classical elements" of air, earth, fire and water. It was not until 1661 that Robert Boyle returned to the concept, arguing that matter was composed of various combinations of different atoms that he called "corpuscles."[26] But even insightful thinkers like Democritus and his Indian predecessors could never have realized the wondrous sub-atomic world that lay within those seemingly solid rocks; a world of electrons orbiting nuclei of protons and neutrons in unimagined spaces, of quarks and leptons, of particle-wave duality and other effects that even now seem to defy common sense. How could they have done so? What process of reasoning could have led even the most brilliant of our distant ancestors to deduce the existence of such things? And, in the absence of our increasingly sophisticated array of technological equipment, what experiences could have revealed them?

Of course, time has marched remorselessly on and we now live in a scientific age offering such marvels as the Large Hadron Collider (or LHC) in Switzerland which in 2012 finally revealed the Higgs boson or "God particle,"[27] a feat some feared would prove catastrophic and others thought would be unattainable. Rumors spread that the high-energy experiment might create a mini black hole that could expand to "dangerous, Earth-eating" proportions. In 2008 a German chemist actually commenced proceedings in the European Court of Human Rights arguing, reasonably enough, that the devouring of the earth would violate the right to life of European citizens and pose a threat to the rule of law.[28] In the following year two eminent physicists suggested that these fears were groundless.

25. McEvilley, *The Shape of Ancient Thought*.
26. Boyle, *The Sceptical Chymist*.
27. Cho Adrian, Higgs Boson Makes Its Debut, 141.
28. Harrell, Eben, "Collider Triggers End-of-World Fears," *Time*, Sept 4 2008.

Their mathematical calculations had shown that nature would "ripple backward through time" to stop the LHC before it could create such a particle. "One could even almost say that we have a model for God," Dr Holger Bech Nielsen, of the Niels Bohr Institute in Copenhagen, suggested, adding that God "rather hates Higgs particles and attempts to avoid them."[29] It is now clear that this presumably playful attempt at divine psychoanalysis proved inadequate but, to plagiarize poor Descartes, we think; therefore we are still here.

But have the dazzling scientific discoveries of the past few generations really provided answers to the more profound questions of life, as some of the more enthusiastic commentators seem to suggest? Has confirmation that there are even smaller particles than Democritus could have imagined cast any light on issues such as the reality of free will or the existence of God? Have we really entered a new age in which all is now clear to those willing to cast off superstition and bask in our newly emerging scientific sunshine?

Sir Isaac Newton (1642–1727) said in his memoirs that "I do not know what I may appear to the world, but to myself I seem to have been only like a boy playing on the sea-shore, and diverting myself in now and then finding a smoother pebble or a prettier shell than ordinary, whilst the great ocean of truth lay all undiscovered before me."[30] If he were alive today and retiring at the pinnacle of an equally distinguished career, would he say anything substantially different? I am sure he would marvel at some of the scientific breakthroughs, reconsider some of his theories to accommodate them, and perhaps even have a shot at resolving some of the great scientific issues of our day. But whilst he might feel that the tide had receded to expose a few more pebbles and shells, I doubt he would be moved to proclaim that the great ocean of truth had now been plumbed and that we had nothing more to learn.

IS CERTAINTY THE ONLY REASONABLE GOAL?

Descartes' quest for certain and indubitable foundations for knowledge may have been understandable, but it was also unattainable. The late, unlamented Chandoux may not have been the most successful orator, or criminal, that Paris had ever seen, but he was right in his contention that science must

---

29. Overbye, Dennis, "The Collider, the Particle and a Theory About Fate," *The New York Times,* October 12, 2009.

30. Brewster, *Memoirs of the Life, Writings, and Discoveries of Sir Isaac Newton,* Volume II. Ch. 27).

be reliant upon probabilities. There is no word in the English language that should cause skeptical eyebrows to raise more quickly than 'certainty'. Some pedant will probably point out my own predilection for declaring that some things are "certainly" true but, as Oscar Wilde famously observed, consistency is the last refuge of the unimaginative. In any event, scientific advances do not proceed as a series of leaps from one undeniable fact to another, but by scientists testing hypotheses and venturing theories that may prove to be invalid. As a leading biophysicist has said, "There are more theories in the graveyard of science than theories that stand the test of time. Why? Because new data is always emerging and theories have to be adjusted."[31] This is true in almost every area of life. We mortals are condemned to draw on the possibilities and probabilities that emerge from whatever evidence may be available to us and, in the lexicons of all but the odd philosopher, words like 'truth' and 'knowledge' often reflect nothing more concrete than beliefs and opinions that are held with substantial confidence.

That may be unfortunate, but it is how we get by. It would be nice to be certain that we do not have cancer, that our marriages and other close relationships are secure, that our children do go to school when we send them off in the morning, that our banks and insurance companies are financially sound, and that a host of other things are as they seem. But how could we ever be sure? We may pursue every avenue of enquiry and congratulate ourselves on our prudence, but certainty will almost inevitably elude us. Even in our courts of law, certainty is not seen as an attainable goal. In criminal cases, allegations must be proven beyond reasonable doubt, but even that falls short of certainty and there are still miscarriages of justice. That is one of the reasons for my opposition to capital punishment; there is an ineradicable risk of wrongful conviction and the execution of the innocent. Who knows? Perhaps even the hapless Chandoux went to his death as an innocent man. If certainty were to be adopted as the only acceptable standard of proof, our courtrooms would soon be left as mausoleums for extinct judicial systems.

So what approach should a skeptic adopt in a world in which truth may be elusive and claims of certainty likely to reflect nothing more than confidence in beliefs that could be wrong? There are a number of possible responses. One could simply give up, accept that truth is unknowable and follow Montaigne, if not by retiring at 38, at least by suspending judgment on any vexing issues and quietly enjoying life. One could accept Descartes' view that only absolute certainties matter and concentrate on death and taxes. One could embrace a cynical approach to anything that seems vaguely

---

31. McLain Sylvia, "Not breaking news".

religious and accept that anything that sounds vaguely scientific must be true. Or one could accept that the essence of skepticism lies in a commitment to pursue the truth, no matter where the trail may lead. This involves asking probing questions, considering the available evidence, addressing any competing arguments and, above all, trying to maintain an open mind. Skeptics are distinguished from their more gullible peers not merely by a propensity for doubt but, more importantly, by a willingness to think for themselves, wrestle with the issues and form their own conclusions, however tentative or qualified.

The aim of any thinking person should not merely be the avoidance of error but the acquisition of knowledge.[32] As a contemporary skeptic has said: "the true meaning of the word 'skepticism' has nothing to do with doubt, disbelief, or negativity. Skepticism is the process of applying reason and critical thinking to determine validity. It's the process of finding a supported conclusion, not the justification of a preconceived conclusion."[33] Or as Carl Sagan put it, "If someone claims a thing happens in a certain way, you do the experiment to check it out, to see if, in fact, it works as claimed. You examine the internal coherence of the idea. You test its logical structure. You see how well it agrees with other things which are reliably known, and only then do you start accepting new ideas."[34]

SHEEP IN SKEPTICS CLOTHING?

Unfortunately, many who call themselves "skeptics" are not really skeptical; merely credulous people who have exchanged one set of dogmatic propositions for another. And, perhaps ironically, there is often a certain naivety in their attitudes. Some will smugly confide that they believe only in the things they can see, hear, taste, smell or touch. If you feel in the mood to tease them, you might ask, "What does that belief look, sound, taste, smell or feel like?" Others seem keen to denounce beliefs they regard as implausible, but uncritically accept contrary views even if they are also dubious or exaggerated. For example, the editors of the Skeptic's Dictionary cheerfully assert that "most skeptics today would agree with Hume's concluding remark on academical or skeptical philosophy:

---

32. See, for example, the discussion by Rescher, *Epistemology*, chapter 3 "Skepticism and its Deficits."
33. Dunning, "What is Skepticism?"
34. Sagan, "God and Carl Sagan: Is the Cosmos Big Enough for Both of Them," 24.

> *When we run over libraries, persuaded of these principles, what havoc must we make? If we take in our hand any volume; of divinity or school metaphysics, for instance; let us ask, Does it contain any abstract reasoning concerning quantity or number? No. Does it contain any experimental reasoning concerning matter of fact and existence? No. Commit it then to the flames: for it can contain nothing but sophistry and illusion.*[35]

If it is true that most skeptics agree with this, then skepticism is in a sorry state, because the passage itself fails the tests it propounds. It contains no abstract reasoning concerning quantity or number and no experimental reasoning concerning matter of fact and existence. Hence, it should presumably be consigned to the flames, along with the rest of the book from which the quote was taken, Hume's other writings and the Skeptic's Dictionary itself, all of which would fail these tests. And it would be quite a conflagration. Books on such topics ranging from logic, philosophy, law, ethics and anything describing concepts or visions for the future would all have to be added, along with the world's collections of poetry and literature. The resulting pyres would make the 'bonfires of the vanities' orchestrated by Savonarola in the 15th century seem like a series of weekend barbecues.

Of course, Hume was not really that stupid. He may have occasionally indulged a penchant for hyperbole, but he made no attempt to organize any book burning soirees and would not have denied the existence of incorporeal things, such as thoughts, emotions, concepts, ideas and even life itself. In fact, despite the apparent vehemence of the passage quoted, Hume's own views on religion are not entirely clear. He has been described as a "non dogmatic atheist."[36] He was certainly critical of religious dogmatism and challenged the so called "argument from design," though acknowledging that the causes of order in the universe bear "some remote analogy to human intelligence."[37] However, he described God as "a Being, so remote and incomprehensible, who bears much less analogy to any other being in the universe than the sun to a waxen taper, and who discovers himself only by some faint traces or outlines, beyond which we have no authority to ascribe to him any attribute or perfection."[38] And, perhaps incongruously, he

---

35. "Skepticism," *The Skeptics Dictionary* (accessed 26 December 2018). For the passage quoted see Hume, David, *Enquiry Concerning Human Understanding*, section 12, part 3, 165.

36. See generally. "Hume on Religion," *The Stanford Encyclopedia of Philosophy*,.

37. David Hume, *Dialogues Concerning Natural Religion*, Part 12, D 12.33, KS 227–8.

38. Hume, *Enquiry Concerning Human Understanding*, section 11 part 27, 145–6.

applauded polytheism which he saw as tolerant of diversity and prone to encouraging virtues of benefit to humanity.[39]

Sadly, there are any number of religious people who seem committed to surpassing the White Queen's claim of believing six impossible things before breakfast.[40] Many examples could be cited, though I am particularly impressed by William Jennings Bryan who made a good pre-breakfast start by proclaiming that "if the Bible had said that Jonah swallowed the whale, I would believe it."[41] But it is not only religious believers who are naive. Some atheists cite the opinions of people like Dawkins or Hitchens as if they were successors to the Delphic oracle, though few seem able to articulate the arguments upon which they rely or to enter into any sensible debate about them. Some make vague, and often inaccurate, generalizations about scientific discoveries, but many seem content to assume that there must be adequate reasons for the oracular pronouncements of prominent atheists, even if unable to say what they might be.

Of course, similar criticisms could be made of countless Christians, Muslims, Jews and other theists, many of whom seem pathetically anxious to believe anything said by their clerics of choice. This point has been so well stressed by atheists that it scarcely needs to be reiterated, though the sometimes accompanying suggestion that religious beliefs can be held only by ignorant, naive or emotionally vulnerable people is a ridiculous stereotype. In any event, skepticism should never be applied selectively. The naive, the misguided, the stupid and even the deranged can all be right, despite the paucity of sensible reasoning, and, conversely, the rational, the shrewd and the cynics can all be wrong. Such truisms once led the eminent biologist, T. H. Huxley, to say that, "I am too much of a skeptic to deny the possibility of anything."[42]

In fact, what some may regard as a skeptical approach can actually blind people to the truth. Soren Kierkegaard offered the following warning:

> . . . one can be deceived in many ways; one can be deceived in believing what is untrue, but on the other hand, one is also deceived in not believing what is true; one can be deceived by appearances, but one can also be deceived by the superficiality of shrewdness, by

---

39. *The Cambridge Dictionary of Philosophy*, 403.
40. Carroll, Lewis, *Through the Looking Glass*, ch 5.
41. Gallagher, *Biblical Prophets, Modern Critics*, 1.
42. Letter to Herbert Spooner, 22 March 1886, in Huxley, Leonard, *Life and Letters of Thomas Henry Huxley*, chapter 8.

the flattering conceit which is absolutely certain that it cannot be deceived. Which deception is most dangerous?[43]

True skeptics heed such notes of caution. They learn what they can of the available evidence and weigh all of the competing contentions, rather than merely embracing views that seem intellectually fashionable. When challenged by difficult questions, they resist any temptation to take refuge in clichés and confront the issues with rigor and integrity. Sagan suggested that we need to maintain "an exquisite balance between two conflicting needs: the most skeptical scrutiny of all hypotheses that are served up to us and at the same time a great openness to new ideas."[44] I would extend this balancing exercise to old ideas that have not been discredited. Wisdom did not spring unexpectedly into human consciousness during the last few years, and science has repeatedly confirmed and explained things that people have believed for centuries if not millennia.

Unfortunately, such an exquisite balance is not easy to maintain and true skeptics sometimes seem to be thin on the ground. So many people who claim to be skeptical seem preoccupied with bolstering faith in their intellectual superiority by ridiculing ideas contrary to their own entrenched beliefs. A true skeptic should have some of the qualities expected of a good judge; fairness, a capacity to put aside any prejudice or presupposition and a determination to weigh the evidence both carefully and objectively. These qualities are not innate; they have to be worked at until they become realities rather than aspirations or pretensions. In the absence of some intuitive flash of brilliance like the one that brought an abrupt end to Archimedes' ablutions, difficult issues need to be approached with an open mind and wrestled through with rigor. And even then our conclusions may prove to be wrong. As Nicholas Rescher has pointed out, many of the great "scientific truths" of earlier generations have now been discredited. Few of the theories advanced by people like Aristotle, Ptolemy, Newton and Maxwell have survived the scrutiny of later scholarship wholly unscathed.[45] If the great thinkers of yesteryear can be wrong, perhaps we too may prove to be fallible.

SO WHAT IS EVIDENCE?

As Rescher has observed: "If we want information—if we deem ignorance no less a negativity than error—then we must be prepared to 'take the

---

43. Kierkegaard, Soren, *Works of Love*, 23.
44. Basil, Robert *Not Necessarily the New Age*, 366.
45. Rescher, *Epistemology*, 57.

gamble' of answering our questions in ways that risk some possibility of error. A middle-of-the-road evidentialism emerges as the most sensible approach."[46] But what is evidence? In a court of law it consists largely of what the witnesses say they saw and heard, but no mortal witnesses were present at the 'Big Bang' or during the vast aeons in which the planets cooled and primitive life emerged. Our ancestors survived from day to day by relying upon their abilities but also upon their experience and instincts. They formed beliefs about the existence of a god or gods and the possibility of an afterlife by observing things like the panoply of stars in the night sky, the outbreak of fire, the miracle of new birth and the phenomenon of death which seemed to involve the life or spirit leaving the body. We now see many of their beliefs as ignorant superstitions, but that is largely because we have the benefit of scientific explanations that they could never have imagined. And if any of them were to suddenly emerge from some sort of time warp, they might ask whether our overall approach is really all that different. They would learn that we scan the heavens with radio telescopes and send out probes to investigate other planets, we have had people land on the moon, and we have learned much of the cosmos that apparently emerged as the consequence of a single cataclysmic event some 13.8 billion years ago. Yet still we look at them with wonder and we still seek understanding by relying on our observations, our experience and occasionally our intuitive leaps of imagination, the validity of which may not be experimentally confirmed for decades, if ever.

Skeptics naturally rely heavily upon science, but this is not the sole domain of reason and experience. Whilst we should be wary of subjective impressions that may the product of reconstruction and imagination, there is no reason to imagine that our beliefs should not be informed by our experiences and those of others, even if they fall outside the parameters of specialized scientific fields such as biology or astronomy. Neither eyewitness observations nor feelings of pain can be sensibly dismissed merely because they have not been confirmed by someone in a laboratory coat, and the commercial and social judgements we make each day are rarely guided by people recognized as scientists. Of course, there is much that people in any discipline may learn from science, but few investors would ignore the advice of their broker merely because his degree was in commerce rather than science. The crucial question that should be asked about any proposition is whether it is rationally supportable.

---

46. Rescher, *Epistemology*, 56.

CAN ONE REALLY APPROACH RELIGION SKEPTICALLY?

There is no obvious reason to exclude religious belief from skeptical examination, but that does not mean that one may rationally leap to the conclusion that everything men and women have believed for centuries is necessarily wrong. Even in this context, skepticism involves examining the evidence and considering the competing arguments. Earlier generations also drew on philosophical reasoning to point the way towards God. Are any of their 'proofs' or theories still persuasive in a more scientific age? And what of religious experience? One may be cynical about anything suggestive of supernatural influences but, when someone says, in effect, "this is what I saw and heard," does the fact that their experiences could be described as 'religious' or 'paranormal' require, *ipso facto*, that they be dismissed as delusional? Has our knowledge of neurology, psychology, and astronomical phenomena, capable of explaining events once seen as auguries, now revealed that religious belief reflects nothing more than a perhaps understandable failure to grasp the truth? Or has our desire to be seen as intelligent and sophisticated led to intellectual tunnel vision?

In the television series, "Star Trek," the captain of the space ship regularly responded to information suggesting that some abnormal situation might lie ahead by crying "On screen!" This conveniently brought into vision a magnified image of that part of the universe he wanted to see. Many people seem to have a similar capacity; things they want to see emerge with crystal clarity, whilst unwanted material never appears on their internal screens.

The world certainly teems with the delusional and those anxious to see supernatural influences in everything. And it seems that there are countless millions who cling to religious beliefs without every questioning them. But this is also true of many who reject any belief in God due to bitterness or some other emotional response to tragedy or hardship they believe a loving God should have prevented. Whether you are inclined towards religious belief or atheism, you can do better than that. Respect for moral integrity may impel one to question the existence of God and other fundamental religious tenets but, conversely, it should also lead one to ask whether atheism really holds the answers. Is this the position which any rational person would hold if not blinded by such factors as ignorance, family upbringing, cultural influences and fear? Or are the arguments of even the most persuasive of its proponents really dependent upon convenient rhetorical constructs, lofty but vague pronouncements about science, and speculative suggestions passed off as proof? Can we even hope to answer such questions? Or must we inevitably settle for a perhaps intellectually satisfying but personally unfulfilling agnosticism?

Such issues can only be approached with a genuine commitment to seek the truth whatever the implications. That can be a frightening prospect, but it is one that must be faced by any who claim to be skeptics unless, of course, "skepticism" for them is merely a self-flattering euphemism for minds closed to anything that may challenge their existing beliefs and prejudices. Skepticism really requires a willingness to question not only our beliefs but also our presuppositions and attitudes, and that can be more difficult than most people seem to imagine.

2

Peering through The Fog

During an earlier life as a judge, I heard an appeal against a mental health order requiring a teenage boy to be detained in a hospital and treated for schizophrenia. Amongst his more enchanting symptoms was the belief that he had lunch with the king of Siam each day. Of course, Thailand is a constitutional monarchy, but his distressed parents doubted that his Majesty had been surreptitiously flying in to dine with their son on such a regular basis. The Mental Health Tribunal had shared their skepticism and, when he refused to take the medication prescribed by a psychiatrist, concluded that involuntary treatment was required. Faced with an obviously delusional person who refused legal assistance, I expected a rambling, irrational diatribe, perhaps punctuated by the odd colorful outburst. I was surprised when he spoke in a calm and steady voice and even more surprised by his lucid and well-reasoned argument.

He began by pointing out that many people have religious beliefs involving the existence of gods and other beings whose existence cannot be scientifically verified and may be disputed by unbelievers. Yet Christian, Muslim or Jewish beliefs rarely prompt psychiatric intervention and no one suggests that Hindus should be locked up or involuntarily medicated merely because others doubt the existence of Vishnu. His situation should not be seen as materially different. Of course, few people claim that the objects of their veneration materialize each day to have lunch with them, and this young man's beliefs were directly attributable to a treatable mental illness. Indeed, he accepted that the antipsychotic medication prescribed for him would dispel his daily fantasies. He refused to accept treatment only because he would miss them. And, he insisted, they should not be taken from him without his consent.

In any event, he pointed out, the law did not authorize mental health authorities to censor the beliefs of others, however unusual. The statutory provision for involuntary treatment applied only when someone would otherwise be a danger to himself or others. In his case, there had been no evidence of either ground, and hence no lawful basis for the order. As I was obliged to explain to his distressed mother and the frustrated health officials glowering in the back of the courtroom, this legal analysis was entirely correct. The famously cynical psychiatrist, Thomas Szasz, once observed that millionaires seemed immune from any diagnosis of insanity[1], but even the irrational poor are generally free to refuse treatment and bask in delusions if they wish. The law regulates behavior; fantasies are optional.

Of course, this legal exposition did little to alleviate his mother's concern and I spent some time trying to persuade him that the enjoyment he gained from these gastronomic trysts was outweighed by the distress his condition was causing her and others who loved him. He responded in tones more sad than defiant. If you truly love people, he said, you accept them as they are and do not impose conditions you know they cannot accept, such as requiring them to forsake their deeply held beliefs. He would not wish to change her to conform to his expectations and she should not seek to change him. In the end I could only uphold his appeal and set aside the order.

What fascinated me about this this troubled but intelligent young man was his apparent recognition that his beliefs were irrational and that he was clinging to them only because they pleased him. One does not expect stark realism from a deluded mind, but despite or perhaps even because of his illness, he revealed striking insight and remarkable candor. And as he left the courtroom, glancing nervously at his watch to ensure he was not keeping the king waiting, I was left wondering whether he was substantially more deluded than those who have less imaginative lunch dates but whose lives are shaped by other self-deceptions.

HOW RATIONAL ARE WE?

Many people would be tempted to endorse the parallel this young schizophrenic drew between his delusional beliefs and the religious beliefs of others. The moral of the story, they might insist, is that even those involved in mainstream religions embrace beliefs in God, not because they are rational, but because they meet their emotional needs. In contrast, atheists claim

---

1. The remark was made during a speech at the Australian National University during the 1980s when we shared the podium.

to eschew flights of fancy, acknowledge the limits of their own mortality and draw their beliefs from science. The more moderate may have some sympathy for those they regard as naive or emotionally stunted, but most nonetheless claim to dwell on a higher intellectual plane. Amused agnostics sometimes cite the old aphorism about pots calling the kettle black. They insist that a dogmatic assertion that God does not exist is as untenable as a dogmatic assertion that he[2] does. In their view, the evidence is insufficient to establish either proposition and vague allusions to science are no more cogent than vague allusions to piety. A truly rational person would simply recognize that human knowledge is limited and smile indulgently at those committed to their competing leaps of faith. But must all who seek the truth about such issues accept being intellectually becalmed? Or can they trim their sails to find enough wind to send them scudding in one direction or the other?

Religious fundamentalists often assert that God has revealed all that is necessary. If you don't understand, then you are obviously one of those who are 'blind because they will not see'. In other words, both the overt disbelief of the atheists and the fence sitting stance of the agnostics are attributable to nothing more than a reluctance to face the truth and the moral implications that it might entail. Most of us remain unimpressed by dogmatic assertions of this kind and they may be rejected by theologians as well as atheists. Yet it is true that people tend to interpret the available evidence in the light of their own inclinations and this phenomenon is not confined to issues of religious belief.

Of course, not all religious believers insist that a lack of faith must be attributable to moral turpitude, not all atheists notionally consign all believers to the same intellectually barren pigeonhole, and not all agnostics scoff at anyone with even a tentative view about the existence of God. Nor does everyone slot neatly into one or other of these categories. People hold varying degrees of belief and the balance between their belief and their skepticism may fluctuate throughout their lives. That is perhaps inevitable. We may like to imagine that our reasoning processes remain unpolluted by extraneous factors, but we cannot escape our humanity. Our opinions are shaped by our experiences and emotions, not just our reason.

---

2. Feminist theologians are asked to curb any incipient outrage at the use of the male pronoun. I am not suggesting that God must be exclusively male. Any deity who created the human race would obviously not be confined to one gender. However, a personal pronoun is obviously required, the gender neutral but plural term "they" might have introduced a potentially distracting suggestion of polytheism and, reduced to two choices, I have opted for the one most commonly used, albeit by the politically unregenerate.

It is easy to recognize this in others. We have all smiled or sneered at those who seem congenitally gullible; the sort of people who always 'take the bait' when being teased or fall prey to practical jokers, salespeople, advertisers or anyone else wishing to exploit them. And the superstitious, like the poor, are always with us. It is easy to raise our eyebrows at the naivety of those who feel shivers of apprehension when black cats cross their paths or let the course of their lives be directed by daily horoscope readings, but many people who reject such superstitions nonetheless seem able to persuade themselves of things incapable of withstanding objective scrutiny. It is good to have the courage of your convictions, but even better when the convictions have some factual basis. Unfortunately, many seem to see this as unnecessary. The Oxford Dictionaries' word of the year for 2016 was "post-truth," a term recognizing that objective facts are less influential in shaping public opinion than appeals to emotion and personal belief.[3] Those confident that few people would be misled by irrational beliefs might reflect upon the results of a survey carried out in 2012 which revealed that 26 per cent of adult Americans believed that the sun orbited the earth and 42 per cent believed that astrology is either "very scientific" or "sort of scientific."[4] You may be relieved to know that none of those who carried out the survey reported lasting ocular damage from rolling their eyes.

But what of us? Are those us who disavow superstition and boldly walk under ladders inherently more rational? Most of us can look back ruefully on beliefs we later attributed to youthful enthusiasm or wishful thinking and perhaps even remember occasions when we shrank from unpalatable truths such as the impending death of someone we loved. But such failings were mere aberrations—lapses from an otherwise invariable pattern of considering things logically—weren't they? Can we now put aside the emotional baggage that influences lesser mortals and rejoice in our capacity to see everything with pellucid clarity? Or must even skeptics make some allowance for their own fears and inclinations, like archers making due allowance for the effect of the wind on their arrows?

Some people may react to such questions with impatience, protesting that the need for objectivity is obvious; it is only the naive and undisciplined that permit themselves to be led astray by presuppositions and emotions. It is true that some of us tend to approach the issues we encounter with greater objectivity than others, whether due to our temperament, common sense or professional orientation. It is also true that we can all try to adopt an objective attitude. Indeed, the plea for such an approach is central to the theme

---

3. Coughlan, "What does post-truth mean for a philosopher?"
4. Henderson, "One in four Americans 'do not know the earth circles the sun.'"

of this book. But can complete objectivity really be slipped on like a freshly ironed shirt? We may assume that our beliefs reflect rational conclusions based upon objective appraisals of the available information, but is this also largely a delusion?

CAN WE SHAKE OFF OUR PRESUPPOSITIONS?

Of course, many presuppositions arise from our education and knowledge. The capacity to learn is one the great strengths of our common humanity and we do so from the cradle to the grave. As children we absorb not merely the knowledge that our parents, teachers, and others try to pass on to us, but also the things they communicate unintentionally, including their prejudices. We also absorb things from the vast panoply of writers, artists, celebrities, and others who affect our beliefs and attitudes. And, of course, we learn from our experience. In theory, at least, all this enables us to draw on reservoirs of accumulated knowledge and wisdom when we face difficult issues. But our presuppositions may also become filters that color and distort our perceptions and have a real, if subconscious, impact upon our capacity to consider issues in an open-minded manner. Even those convinced of their ability to avoid prejudgment and act with undiluted objectivity might be surprised to find how readily even intelligent people succumb to the perhaps unrecognized influence of things they would consciously dismiss as irrelevant.

Research has shown that people are twice as likely to select information that supports their own point of view than to consider an opposing idea and that they are even more resistant to new points of view when the ideas are associated with political, religious or ethical values.[5] Longer explanations tend to be regarded as more plausible than short ones. Those that point to a goal or reason for things happening tend to be accepted as more credible, even if they actually cast little light on the phenomenon being explained. And there is a "seductive lure effect" when some psychological explanation contains "logically irrelevant neuroscience information."[6] These factors seem to resonate with subconscious presuppositions that certain types of information tend to be reliable. Presuppositions arise in many ways and their impact can be disturbing.

---

5. See generally, Hart et al, "Feeling Validated Versus Being Correct: A Meta-Analysis of Selective Exposure to Information," (2009) *Psychological Bulletin*, Vol. 135, No. 4, 555–588.
6. Loria, "Scientists discovered an absurdly easy way to seem convincing."

The results of one study suggested that the fate of a criminal defendant might depend on where he was required to sit, with 60 per cent of mock jurors opting for a conviction when he was confined to a glass dock, 47 per cent when in an open dock, but only 36 per cent when permitted to sit with his lawyer at the bar table.[7] These are startling figures. We trust juries to deliver verdicts based on a fair and careful assessment of the evidence. Few lawyers would have imagined that the seating position of the defendant could have proven to be the decisive factor for almost a quarter of the participants. The most likely explanation is that the different placements gave rise to different presuppositions, with confinement in the glass dock most strongly suggesting that the defendant was a dangerous criminal, and that this influenced the overall impressions some jurors formed of the evidence. As the leading researcher ruefully concluded, "People think they can detect their own prejudices. In fact, all the psychology evidence is they can't and you need to do a randomized controlled trial to see how people actually behave as opposed to how they think they behave."[8]

Other studies have shown that jurors tend to find confident expert witnesses more credible,[9] though, conversely, errors by confident witnesses apparently have a greater impact on their credibility,[10] and "likable" expert witnesses were perceived to be more trustworthy.[11] Research has also shown that people tend to trust those who are physically attractive. The appointment of beautiful or handsome CEOs actually tends to boost the share prices of their companies.[12] This phenomenon, sometimes called the "halo effect," has a negative corollary; people tend to expect the worst from those who are unattractive. Both trends are reflected both in childhood cartoons and adult fairytales provided by Hollywood; the good princes are invariably handsome, the princesses beautiful and the witches ugly.[13] Of course, even

7. Tait, "Juries can be influenced by where defendants sit in a courtroom, Australian study finds." See also the discussion in Tait, "Deliberating about terrorism: Prejudice and jury verdicts in a modern terrorist trial.."

8. Tait, "Juries can be influenced by where defendants sit in a courtroom, Australian study finds."

9. Cramer, R.J. et al, "Expert witness confidence and juror personality: their impact on credibility and persuasion in the courtroom," *J Am Acad Psychiatry Law,* 37(1) (2009) 63–74.

10. Tenney et al, "Calibration trumps confidence as a basis for witness credibility," *Psychological Science.*18(1):46 – 50, February 2007.

11. Brodsky et al, "Credibility in the courtroom: how likable should an expert witness be?" *J Am Acad Psychiatry Law,* 37(4) (2009) 525–32.

12. Halford and Hsu, *Beauty is Wealth: CEO Appearance and Shareholder Value,* December 19, 2014, https://ssrn.com/abstract=2357756.

13. Stanger, "Attractive People Are Simply More Successful," *Business Insider,*

the beautiful people cannot win them all; jealously leads some to resent those who are very attractive.[14]

Even our visual perceptions of others may be influenced by bias and presupposition. An American study seems to have provided computer-generated confirmation of the old adage that we may see people through "rose-colored glasses." As bizarre as it may seem, the experiments actually revealed that people who supported the political party of biracial candidates tended to see their skin color as lighter than it actually was, whilst those opposed to that party tended to see it as darker than it was.[15] Our western societies may overtly condemn racism, but subliminal connections between skin color and virtue apparently linger. Perhaps that is why Republican advertisements targeting Barack Obama in 2008 depicted him with a very dark skin.[16]

Religious beliefs are influenced and buttressed by history and culture as well as by family upbringing. That is reflected in the distribution of the world's major religions. For example, Iran is predominantly Muslim whilst neighboring Armenia is predominantly Christian. Children growing up within communities or families with a strong religious ethos naturally absorb the beliefs and attitudes in which they have been raised and they may become deeply engrained. Even those willing to question them will inevitably approach the relevant issues with presuppositions that subtly shape their conclusions. But it is not only religious belief that is shaped by presuppositions and biases. Those who have long regarded all religious beliefs as naive fantasies will also be influenced by their presuppositions. No one approaches questions of this nature with a clean slate.

CAN WE REALLY PUT ASIDE OUR EMOTIONS?

Even staunch atheists would generally concede the validity of Jesus' famous observation that there are none so blind as those that will not see, but even those conscientiously seeking the truth may be misled by their feelings. More than half a century ago, an English barrister, Sir Malcolm Hilberry QC, recognized that juries were largely swayed by feelings but were unaware

---

October 10, 2012, https://www.businessinsider.com.au/attractive-people-are-more-successful-2012-9?r=US&IR=T.

14. Stanger, "Attractive People Are Simply More Successful."

15. Caruso et al, "Political partisanship influences perception of biracial candidates' skin tone." *Proceedings of the National Academy of Sciences*, 106, (2009) 20168–20173.

16. Ehrenfreund, "Obama's skin looks a little different in these GOP campaign ads," *The Washington Post*, December 29, 2015.

of it. He thought that, the less training and capacity for reasoning people had, the more likely they were to pride themselves on being susceptible only to logic and impervious to mere emotion, but added, "the fact is that reason is a new human toy, while emotions have been the mainspring of men's thoughts and acts since man first appeared in the morning of time."[17]

The impact of emotions on perceptions has long been recognized. Julius Caesar said "men willing believe what they wish"[18] and the phrase "wishful thinking" is now embedded in our contemporary vernacular.[19] But self-interest is not the only thing that may distort the paths of reason; there are other emotional culprits, such as loyalty, compassion, bitterness, resentment, guilt and fear. And our responses may vary, according to our character, personality, and even our mood. Most of us are familiar with stereotypes such as the romantic dreamer, the 'hot head', or the 'panic merchant', but none of us are immune. One person may absorb the beliefs and values of a strict religious upbringing whilst another may rebel against them, but both will have been affected by them. Two children may pray for critically ill mothers. One may recover and the other die, but neither will remain uninfluenced by their experience. We may think that our beliefs are the product of rational analysis, but even our rationality is affected by our emotions.[20]

Perhaps understandably, many people are wary of others whom they fear may be 'carried away' by their emotions and blinded to realities that would be obvious to those with cooler heads. Hence, as the psychologist, Erich Fromm, has observed, in the eyes of many, "to be 'emotional' has become synonymous with being unsound or unbalanced."[21] On the other hand, Robert Solomon has rejected the idea that that emotions are merely unruly elements of our nature that distort our thinking. He maintains that whilst they may mislead, they may also illuminate. As Solomon explains, "emotions lend a keenness to our perception and sometimes to our judgment that is not available to the disinterested, and, where most matters

17. Hilberry, *Duty and Art in Advocacy*, at 33. The passage was written before the rise of feminist concern about the use of language expunged the generic use of the male pronoun from professional discourse and also at a time when jurors were predominantly male.

18. In Latin: *Fere libenter homines id quod volunt credunt*, Caius Julius Caesar, "*De Bello Gallico and other commentaries*" Project Gutenberg ebook loc 1201 (Jan 9 2004) ebook #10657.

19. For a discussion of such phenomena see Bastardi et al,"Wishful Thinking: Belief, Desire, and the Motivated Evaluation of Scientific Evidence." *Psychological Science* 22 (6) (April 22 2011) 731–732.

20. For a succinct discussion of the relationship between emotion and rationality see Pham, "Emotion and Rationality."

21. Fromm, *The Fear of Freedom*, 211.

human are concerned, a readiness for insight and understanding that the most brilliant social scientist may not be able to approximate."[22] He cites Jean-Paul Sartre's claim that emotions involve "magical transformations of the world."[23]

It may be easy to dismiss such flamboyant, linguistic flourishes, but neurological studies have shown that judgments are often made at a "gut" or emotional level. That is evident from patients with lesions of the ventromedial sector of the prefrontal cortex which interfere with the normal processing of the "somatic" or emotional signals within the brain. This impairs decision-making processes, even though most of the basic cognitive functions remain unaffected.[24] More recent fMRI[25] studies on people with no brain injuries have also confirmed that emotional states can impair performance in reasoning tasks.[26] Even those who shrink from Christopher Hitchens' contention that our species is only partially rational,[27] cannot doubt that our emotions are highly influential. We may strive to suppress them in the interests of objectivity, but they cannot be confined to an intellectual cupboard and brought out only on appropriate occasions. Whether we acknowledge it or not, they influence our perceptions and our judgments.

That is why we can suddenly become acutely aware of things we had previously known but have been able to overlook. Solomon refers to an acquaintance who bought a sports car "for the price of 250,000 Ethiopian dinners."[28] Unfortunately, I read this damning comparison immediately after buying a sports car of my own. I did not know whether to repent in sackcloth and ashes or send Solomon a poison pen letter with some brochures from the nearest Porsche dealer. Of course, such reactions occur nor merely because someone has chided us for our extravagance, but also because we have been made to think about the plight of others and our capacity to have eased their suffering by diverting our money to their aid. Our consciences may be pricked, but our perceptions have also been changed and, I might add defensively, such perceptual epiphanies affect more than the odd sports car owner.

22. Solomon, *A Passion for Justice*, 220.
23. Solomon, *A Passion for Justice*, 220.
24. Bechara, "The role of emotion in decision-making." See also Bechara, Damasio. & Damasio, "Emotion, decision making and the orbitofrontal cortex," and Emonds et al, "Comparing the neural basis of decision making."
25. Functional magnetic resonance imaging.
26. Brunetti et al, "Framing deductive reasoning."
27. Hitchens, *God is not Great*, 8.
28. Solomon, *A Passion for Justice*, preface at xiii.

Imagine for a moment the kind of arguments politicians sometimes use to justify curtailing foreign aid to poor African countries. There is a standard line of patter; much of it is spent on administration, more is siphoned off by corrupt governments, some might even be spent on weapons and, in any event, patronizing handouts do not address the underlying problems. Anyway, doesn't charity begin at home? Isn't our first responsibility to our own people? Then imagine traveling to such a country, looking into the haunted eyes of a starving child with emaciated limbs, a swollen belly and skin covered in sores, and then explaining why you think we should leave her to her fate. The moral implications of such a scenario may be obvious, but what of your rational assessment of the worth of foreign aid? Would that remain unaltered? Some facts may become fully visible only when we are confronted by them in some vivid and inescapable manner. One need only consider the chilling aphorism attributed to Stalin: "the death of one man is a tragedy, the death of millions is a statistic."[29] So many atrocities in the world are ignored not because of insufficient information but because of a failure of imagination. As contrived as it may seem, experiments have shown that simply asking people to close their eyes whilst thinking about a certain situation actually affects the ethical judgments they make.[30]

How pervasive are emotional influences? Was Hilberry right in suggesting that it is really only those with little capacity for reasoning whose emotions are likely to divert them from the paths of logic? Are training and intellectual rigor sufficient to ensure due objectivity? Or are even professional and scientific opinions affected by the subtle and largely unrecognized influences of our feelings and presuppositions? An Australian barrister took a more realistic approach, ruefully warning his colleagues that "the temperament, the imagination and the feelings may all mislead us in the chase."[31]

Some may protest that this may be true of lawyers, but that is because the predominant objective of the chase is not to find the truth but to obtain the best result for their clients.[32] What of others, whose lives remain unsullied by loyalty to clients? Roger Fisher, then Director of the Harvard Negotiation Project, regularly conducted exercises in which law students were given identical facts about a hypothetical company and asked to negotiate its sale, with half representing vendors and half representing purchasers.

29. The attribution has been disputed. Russian historians apparently claim to have have no record of Stalin making such a comment. Solovyova, "Mustering Most Memorable Quips."

30. Caruso, Eugene M. and Francesca Gino "Blind ethics."

31. Reynolds, R.G., "The Principles of Advocacy," 19.

32. For a digression into legal ethics and the search for truth within an adversarial system of justice see Crispin, *The Quest for Justice*, 63 et seq.

Before negotiations commenced each student was asked to make an objective estimate of the actual value of the company. Fisher found that those asked to represent vendors routinely nominated higher figures than those asked to represent purchasers. Harvard skims the intellectual cream of aspiring students, and these highly intelligent young people were allocated their roles on a random basis. Their "clients" were hypothetical entities, not real people for whom they might have felt loyalty or sympathy and they had no obvious 'axe to grind' in representing them. Yet, year after year, the results revealed the same pattern. The mere allocation of partisan roles was sufficient to distort their assessments.[33]

Beliefs about such issues as the existence of God and the possibility of an afterlife are influenced by emotions vastly more powerful than any likely to affect students notionally representing fictitious clients. Christians maintain that we have been created by God for a purpose, our lives are in his hands, our sins can be forgiven and we may die only to begin a new life in which there will be no more fear or pain and we will be reunited with those we love who have 'gone before' us. Even those committed to seeking the truth, whatever the cost, may well be influenced by the subconscious desire for all this to be true and, perhaps, by fear of failure to heed the call to faith.

DO SCIENTISTS DWELL ON A MORE OBJECTIVE PLANE?

What of scientists? Many work in corporate environments where loyalties and self-interest may subtly undermine their objectivity but, in theory at least, they chase only truth. Science has been described as "a method or procedure that has characterized natural science since the 17th century, consisting in systematic observation, measurement, and experiment, and the formulation, testing, and modification of hypotheses."[34] Adherents understandably claim to labour in disciplines characterized by objectivity and rigor. Of course, not everyone is impressed. Some reject findings they find unpalatable, whether due to self interest or ideology, and others worry that scientific curiosity and ambition will lead us all into areas of danger or dubious ethical probity. Then there are those who seem convinced that their own opinions, however ill-informed, are as valid as those of the most

---

33. Fisher, "He who pays the piper," 152.

34. From the Oxford English Dictionary definition for "scientific." Whilst perhaps hallowed by time, this definition is now being challenged, particularly by theoretical physicists and others who insist that it should be amplified to embrace theories that may not be verifiable or falsifiable. This is discussed in chapter 3.

highly qualified experts. Of course, such views are held selectively—few people adopt a DIY approach to a troublesome gall bladder or ruptured appendix—but they are reflected in widespread rejections of public health warnings and other flights from reality. In this context, scientists are often the calm, if frustrated, voice of reason.

Yet the great scientific breakthroughs have been the achievements of potentially fallible men and women, not automatons driven by remorseless logic unaffected by human emotions. Of course, few people may doubt that the personal lives of scientists involve the same emotionally fueled responses that beset the rest of humanity, but there does seem to be a widespread assumption that they don complete clinical detachment along with their white coats. I have cross-examined scientists who also seemed to share this assumption, but it is almost invariably unrealistic.

Any scientist reduced to spluttering indignation by this statement should take a moment to reflect on Albert Einstein's decision to introduce a cosmological constant into his general theory of relativity. Whatever the subsequent justification for the concept,[35] it seems clear that he used it to fudge the results of his equations so they would accord with a static universe. He realized the error only when Edwin Hubble discovered that the distant galaxies are expanding away from each other. He is said to have described this as the "biggest blunder" of his life.[36] It is true that astronomers had previously been unable to detect such widespread expansion, but why did he not heed the evidence provided by his own equations? The only explanation seems to have been a philosophical bias;[37] his presupposition of a static universe was too strong to be dispelled by equations alone.

Of course, Einstein was not the only scientist to fall into error for that reason. Problems with the accuracy of astronomical observations were first noted in 1795 and by the 1830s astronomers had recognized that errors were reflecting predictable individual tendencies and developed what they called "personal equations" to adjust for them.[38] Isaac Newton apparently failed to see any absorption lines in the prismatic solar spectrum even though they

---

35. It has recently been suggested that a cosmological constant may be a form of energy that explains a number of matters including the acceleration in the rate of the universe's expansion, the magnitude of the extrapolated age of the universe and the distribution of galaxies and clusters. See, for example, National Aeronautics and Space Administration, "What is a Cosmological Constant?"; Goldsmith, *Einstein's Greatest Blunder?* and Moskowitz, Clara , "Right Again Einstein!"

36. Gamov, *My World Line*, 44.

37. Dodson, Brian, "Einstein's biggest blunder" beats dark energy."

38. Boring, *A History of Experimental Psychology*, 134–138.

should have been visible to him through the equipment he used.[39] These failures pale into relative insignificance when, conversely, other scientists reported detecting a form of radiation called "N-rays" which were supposed to emanate from most substances, including the human body. The observations were described in about 300 published articles[40] and this flow of literature ceased only when it was realized that N rays did not exist.[41] Observer errors have been found in reading scales,[42] counting blood cells,[43] examining X rays[44] and in other areas of science.[45] Many seem to reflect a tendency to see things through lenses of expectations.[46]

In fact, scientists have sometimes adhered to false beliefs in the face of undeniable evidence to the contrary. Arthur C. Clarke famously observed that at the beginning of the twentieth century scientists were almost unanimous in declaring that heavier-than-air flight was impossible, and that anyone who attempted to build an airplane was a fool.[47] Perhaps the most striking thing about this conviction is not that it was unfounded, but that it was maintained despite the obvious fact that these doyens of scientific realism would have seen heavier than air birds in flight.

It is not surprising that Thomas Kuhn, Norwood Hanson, Paul Feyerabend, and others have all questioned the assumption that scientists can shield their observations from biases due to presuppositions and theoretical commitments.[48] In fact, some do not seem to see the need. The cosmologist, Sir Arthur Eddington, once cheerfully encouraged his colleagues with the line, "Don't worry if your theory doesn't agree with the observations, because they are probably wrong."[49] Fortunately, few seem to have been quite so sanguine. The prevalence of errors led to numerous investigations,[50] and

39. Boring, "Newton and the Spectral Lines," 600–601.
40. Lagemann, R.T.. "New light on old rays."
41. Kohn, Alexander, *False Prophets,* 18–20.
42. Yule, G. Udny, "On Reading a Scale," 570.
43. Joseph Berkson et al, "The Error of Estimates of the Blood Cell Count," 322.
44. Johnson, M.L., "Seeing's Believing."
45. Kohn, *False Prophets;* Risinger, "The Daubert/Kumho Implications."
46. Sackett, D. L., "Bias in analytic research." For examples of this effect, see Rosenthal, *Experimenter Effects in Behavioral Research*: Saks, "The Daubert/Kumho Implications of Observer Effects in Forensic Science"; Krane, "Sequential unmasking."
47. Clarke, *Profiles of the Future,* 10.
48. See, for example, the discussion in Bogen, James, "Theory and Observation in Science."
49. Quoted by Hawking, *"The Beginning of Time."*
50. For a general discussion see Rosenthal, *Experimenter Effects in Behavioral Research.*

from this process emerged stringent protocols, such as double blind trials and peer review. These measures may have reduced the the risk of error, but they have not proven to be a panacea for all scientific ills.

Randomized double blind trials are frequently lauded as the "gold standard" and they can be of great value in providing an objective means of testing new drugs or other forms of medical treatment. Their reliability has sometimes been jeopardized when participants have been inadvertently given subtle clues[51] or otherwise been able to discriminate between active and placebo medications.[52] Of course, such obvious pitfalls are usually avoided by strict adherence to protocols, but, even when the trials are rigorously undertaken and validly assessed, further investigation may still sometimes reveal that the conclusions were incorrect.[53] One disaffected epidemiologist has actually suggested that "gold calf" might be a more appropriate description than "gold standard" and suggested that some "facts" may not exist "independent of the apparatus of their production."[54] This splendidly overblown allusion to the golden calf may rather overstate the risk of error in a generally reliable procedure. However, double blind trials are not always possible. An astronomer seeking to explain reports of an apparently unique event in the cosmos cannot simply ask God to keep repeating it, preferably with his eyes shut.

Peer review generally determines which grants are allocated, papers published, academics promoted, and even Nobel prizes awarded, but the International Council for Science has warned of the risk of outcomes being affected by bias.[55] Articles challenging the status quo may be reviewed by referees who have spent their professional lives defending it and are not keen to permit some 'whiz kid' to demonstrate that they have been wrong. Researchers who carried out a systematic review in 2002 concluded that "the practice of peer review is based on faith in its effects, rather than on facts."[56] Others have suggested it may be "a game of chance."[57] A former editor of the British Medical Journal has been even more scathing: "In addition to being poor at detecting gross defects and almost useless for detecting fraud it is slow, expensive, profligate of academic time, highly subjective, something

---

51. Rosenthal, *Experimenter effects in behavioral research*, 464.
52. Morin et al, "*How 'blind' are double blind placebo-controlled trials*."
53. Lerner, "The Mysterious Decline Effect".
54. Kaptchuk,"The double-blind, randomized, placebo-controlled trial."
55. International Council of Science, *Advisory Note* "Bias in science publishing." See also McGauran et al, "Reporting bias in medical research—a narrative review."
56. Jefferson T. et al, "Effects of editorial peer review: a systematic review."
57. Neff and Olden, "Is Peer Review a Game of Chance?"

of a lottery, prone to bias, and easily abused."[58] Randy Schekman has even called for a boycott on leading academic journals, complaining that they are creating a toxic culture by using frequency of citation as an indicator of quality when, in reality, "a paper can become highly cited because it is good science—or because it is eye-catching, provocative, or wrong."[59]

Of course, the problem of subconscious bias is not confined to peer review and it may be ineradicable. Studies have actually shown that "bias blindness" can persist even when judgments are based upon explicitly biased strategies or techniques.[60] and those who work within an ethos in which objectivity often seems to be taken as a "given" may be less alert to the risk than others. At the risk of being burnt at a bunsen burner for what some may see as secular blasphemy, I must say that I have seen no evidence that scientists, alone amongst all humanity, are immune from the human frailties that expose other mortals to the risk of error. In fact, there are some psychological factors that may be seen as potential Achilles' heels that scientists ignore at their peril.

Daniel Kahneman, the Nobel Prize winning psychologist, has warned of "theory induced blindness." He explains that 'Once you have accepted a theory, it is extraordinarily difficult to notice its flaws. As Daniel Gilbert has said, "disbelieving is hard work."[61] It may be difficult for any of us to admit we have been wrong, but that may be particularly taxing for scientists who believe they have adopted theories on logically compelling grounds. Of course, the converse may also be true. Enthusiasm for a new theory may also influence the manner in which the available evidence is interpreted. This may emerge with striking clarity in our courts where expert witnesses are cross-examined about their views and confronted by contrary evidence. Despite oft-repeated folklore about dirty tricks,[62] this approach does tend to uncover any obvious flaws and some theories prove to be dependent upon surprisingly flimsy grounds.

---

58. Smith, Richard, "Peer review: a flawed process at the heart of science and journals."

59. Quoted by Sample, Ian, "Nobel winner declares boycott of top science journals."

60. Hansen et al, "People Claim Objectivity After Knowingly Using Biased Strategies."

61. Kahneman, Daniel, "Bias, Blindness and How We Truly Think." See also Kahneman, *Thinking Fast and Slow*.

62. Lawyers have been derided by various epithets reflecting this view. Marvin Frankel, an American judge and legal academic, has cited "mouthpiece," "hired gun," "mercenary warrior" and "shyster" before offering his own formulation of "an all purpose, surrogate villain, doing everybody's dirt work—obstructing, perverting, distorting, blocking the high road to justice." See Frankel, *Partisan Justice*, 3.

But the concept of theory-induced blindness may have a broader application than Kahneman suggests. Scientists have often seemed unable to accept apparently well researched and logically compelling propositions falling outside prevailing "paradigms," a term initially used by Thomas Kuhn to describe strong networks of commitments, concepts, thought patterns, methods and standards that shape the practice of science within a particular field.[63] Paradigms inevitably give rise to strong presuppositions about what should be studied, what questions should be asked, how they should be investigated and how results should be interpreted. Common understandings and expectations within a profession may exert a strong, almost gravitational pull towards conformity. This may be strengthened by other psychological factors, including identification with others in the same group and absorption of its values and beliefs.[64] When any cohesive groups are substantially insulated from dissenting views, even their more independently minded members may fall prey to "groupthink,"[65] a tacit consensus that may make it difficult for scientists to think 'outside the square'.

Take the case of Dr Barry Marshall, who shared a Nobel Prize in 2005 for discovering that stomach ulcers were caused by a germ, the Helicobacter pylori bacterium. This was a crucial finding capable of saving many patients from invasive surgery and perhaps death. But the presuppositions of his colleagues initially prevailed. Gastroenterologists dismissed the suggestion, insisting that they already knew what caused ulcers; it was stress. Marshall later said that "to gastroenterologists, the concept of a germ causing ulcers was like saying that the Earth is flat." The results he presented were disbelieved, "not on the basis of science but because they simply could not be true." He was refused permission to run human trials on existing patients and was finally driven to deliberately infect himself in order to prove the effectiveness of antibiotics. Even then another decade was to pass before a consensus meeting of the National Institutes of Health in Washington DC publicly accepted that the key to treatment of duodenal and gastric ulcers was detection and eradication of this germ.[66]

---

63. Kuhn, Thomas S, *The Structure of Scientific Revolutions*. The influence of paradigms is now well recognized in other fields. See, for example, Barker, J A, *Paradigms*.

64. For a general discussion of such factors see Aronson, *The Social Animal*, 13–55.

65. The term was coined by Irving Janis and describes a mode of thinking that emerges when "concurrence seeking becomes so dominant in a cohesive ingroup that it tends to override realistic appraisal of alternative courses of action." Janis, "Groupthink." See also Whyte, "Groupthink Reconsidered."

66. Weintraub, Pamela, "The Dr. Who Drank Infectious Broth, Gave Himself an Ulcer, and Solved a Medical Mystery." See also Marshall, "Barry J Marshall—Biographical."

This was not the first time paradigm-induced blindness had delayed due recognition of the cause or nature of illness. Whilst feminists and others were suggesting new perspectives about the nature of anorexia nervosa, doctors who turned to the flagship journal, "Psychosomatic Medicine," during the 1970s found that this condition had apparently been reduced to "the anorexic body."[67] Why? There are some physical conditions that cause sustained weight loss, but there was no sensible reason for ignoring psychological causes. How could the medical profession have discounted the maelstroms of emotional factors others had recognized were relevant? The most likely explanation is the professional paradigm that emerged from the focus on the 'visible' body, as distinct from the 'invisible mind', as modern medicine was increasingly recognized as a 'scientific' domain.[68] Emotions could neither be seen nor measured and were apparently dismissed as unscientific.

Of course, subconscious biases may arise from factors such as empathy or conflicts of interest,[69] and, like the potential student negotiators mentioned earlier, even eminent experts are affected by the roles they are asked to play. This problem is also evident in legal proceedings where expert witnesses sometimes display "instruction bias," the tendency for doctors and other scientists to produce reports favorable to those retaining them. This is sometimes obvious in personal injury cases where medical specialists retained by insurance companies frequently conclude that injured plaintiffs are less disabled than the specialists retained by the plaintiffs believe. Similar problems may also occur in criminal cases, particularly when forensic scientists work within police forces or in close contact with investigative officers. Circumstances of that kind inevitably lead to the provision of information suggesting the guilt of defendants and perhaps a sense of being part of the same 'team'. This can lead to "confirmation bias" and, in some cases, a perception that the ultimate goal is to prove the prosecution case rather than simply report what the evidence reveals.[70] As the head of one forensic science body ruefully conceded, when scientists set out to confirm predetermined theories there is always a risk that they will mislead themselves.[71]

Enthusiasm for cherished theories can also lead scientists to overlook deficiencies in the evidence said to support them. Identification evidence

---

67. Mizrachi, "Epistemology and legitimacy in the production of anorexia nervosa".

68. Mizrachi, "Epistemology and legitimacy in the production of anorexia nervosa"

69. MDU, "Bias in medico-legal decisions," *MDU Journal*, November 2012.

70. Moser,"Confirmation Bias: The Pitfall of Forensic Science."

71. The comment was made by Tony Raymond, then Biology Division Manager, of the State Forensic Science Laboratory, Victoria, in private conversation during 1985.

based upon comparisons of hair samples was admitted in American courts for more than 150 years. In 1977 the FBI actually issued a manual,[72] touting the value of "scientifically examined physical evidence by the crime laboratory" and referring to criteria such as color, diameter, cuticle, scales, pigment, medulla and cortex. Yet there had been no databases with which allegedly incriminating samples could be compared and a comprehensive review authorized by the National Research Council in 2009 found that there had been "no scientific support" for such comparisons in the absence of DNA analyses.[73] It was not until April 2015 that the FBI and Department of Justice formally acknowledged that flawed evidence had been given in many criminal trials, including 32 that had resulted in death sentences, 9 of which had apparently been carried out.[74]

Unfortunately, many people seem to regard anything said by a scientist in vaguely esoteric terms as a "scientific fact." This naive acceptance, sometimes dubbed the "CSI effect," can lead people to overlook alternative explanations and dismiss evidence to the contrary. As one sociologist has warned, "a scientific basis stamps the professional . . . with the legitimacy of a general body of knowledge and a mode of cognition, the epistemological superiority of which is taken for granted by our society."[75] To some extent at least, this is true not merely of individual scientists, but of the entire field of science, which is sometimes seen as a general body of knowledge embracing all reality. Hence, to describe a proposition as "scientific" is to affirm that it is rational and, conversely, to describe it as "unscientific" is to damn it as irrational or fanciful. Perhaps that is why some people seem reluctant to accept that some issues may lie beyond the reach of science. Scientists themselves sometimes complain that even qualified statements of opinion are treated as factual statements by which the credibility of any other evidence may be weighed. Michael Polanyi once said:

> In the days when an idea could be silenced by showing that it was contrary to religion, theology was the greatest single source of fallacies. Today, when any human thought can be discredited by branding it unscientific, the power exercised previously by

---

72. Hicks, *Microscopy of Hair. A practical Guide and Manual*, FBI, January 1977.

73. Committee on Identifying the Needs of the Forensic Sciences Community, National Research Council, *Strengthening Forensic Science in the United States*.

74. Pilkington, 'The man who was jailed for 22 years—on the fantasy evidence of a single hair'.

75. Larson, *The Rise of Professionalism*, 40–41.

theology has passed over to science; hence science has become the greatest single source of error.[76]

This splendidly provocative claim has no doubt irritated theologians and scientists alike, and I am sure it was written with a mischievous smile. Polanyi was a polymath who served as professor of chemistry at Manchester University and was elected to both the Royal Society and the American Academy of Arts and Science. His comments should not be taken to reflect some Luddite view that science is constantly seducing innocent souls into error. Nonetheless, they convey a disturbing truth. It is one thing to say that some proposition has been refuted by scientific investigation and another to merely deride it as "unscientific."

Whilst it may seem unkind to question the faith of those looking forward to a Utopian society in which priests wearing white coats rather than black robes will reveal every hidden truth, that is not a present reality. Science has opened our eyes to previously unimagined horizons, dispelled ignorance and superstition, reduced human suffering, increased our longevity and brought us lifestyles to which earlier generations could not have aspired. And this has not occurred merely because the odd Archimedes has had an occasional "Eureka' moment, but also because countless men and women have spent their professional lives conscientiously struggling to find the truth. Nonetheless, scientists share our common humanity and they too are influenced by their presuppositions and emotions.

CAN MATERIALISM BE A SACRED COW?

One of the more common paradigms in science is a philosophical and emotional commitment to materialism. The essence of this paradigm, also referred to as 'physicalism', is the theory that "physical matter is the only or fundamental reality and that all being and processes and phenomena can be explained as manifestations or results of matter."[77] Whilst this belief is still widely held there is little, if any, real evidence to support it. Furthermore, the underlying assumption that everything is ultimately reducible to fundamental sub-atomic particles now seems to have been fatally undermined by the discovery of quantum fields.[78] The paradigm is usually defended by attempts to demonstrate that apparently non-physical things like thoughts, concepts, beliefs and consciousness could be epiphenomena

---

76. Polanyi, "Scientific Outlook: Its sickness and cure," 480.
77. Merriam-Webster, "Materialism."
78. See the discussion in chapter 5 under the heading "The first cause."

that supervene upon the actions of physical brains. These attempts often rely upon apparently valid scientific observations, but involve interpretations of the evidence that seem shaped by presupposition, if not wishful thinking. There are surprising distortions in logic, some of which are discussed in subsequent chapters, and many seem due to an emotional commitment to materialism and a concomitant aversion to religious belief. The noted geneticist, Richard Lewontin has explained that:

> *It is not that the methods and institutions of science somehow compel us to accept a material explanation of the phenomenal world, but, on the contrary, that we are forced by our a priori adherence to material causes to create an apparatus of investigation and a set of concepts that produce material explanations, no matter how counter-intuitive, no matter how mystifying to the uninitiated. Moreover, that materialism is absolute, for we cannot allow a Divine Foot in the door.*[79]

Some people experience strong emotional reactions if their materialistic paradigm is threatened, whether by religion, philosophy, or even their own experiences. Take one example. In 1973 John Taylor, a distinguished physicist who was then professor of mathematics at King's College, London, began a scientific study of claims by the famous psychic, Uri Geller, to be able to engage in telepathy and to bend spoons by mind power alone. After conducting hundreds of tests under strictly controlled conditions he found, to his considerable surprise, that Geller seemed able to do things that Taylor could not explain, whether by fraud or any methods known to science. For present purposes, I am not concerned with the nature of the tests or the validity of Taylor's conclusions, but rather with the emotional responses they elicited. One might have expected skepticism and perhaps some discussion about the adequacy of his protocols, but assumed that the calm, objective attitude that is supposed to pervade scientific circles would have remained unruffled. Instead they seemed to unleash torrents of emotion. Taylor himself was deeply disturbed by his findings. He described the effect as "overpowering" and said that "I felt as if the whole framework with which I viewed the world had suddenly been destroyed. I seemed very naked and vulnerable, surrounded by a hostile, incomprehensible universe. It was many days before I could come to terms with this sensation."[80]

This emotional response does not seem to have been very different in nature or intensity from what might have been expected from a devoutly

---

79. Lewontin, "Review of 'Carl Sagan's The Demon-Haunted World: Science as a Candle in the Dark.'"

80. Taylor, *Super Minds*, 56.

religious person who had found the foundations of his faith suddenly swept away. Some of his colleagues avoided the risk of similar emotional reactions by simply refusing to attend any demonstration of the phenomena he had observed. At least one would not hear of the results being possible and another, a Nobel Prize laureate, insisted that the metal bending could only have been attributable to fraud.[81] Taylor ruefully ventured the suggestion that, whilst the position taken by these fellow scientists may have been understandable, it did not augur well for the future of science.

I have no brief to defend Geller and I bend no spoons, though I have been known to break the odd glass whilst cleaning up after dinner. Nor do I see cutlery bending as the next frontier to be conquered in the research laboratories of advanced nations. Nonetheless, it would be difficult to argue with Taylor's latter observation. Science is advanced by questioning existing beliefs and testing them by experiment and observation; not by mindlessly defending them, turning blind eyes to carefully devised testing regimes, and refusing to accept that the results could have been as reported. Taylor's colleagues had not been asked to consider the claims of a religious zealot or crackpot venturing impetuously into an alien discipline, but the reports of a senior academic colleague who had personally carried out hundreds of tests. And he had not been urging his colleagues to embrace anything supernatural, but to assist him in finding the rational explanation he believed that science "should be able to give."[82] Why did they not respond?

The intensity of Taylor's emotional reaction to the results and the obdurate refusal of his colleagues to look at the evidence that had so unsettled him, raise questions about the capacity of people whose lives have been shaped by commitments to a purely materialist paradigm to bring an open mind to any issues relating to religion or spirituality. Atheists often cite the fact that many eminent scientists reject religious beliefs, but does this really reflect anything more than a world view that cannot accommodate them?

CAN SCIENCE ANSWER RELIGIOUS QUESTIONS?

One may also ask whether science is even capable of addressing questions about the existence of God or other religious issues? Or are techniques devised to investigate the physical universe as impotent to detect anything on a spiritual or immaterial plane as Newtonian physics were to reveal the secrets of sub-atomic particles? It is true that science has provided a factual substratum upon which intellectual edifices have been constructed

81. Taylor, *Super Minds*, 56 and 163.
82. Taylor, *Super Minds*, 56.

by theists and atheists alike. But are scientists really equipped to provide answers to questions about the existence of God, the meaning of life, and the possibly of life after death?

Stephen Jay Gould has suggested that science and religion are 'non-overlapping magisteria' ('NOMA'). In his view, science is concerned with the factual nature of the natural world and religion is concerned with human purposes, meanings, and values.[83] Whilst this formulation may suggest a neat division between facts and values, it has been suggested that the magisteria would inevitably overlap to some extent.[84] Gould himself believed that issues such as the existence of the soul fell into the latter magisterium and explained that his world could neither prove nor disprove such a notion.[85] Richard Dawkins rejects the concept of NOMA altogether, arguing that religion cannot be separated from either the natural world or science.[86] In some respects this may be true, but the supernatural realm, if it exists, is unlikely to be examinable by the techniques that science has designed to investigate the natural world, and scientists are unlikely to wheel out a god detection machine any time soon.

Some things may forever remain beyond the reach of our human faculties. We acknowledge that there are colors we cannot see and sounds we cannot hear. of course, the marvels of modern science have enabled us to surpass the limitations of our physical capacities in the acquisition of knowledge, but even the reach of science is limited. We cannot hope to ever know what is beyond the cosmic horizon, the distance beyond which information could not be retrieved due to properties of general relativity, expansion and physics. Other limitations are suggested by features of quantum mechanics.[87] But could we also have intellectual limitations? Some seem convinced that, given a sufficient window on the cosmos, they would have the capacity to resolve the most profound mysteries and plumb the depths of ultimate reality. Is that realistic? Or was Hitchens right in his suggestion that "some problems will never be resolved by the mammalian equipment of the human cerebral cortex"?

The rich mixture of humanity on this beautiful but beleaguered planet of ours offers an amazing diversity of characters, personalities and abilities. We run the whole gamut from retardation to genius, from naivety to

83. Gould, *Rocks of Ages: Science and Religion in the Fullness of Life.*
84. Collins, *The Language of God,* 95 and 165.
85. Gould, "Nonoverlapping Magisteria."
86. Dawkins, *The God Delusion,* 65.
87. See, for example, Cowan, and Tumulka, *Epistemology of Wave Function Collapse in Quantum Physics.* See also Brooks,"What we'll never know."

cynicism, from unimaginative to visionary. Some are practical types and others seem to spend their days communing with the fairies. Some are mired in superstition and others in intellectual conceit. Most of us like to think that we approach the important issues of life in a rational and well considered manner, and those who have devoted their lives to the pursuit of scientific truths may have more grounds for optimism than most. Yet none of us live in some Elysian field of intellectual purity, but in the real world where our intellect is constantly buffeted by our existing beliefs and feelings. Yes, this is also true of atheists as well as religious believers. During an interview in 2011 Hitchens told Dawkins that: "The reason why most of my friends are non-believers is not particularly that they were engaged in the arguments you and I have been having, but they were made indifferent by compulsory religion at school."[88] Our presuppositions, biases and other emotional baggage affect us in many ways. They may enshroud the truth or, as this observation suggests, even prevent us from looking for it.

Those of us who really want to know the truth may have to seek answers, not in inherited beliefs, fashionable concepts or the pronouncements of a celebrity de jour, but in the more challenging process of conscientiously wresting with the issues. They may have to follow the evidence wherever it may lead, recognize that objectivity is a goal to be striven for amidst the clamor of competing thoughts and feelings and be willing to ask the simple but profoundly important question: 'could I be wrong?'

---

88. Dawkins, Richard, "Never be afraid of stridency."

3

Fundamentalism and Other Distractions

A latter day Odysseus, doing his or her best to peer through the fog, will inevitably be confronted by the emerging shapes of religious fundamentalism and the 'new' atheism. They may loom on opposing sides of the intellectual stream, like Scylla and Charybdis besetting the Strait of Messina, but both pose dangers for the unwary and there are some striking parallels. In particular, both offer certainty and a sense of superiority. Of course, dogmatic atheists cannot offer such alluring prospects as the forgiveness of sins or eternal life, but certainty itself can be a beguiling goal and some people seem to rejoice in their assumption of intellectual superiority whilst others draw consolation from the belief that they have found the courage to face the truth.

RELIGIOUS FUNDAMENTALISM —A REASON FREE ZONE?

The term 'fundamentalism' originally meant nothing more than adherence to the fundamental tenets of a religion,[1] but it has become associated with believers who adopt a literal interpretation of the Bible, the Qur'an or other sacred writings. Fundamentalists generally insist that all the really impor-

---

1. The term seems to have been coined to describe a distinct version of evangelical Christianity that emerged during the early part of the 20th century to defend the "fundamentals of belief" against modernism and liberalism. It was characterized by millenarianism and belief in biblical inerrancy. See, for example, the discussion in Marsden, *Fundamentalism and American Culture*, 4–5.

tant questions of life were answered many centuries ago in these sacred texts. God created the world, formed us, told us what to do and explained the consequences. There is no need for discussion. What more could you need to know? Whilst their commitment to scriptural statements concerning moral issues may lead others to accuse them of inflexibility or even bigotry, many are warm hearted and decent people. Whilst they might regret the fact that not everyone shares their faith, they tend to pray for others rather than sally forth to smite them.

Unfortunately, not everyone who adopts a dogmatic approach to religious texts has such a benevolent attitude. In recent years the fierce intolerance of Islamist terrorists and others described as fundamentalists has changed public perceptions. Some, who would once have described themselves as fundamentalists, would now protest that the term has been debased by its application to people whose hatred and cruelty seem shockingly antithetical to the religions they claim to serve. Yet even groups of believers who deplore such violence as sins against God sometimes exhibit an implacable conviction that they alone adhere to the whole truth. They tend to have strong, authoritarian leaders who proclaim the will of God, often with seemingly boundless confidence. Outsiders may be invited to join them, and they may even seek to recruit them by evangelistic programs of various kinds, but the groups are nonetheless exclusive. You are either in the fold or out of it. There is little tolerance of debate. People who do not share their beliefs may be assumed to be amongst those who are blind because they will not see. Protests about particular aspects of their dogma are likely to be dismissed as defensive quibbles that have no place in a believer's life. One must believe and obey. This may not seem like a great sales pitch, but fundamentalists often draw ardent followers. They articulate a clear call to piety that resonates through the ether of complex, confusing and often competing messages that pervade our modern societies.

Of course, most believers accept the authority of the Bible, the Qur'an or some other holy book, but many interpret particular passages by reference to the contexts in which they were written and in the light of other passages concerning the compassionate nature of God. Hence, few Christians would doubt that Jesus was speaking figuratively when he said that "If anyone comes to me and does not hate father and mother, wife and children, brothers and sisters—yes, even their own life—such a person cannot be my disciple.[2] Fundamentalists generally insist that scriptural passages be interpreted literally, irrespective of the consequences. Some support their obduracy by citing texts, such as "the wisdom of this world is foolishness in

---

2. Luke 14:26.

God's sight,"[3] though it is unlikely that St Paul meant that reason is useless, if not morally seditious, or that it is the mindless, rather than the meek, who shall inherit the earth.

Most religions actually maintain that the ways of God are beyond human understanding. Adherents generally agree that he has chosen to reveal some crucial truths, but there is a wide diversity of beliefs about the nature and content of that revelation. In any event, skeptics who have not been conscious of a call to faith are bound to be nervous about claims that certain things must be true because long dead people were inspired to write them down. The astronomer and cosmologist, Carl Sagan vividly protested that ". . .if God wanted to send us a message, and ancient writings were the only way he could think of doing it, he could have done a better job. And he hardly had to confine himself to writings. Why isn't there a monster crucifix orbiting the Earth? Why isn't the surface of the Moon covered with the Ten Commandments? Why should God be so clear in the Bible and so obscure in the world?"[4]

Sagan might have gone further and asked why God did not bypass any reliance upon messages altogether and simply hardwire knowledge of his existence and commandments into our brains. Of course, any argument based upon speculation about how a supernatural being might be expected to behave itself involves stepping onto very thin ice. We may perhaps engage in some fanciful musing about how we would deal with the human race if we could could take over the running of the universe for a while, but anthropomorphic projection is always a dubious exercise. Any number of dog owners seem convinced that their furry friends are intimately attuned to their feelings and share their views on everything from the morality of the cat next door to nuclear disarmament. But suppose the position were to be examined from the dog's perspective? Could even the most empathic dog really make valid judgments about human behavior based upon its own experience? Faced with waiting outside a butcher's shop, would poor, faithful Slobberchops deduce that a butcher was inside handing out meat to people waving a piece of plastic across a tiny electronic device? Or would he protest that such a person would obviously have locked the door and spent the day eating his own raw sausages? We enjoy many advantages denied to our canine companions but, since the intellectual gulf between us and God would presumably be even greater than that between us and them, are our attempts to use our own experience as a guide to how he should have acted likely to be any more reliable?

3. I Corinthians 3:19.
4. Sagan, *Contact*, 170.

Many religious fundamentalists embrace the concepts of an omnipotent God and a limitless existence to come, but their conception of the universe they currently inhabit is often confined by a self-imposed and staunchly defended myopia. Literal interpretations of specific texts and constant resort to metaphors drawn from earlier ages seem to leave some clinging to pre-medieval world views. They may accept that God made a few other planets and comets to whiz about and lend interest to the sky, but they often seem nervous about any suggestion that the universe may be larger or older than they had imagined. Sagan was clearly bewildered by this attitude. He asked: "How is it that hardly any major religion has looked at science and concluded, 'This is better than we thought! The Universe is much bigger than our prophets said, grander, more subtle, more elegant?' Instead they say, 'No, no, no! My god is a little god, and I want him to stay that way.'"[5]

This criticism of the world's religions was obviously painted with too broad a brush; not all religious believers conceive of God as an elderly man with supernatural powers and not all religious institutions are reluctant to embrace modern scientific discoveries. David, the Old Testament king and psalmist, wrote that "the heavens declare the glory of God"[6] and I suspect that most believers are happy accept that the grandeur of his creation is greater than earlier generations could have known. Unfortunately, some fundamentalists do seem anxious to retain an understanding of the universe that accords with their limited image of God. They may not want God to be 'little,' but they may find it difficult to wholly suppress a fear that a universe as old and expansive as modern cosmology suggests could only have been created by a God who was a master architect, preoccupied with the vast sweep of countless galaxies and perhaps too busy to be concerned with our small tawdry lives. Whatever the reasons, many seem to be afflicted by an intellectual tunnel vision from which they have no wish to be healed. That is unfortunate because, as Sagan suggested, any credible concept of God must be compatible with all we now know of our spectacular universe.

Whilst many theists have offered rational arguments for the existence of God, fundamentalists often seem deeply uncomfortable discussing them and quickly fall back to citing texts. Of course, skeptics find it difficult to grapple logically with a person whose entire argument is effectively encapsulated within the words, 'Thus saith the Lord', a claim that is unlikely to help anyone who doubts that there is a lord to saith anything. Those unpersuaded by such claims may need to look elsewhere for coherent arguments about his existence.

---

5. Sagan, *Pale Blue Dot: A Vision of the Human Future in Space*, 50.
6. Psalm 19:1.

A RESPONSE—EQUAL AND OPPOSITE VEHEMENCE?

Even if one ignores those temperate souls who may think they are atheists when I have classified them as agnostics, the ranks of those convinced there is no god obviously include a wide diversity of people (though most would probably baulk at describing atheism as "a broad church"). Almost all would claim that atheism represents a triumph of reason over superstition and few would concede that their beliefs may be anything but the product of a rational approach to the truth, wholly uninfluenced by presuppositions or emotional considerations. In the face of such conviction it may seem churlish to remind them that they share the same human frailties as those who embrace religious beliefs, but a skeptic might doubt that they alone form their beliefs in an emotional vacuum. Some express their views in tones suggestive of a detached, even vaguely apologetic, objectivity, but emotions do not sway only the volatile and aggressive; they may subtly influence even the most erudite and apparently phlegmatic. And there are many atheists whose emotional reactions seem to permeate everything they write or say about their beliefs.

Some seem to have embraced atheism as an emotional reaction to life experiences and live behind staunchly maintained palisades from which any challenges to their beliefs may be rebuffed with vehemence, derision, and patronizing non sequiturs. I am never quite sure whether some of the more aggressive discount the possibility of God due to some sort of logical analysis or whether they are just too angry with him to acknowledge his existence. One avowed atheist told me, "I curse God every day." He was not mollified by the suggestion that this meant he was not an atheist at all; merely a theist who was grumpy with God. But it is not only the odd irascible character whose atheism seems to reflect antagonism to the very concept of God. The influence of emotion is often revealed in contemporary, atheistic literature. One of the more clearly articulated expressions of antipathy has been provided by the well known philosopher, Thomas Nagel:

> "... I want atheism to be true and am made uneasy by the fact that some of the most intelligent and well-informed people I know are religious believers. It isn't just that I don't believe in God and naturally hope there is no God! I don't want there to be a God; I don't want the universe to be like that."[7]

One can almost feel the anxiety seeping through the intellectual defenses he has erected. Yet this was a remarkably candid statement made by an

---

7. Nagel, *The Last Word*, 130–131.

intelligent man who was acutely aware of the strength of his feelings. Sadly, there are many others who are less self-analytical and more contemptuous of anyone who professes some form of religious belief.

The current fervor is actually more than a little bemusing. Yes, I know the rationale; it's all supposed to be about upholding the truth, liberating the innocent from the chains of superstition and undermining the bases for religiously motivated violence and other evils. But there is such a note of faith and ardor about it all. Many of the more evangelistic atheists claim the intellectual high ground and dress up their articles of faith with well articulated phrases, but they display the same emotional commitment as the most fervid holy rollers. And some of it is charmingly naive. Even Richard Dawkins asks us to join John Lennon in imagining, if not singing about, a world without religion in which everyone would "live in peace" and "be as one." I like the song, but I am not persuaded that religion is the source of all evil, that atheists are in a state of innocence like Adam before he sank his teeth into the apple, or that people do not resort to violence over other issues such as sex, money or power. What about the survival of the fittest? Was all that biting and snarling due to religion polluting the genetic soup? Would the predators have otherwise morphed into vegetarians and shared their salads with the deer and the rabbits?

It is undeniable that horrendous things have been done in the name of religion. Writers, including Dawkins, Christopher Hitchens, and Daniel Dennett, have produced numerous pages belaboring this point with due vehemence. And they have had no need for exaggeration. No one with any integrity and knowledge of history could sensibly defend the world's religions from the chronicles of violence and repression they have sometimes spawned. The dangers posed by the some of the more extreme forms are well known: the demonization of unbelievers, the murder of dissidents, the subjugation of women, and terrorism.[8] The underlying premise of many so-called 'jihadis' seems to be that fidelity to a god of love and mercy is best expressed in murder and unspeakable cruelty. Social commentators suggest that we now live in "a different world," but terrorism is not a new phenomenon and the cycle of bloodshed they rightly decry is merely the current chapter in a long history of religiously based violence. Such irrational cruelty has not been confined to the adherents of any one religion. Incas, Mayans and others engaged in human sacrifice. The Thuggee sect in Asia murdered perhaps 2 million people as sacrifices to appease the goddess Kali. Christians slaughtered thousands in the crusades and introduced the

---

8. Vorster, "Perspectives on the Core Characteristics of Religious Fundamentalism Today."

horrific tortures of the Inquisition. Hindus followed the practice of sati in which a widow was expected to burn herself to death on her husband's pyre. Whilst such acts may have been contrary to central tenets of the religions they were supposed to have served, they were not mere aberrations, but practices maintained for centuries and, despite their diversity, they reflected common assumptions that cruelty can be justified or even required by religion.

Nor can this chronicle of violence be dismissed as the product of earlier ages that has no continuing relevance. Our contemporary news bulletins provide daily reminders of horrors such as religiously motivated terrorism, genital mutilation or the shocking abuse of children entrusted to people claiming to serve God. These are appalling crimes and they cannot be justified or condoned by apologetic phrases like "honor killings"—an obscene euphemism for murdering one's own children or other family members due to embarrassment at their behavior—or by politically trendy but ultimately shameful appeals to history and culture. It is undeniable that some of the worst examples of brutality and depravity the world has ever witnessed have been committed by those ostensibly worshipping a god of love.

On the other hand, atheists sometimes single out religion as if it were the sole cause of conflicts actually driven by many factors including nationalism, tribalism, territorial disputes and historic grievances.[9] In fact, the world often reels from violence that has little, if anything, to do with religion. Neither of the world wars fought last century were crusades against enemies perceived as infidels. Nor were the Korean or Vietnam wars. Even John Lennon would probably have acknowledged that Stalin was as evil as Torquemada and the gulags and concentration camps run by overtly atheistic regimes have never reflected the peace and unity he envisaged. Ironically, Lennon, who famously suggested that without religion there would be "nothing to kill or die for," was himself murdered by by someone who had found something else to kill for: notoriety. His assailant had thought that by killing Lennon "he would become somebody."[10]

Those interested in a balanced view of history might also point out that religious people founded the first poorhouses, orphanages, homes for the aged, hospitals and other facilities such as leper colonies to care for the sick and dying. They established schools and universities that were the only

---

9. For a discussion of this issue see Armstrong, *Fields of Blood: Religion and the History of Violence*.

10. Wilkinson, Matt, "John Lennon's Murderer Reveals Motive Behind Fatal Shooting," *NME*, September 17, 2010, https://www.nme.com/news/music/john-lennon-55-1299752.

cradles of education for many centuries and they took leading roles in many campaigns for social reform such as the fight against slavery.

There is also the obvious objection that, in railing against atrocities attributed to 'religion', there is a perhaps understandable tendency for atheists to conflate all religions and all who hold some form of religious belief. The protestations of religious believers who are just as incensed at such conduct as Hitchens, Dawkins et al tend to be ignored, apparently on the basis that anyone who is not an atheist must be taken to have joined with the terrorists and other depraved fanatics in a common cause or, at least, to have contributed to an atmosphere in which violence could be fomented. On this unstated but clearly implicit line of reasoning, committed pacifists like the Quakers must be blamed for the violence they have consistently opposed and, presumably, even the victims, most of whom also believe in God, must share the blame for their own misfortune.

Of course, none of these observations offer any excuse for the appalling levels of religiously-based violence in many parts of the world or for the oppression under which so many are forced to live out their meagre lives. Nor do they provide any excuse for those who remain silent. No matter what our religious views may be, we should all stand against such blatant injustice.

But what is all this supposed to prove? That there can't be a god because some believers are bad people? Or that belief in a god must be delusional because it has sometimes led people to do bad things? Even Hitchens seems to flirt with arguments of this kind. One of the "provisional conclusions" he draws from the maltreatment of children by religious people and institutions is that religion is manufactured.[11] This is strikingly illogical. There were sun worshippers who engaged in human sacrifices. Is there no sun? Terrible crimes were committed in the name of the British monarchy. Is Queen Elizabeth a myth dreamed up to placate some psychological need the English have for pageantry? Hitchens was a wonderfully intelligent and articulate man who, in any other contexts, would have recognized a non sequitur when he saw one. But none of us are immune from the seductive influence of emotional reactions and, when it comes to religion, it is not only believers who lose objectivity.

In fact, whilst atheists have often taken delight in refuting arguments said to prove the existence of God, few seem to question the validity of the arguments they seem to think underpin their own beliefs. Many react with what seems to be a real sense of grievance when asked to go beyond oft-rehearsed criticisms of religious beliefs and defend their own position by

11. Hitchens, *God is not Great*, 52.

explaining why they are convinced that there is no god. Some seem to feel that this is an unfair request. If pressed, they may offer airy platitudes about rationalism and science, but there is often a disturbing paucity of logical reasoning. Of course, this observations could also be made of many religious adherents, but atheists insist that their beliefs are driven by reason and logic alone. So, when put on the spot, how do they defend them?

ARE ATHEISTS REALLY SUPERIOR BEINGS?

First, many simply lean back in their chairs, clasp their hands together behind the heads, smile condescendingly and explain that it is all obvious to them. This attitude also permeates much of the literature. There may be confident statements about Darwin's theory of natural selection, perhaps supported by accounts of how scientific attitudes emerged from superstition and dogma, and occasional references to psychological factors said to explain why the naive believe in God, but the validity of atheism tends to be assumed as obvious, at least to the intelligentsia. Whilst Christians and others who believe in God are sometimes accused of displaying a "holier than thou" attitude, atheists often adopt a "smarter than thou" attitude; tacitly implying that you would see the light if only you were as intelligent as they are. In fact, Dawkins has put this quite explicitly: "Highly intelligent people are mostly atheists. Not a single member of either house of Congress admits to being an atheist. It just doesn't add up. Either they're stupid or they're lying."[12] That seems to reflect the way many atheists see humanity; those who agree with them, even if willing to lie rather than admit it, are intelligent and everyone else is stupid. Some, including Dawkins and Dennett, have actually suggested that atheists should be called 'brights'. Despite his own fervent atheism, even Hitchens described this self-congratulatory proposal as "cringe-making"[13] and it seems more likely to attract derision than plaudits, though a fair-minded person should perhaps acknowledge their modesty in declining to go further and call themselves "sunbeams."

In most cases this assumption of intellectual superiority is expressed in relatively benign ways. Atheists may be smug and they may patronize anyone with religious beliefs, but their condescension is sometimes leavened by sympathy for those they see as enmeshed in superstition and potentially damaging dogma. The desire to help people shrug off chains they feel have been forged from such factors can be an endearing quality, as anyone who has reflected upon the plight of women and girls under rule of the

---

12. Quoted by Wolf, in "The Church of the Non-believers".
13. Hitchens, *God is not Great*, 5.

Taliban should readily acknowledge. At the other extreme are those who seem determined to demonstrate that bigotry is not confined to religious fundamentalism. The vehemence of their denunciations sometimes betrays deep resentment towards those outside the atheistic fold. Some seem to relish trampling over their sensibilities of others, openly sneering at their deeply held beliefs with intentionally offensive phrases such as "your invisible friend" and otherwise suggesting that anyone who clings to religious beliefs should be flagellated for refusing to see the light.

Such is the depth of hostility that even other atheists are not exempt from their bile. Following the publication of his book, "Religion for Atheists: a Non-Believer's Guide to the Uses of Religion" Alain de Botton was treated to tirades of abuse and even threats of violence. His crime? He had dared suggest that atheists might learn from some aspects of religious practice, such as the importance of community and emphases on love and compassion. As an agnostic writer observed, this was "enough to bring the full force of a neo-atheist fatwa crashing down on his head."[14] Many people sometimes find that they can learn more from those who disagree with them than from those who share their views, but Botton's vitriolic critics apparently saw any such suggestion as a scandalous heresy. This startling outburst left many bemused. Sayeeda Warsi, the first Muslim to become co-chairperson of the British Conservative Party, asked "Why are the followers of reason so unreasonable?"[15] There was no wholly reassuring reply.

A few also claim the high moral ground, most notably by claiming that atheists are braver than lesser mortals. They suggest that you too would see the light if, like them, you had the courage to face the truth and live with the implications of a godless universe. It would require courage to accept that one is an orphan within a pitiless universe and that death will bring nothing but eternal oblivion, but that does not demonstrate that atheism is well-founded.

In fact, the rising tide of fervor has troubled many atheists. Joseph Hoffmann has warned his fellow atheists that they run the risk of "turning their social solidarity into tent revivals or support groups." Yet even he suggests that atheism tends to be associated with virtuous qualities, including courage, imagination and, perhaps ironically, social tolerance.[16] The last point may have been lost on poor, shell-shocked Botton, but the overall message is clear: one is asked to accept that atheists must be right because they are superior people.

14. Appleyard, "The God Wars."
15. Appleyard, "The God Wars."
16. Hoffmann, "Five Good Things about Atheism."

A BURDEN OF PROOF?

Second, there are arguments based on an assumption that if the available evidence doesn't prove that something exists, then the converse must true: QED God doesn't exist. Yes, there really are people who seem to believe there is no need to prove a negative proposition. Of course, most people who believe in God maintain that there is ample evidence of his existence and I will discuss that claim later but, for present purposes, I am content to echo the truism that "absence of evidence is not evidence of absence."[17] That should be obvious to even the most emotional atheist. If arguments based solely upon the perceived insufficiency of evidence were valid, earlier generations of Europeans would have had no difficulty in proving the non-existence of America or Australia.

Some of the more erudite atheists have tried to rationalize this approach by claiming that those who assert the existence of God bear a burden of proof,[18] and that, if it is not discharged, the contrary may reasonably be assumed. Hitchens has succinctly crystallized this proposition: "what can be asserted without evidence can be dismissed without evidence."[19] This couplet, now known as "Hitchens' razor," is presumably a gloss on the old Latin proverb *"quod gratis asseritur, gratis negatur"*[20] (what is asserted gratuitously may be denied gratuitously). Richard Dawkins has also taken up this theme, arguing that "the onus is on you to say why, the onus is not on the rest of us to say why not."[21] These aphorisms are concise, pithy and, in the context in which they are invoked, arrant nonsense. The objective truth or falsity of a factual proposition is not like a candle whose flame leans in one direction or the other according to a rhetorical breeze labelled an "onus of proof."

As other atheists have readily conceded, such a proposition is not recognized in the sciences.[22] It is true that in legal proceedings the general rule is that "he who asserts a wrong has been committed must prove it."[23]

---

17. Garvey, Brian, "Absence of Evidence, Evidence of Absence, and the Atheist's Teapot," 9.

18. This is an old claim. See, for example, Fury, *History of Freedom of Thought*, 20. It is developed in Flew, *The Presumption of Atheism and Other Philosophical Essays on God, Freedom, and Immortality*.

19. Hitchens, *God is not Great*, 150.

20. Stone, *The Routledge Dictionary of Latin Quotations*, 101.

21. Dawkins Richard, *Militant Atheism*—ted.com. February, 2002, https://www.ted.com/talks/richard_dawkins_on_militant_atheism.

22. Lowder, "Is a Sound Argument for the Nonexistence of a God Even Possible?"

23. See, for example, the judgment of the House of Lords in *Royal Bank of Scotland*

This is an indispensable element of both criminal and civil trials, though in the latter proof is required only on the balance of probabilities rather than beyond reasonable doubt. But this rule is not rooted in logic; it is rooted in human rights and fairness. It reflects a fundamental principle that no one should be convicted of a crime or have their property taken from them unless the allegations against them have been proven to be true. These well-known legal rules obviously have no application to everyday discussions or arguments and they certainly offer no justification for anyone to proclaim, "I must be right unless you can prove I am wrong." One can well imagine the reception that Dawkins might receive if he said something like that at a scientific conference whilst debating a controversial proposition in his field of genetics.

If you do not know whether something is true, recourse to an imagined onus of proof will not change the objective reality, dispel your ignorance or make it safe to rely upon an unfounded assumption. This proposition should be obvious to anyone, let alone to people lauded as intellectuals. And in reality, of course, it is. Even the most devoted acolytes of Hitchens or Dawkins would baulk at leaving their homes uninsured on the basis that there is no evidence that they are about to be burgled. Scientists spend their lives seeking new discoveries, not merely dismissing any still unproven possibilities. The world's great explorers set sail in the hope of finding new lands when no one had satisfied an onus of proof as to their existence. And America and Australia did not wink into existence only when the native inhabitants discharged some imaginary onus of proving they were actually there. It is absurd to have to belabor such an obvious point, but a surprising number of atheists seem to take this nonsense about an onus of proof seriously. So let me put this simply: if you cannot ascertain the truth, then you have to live with the resultant uncertainty, not simply declare that one possibility must be true because no one has proved the other. The relevant question is not who must carry the burden of proof in some hypothetical debate but what, if anything, does the evidence reveal?

WHO NEEDS EVIDENCE?

Yet Bertrand Russell went even further, dismissing the need for evidence altogether. Why? Well, he explained, if he were to suggest that a teapot was revolving around the sun in an elliptical orbit, nobody would be able to disprove it. Nonetheless, no sensible person would think that this would

---

v *Etridge*, paragraph 13.

be sufficiently likely to be taken into account.[24] Hence one may dismiss any possibility that God exists. Russell was perhaps the most famous philosopher of his generation and it is surprising that he felt driven to rely upon a derisive analogy—a somewhat ironic approach given that Copernicus and other scientific pioneers were initially subjected to ridicule and derision by religious people.[25] Of course, there is nothing intrinsically wrong with resort to an analogy provided it offers a reasonable parallel to the relevant features of the scenario in question and explains or illuminates a genuine argument, but Russell's analogy fails to meet either of these conditions. It is merely an exercise in hyperbole, invoked to emphasize his subjective impression that the existence of the Christian God was unlikely.[26] Another atheist, Sigmund Freud, once observed that analogies prove nothing, but they can make one feel more at home.[27] Perhaps Russell hoped that his hypothetical teapot would make others feel more at home accepting an assertion unsupported by evidence.

Despite its obvious lack of cogency, Dawkins and others have jumped onto this rickety bandwagon and added other silly analogies such as giant green lobsters and a flying spaghetti monster.[28] Such absurd scenarios again seem intended to lend rhetorical impact to opinions that the existence of God is unlikely, but Dawkins goes further, venturing the suggestion that Russell's teapot actually "demonstrates that the ubiquity of the belief in God, as compared with belief in celestial teapots, does not shift the burden of proof in logic." This is one of the most illogical appeals to logic I have ever read.

At the risk of again belaboring the obvious, one may wonder whether Dawkins and others who seem impressed by this nonsense would have been equally enthusiastic if Russell had compared his hypothetical floating teapot with the possibility of quasars, quarks, the HIV virus or other things the existence of which had not been verified at the time he was writing. Or if a latter day Russell were to dismiss multiverse concepts as no more credible than an infinite array of orbiting teapots. Courtrooms often resound with the 'forensic flourishes' of advocates addressing juries and many rely on analogies, but few would risk undermining the credibility of their arguments by suggesting that A could not exist because it would be ridiculous to

---

24. Russell, Bertrand,"Is There a God?," 548.
25. Padmanaghan, "Dawn of Science: 14 The Galilean World."
26. Garvey, "Absence of evidence, evidence of absence, and the atheist's teapot."
27. Cited by Nordquist,"The Value of Analogies in Writing and Speech."
28. Dawkins, *The God Delusion*, 76.

imagine B. Opinions must stand or fall on the basis of evidence and rational argument; not by analogies that add neither cogency nor clarity.

THE NEED FOR RATIONAL ASSESSMENT

It is often suggested that the rising tide of scientific information has swept aside the basis for religious belief like incoming waves swamping the sand castles left by optimistic children. Yet many of those who are keen to promote this view seem unable to move beyond emotive responses, rhetoric and defensive sophistries. Whilst some advert to the theory of natural selection and others to the problem of human suffering, many who dismiss religious beliefs as superstition seem to just embrace atheism as if it were the default position. On the other hand, many Christians and other religious believers adhere to beliefs they have held since childhood and are central to their sense of security and even self identity. For them, the call to faith may be a moral imperative. They belong to church communities of like-minded people who affirm the truths of the scriptures and insist that the truth has been divinely revealed. Many would insist that they know the reality of God from the "inner witness" within their own lives and would think that a debate with those who question their beliefs would be as pointless as a debate with strangers about whether family members love them. Some fundamentalists are keen to keen to defend their views that we live in a universe only a few thousand years old and there are some scholarly books written in defense of belief in God. But few people seem to make any serious attempt to approach the great questions of life with a commitment to considering the issues in a fair and objective manner and asking whether there is any real evidence that God exists or, conversely, whether we live in a godless universe.

4

The Case for Atheism

Atheists are neither thin on the ground nor reticent about their opinions, and an abundance of literature has been produced since people like Diagoras of Melos, Theodorus of Cyrene, and the Roman poet, Lucretious, first expressed their disdain for religion in the centuries prior to the birth of Christ. But this is not an academic treatise and I feel no need to drag you through an ideological pub crawl to taste countless brews of substantially the same ale. Instead, I will concentrate on the arguments advanced by Richard Dawkins whom I have chosen for a number of reasons: he is an eminent scientist, a competent writer and the most prominent of the contemporary atheists. Furthermore, he has attempted to encapsulate the case for atheism in a single chapter, optimistically entitled, "Why there almost certainly is no God."[1]

It is an interesting chapter and one well worth reading but, at the risk of offending his more ardent followers, I must say that the most striking thing about it is its obvious failure to fulfill the promise implicit in the title. His scientific knowledge is impressive and he has obviously given much thought to the issues covered, but his arguments offer surprisingly little support for this contention. Much of the chapter is devoted to defending natural selection, an exercise undertaken in more detail in his subsequent book, *The Greatest Show on Earth* (2009), and in attempting to refute arguments that some people have advanced in support of their beliefs that God does exist. The few arguments intended to prove the converse are surprisingly limited and, whilst some of the factual bases for them are well articulated,

---

1. Dawkins, *The God Delusion*, 137.

the inferences he seeks to draw from them are often tenuous, if not wholly invalid. But do not accept my opinion; judge for yourself.

A CURIOUS CLAIM ABOUT PROBABILITY

Dawkins begins with an argument from improbability which, he suggests, is seen by many theists as convincing evidence for the existence of God when, "properly deployed," the argument actually "comes close" to proving that God does not exist. He follows this assertion with a curious statement: "My name for the statistical demonstration that God almost certainly does not exist is the Ultimate Boeing 747 Gambit."[2] This name is taken from a phrase attributed to Sir Fred Hoyle, who expressed the view that the probability of life originating on earth is no greater than the chance that a hurricane sweeping through a scrapyard would result in the assembly of a Boeing 747. Dawkins describes this as "the creationist's favorite argument," but says that it is "an argument that could only be made by somebody who doesn't understand the first thing about natural selection; somebody who thinks natural selection is a theory of chance whereas—in the relevant sense of chance—it is the opposite." Whilst I have considerable respect for Dawkins' contribution to knowledge as a scientist, I must say that at least some of these assertions are nonsense.

First, it is ridiculous to suggest that Hoyle did not understand the concept of natural selection. In fact, Hoyle was a distinguished astronomer and mathematician who was Plumian Professor of Astronomy and Experimental Philosophy at Cambridge University, a member of the Royal Society and founding director of the Institute of Theoretical Astronomy. He was also the first to establish the concept of nucleosynthesis in stars.[3] Many were surprised that he did not share the Nobel prize later awarded to two of his colleagues,[4] an omission that Dawkins himself describes as mysterious.[5] He was also an atheist.[6] When working on the mechanics of stellar nucleosynthesis he realized that the triple alpha process by which helium-4 nuclei (or alpha particles) are transformed into carbon would require specific reso-

2. Dawkins, *The God Delusion*, 137.

3. Fowler, "William A. Fowler—Autobiography."

4. McKie, "Fred Hoyle: the scientist whose rudeness cost him a Nobel prize." There was some suspicion that Hoyle was denied the third place in the prize because of an earlier public disagreement with the prize awarded in 1974. Mitton *Fred Hoyle a life in science*," 301–305,

5. Dawkins, *The God Delusion*, 171.

6. Gregory, *Fred Hoyle's Universe*. Oxford, 143.

nance energy and spin. Subsequent experiments confirmed his predictions about the energy levels in the carbon nucleus, but he calculated that their spontaneous occurrence would have been highly improbable statistically. It was this observation that first led him to suggest that "some super-calculating intellect" must have designed the properties of the carbon atom,[7] a thought that left him "greatly shaken."[8]

Second, natural selection does not offer a wholly satisfactory answer to the concerns Hoyle raised. He argued that life on earth could not be attributed to abiogenesis, that is by spontaneous generation from inanimate matter. It was the implausibility of abiogenesis as an explanation for the origin of life on earth that Hoyle compared with the chance assembly of a Boeing 747,[9] not the "alleged improbability" of natural selection as Dawkins has suggested.[10] The theory of natural selection is obviously concerned with the evolution of living organisms from earlier life forms. It does not offer any explanation for the emergence of life itself. Abiogenesis was not addressed by Darwin in his ground breaking book, *On the Origin of the Species*, and whilst he later ventured a very tentative suggestion that life may have begun in a "warm little pond" he never incorporated it into his theory.[11]

Hoyle famously said that, "If one proceeds directly and straightforwardly in this matter, without being deflected by a fear of incurring the wrath of scientific opinion, one arrives at the conclusion that biomaterials with their amazing measure or order must be the outcome of intelligent design."[12] Of course, some have disagreed with his conclusions,[13] but others have come to a similar view. For example, Hugh Ross, has calculated that the chances of life emerging by chance from the processes triggered by the Big Bang were less than one in a trillion trillion trillion trillion trillion trillion trillion trillion trillion trillion.[14] Yet, rhetoric aside, Dawkins seems to offer nothing in response to Hoyle's conclusion about abiogenesis, except the obvious non-sequitur that seemingly improb-

---

7. Hoyle, "The Universe: Past and Present Reflections."

8. Hoyle, "The Universe: Past and Present Reflections." See also Hoyle, *The Intelligent Universe*.

9 See the discussion under the heading, "Life," in chapter 6.

10. Dawkins, Richard, *The Blind Watchmaker*, London: Penguin, 2006, 233–4.

11. See the discussion under the heading, "Life," in chapter 6.

12. Hoyle, Evolution from Space, Omni Lecture. See also Hoyle, Fred, Evolution from Space, 27–28.

13. See for example, Musgrave, Ian, "Lies, Damned Lies, Statistics, and Probability of Abiogenesis Calculations"; and Smith, *The Problems of Biology*, 49 et seq.

14. Ross, Hugh, *The Creator and the Cosmos*, Colorado Springs,: NavPress, 2001, 198.

able things may evolve as a consequence of natural selection. He does not challenge Hoyle's calculations and does not attempt to explain how natural selection could explain the phenomena that shook Hoyle's atheism and led him to speculate about the existence of a higher intellect.

Third, Dawkins' suggestion that Hoyle's metaphor almost proves that God does not exist would defy even the most imaginative feat of mental gymnastics. Evidence that an event did not occur by chance, rationally suggests that someone caused it to happen. It does not almost prove that no such person or being exists. Neither Hoyle's opinion about the extraordinary improbability of terrestrial life arising by abiogenesis, nor his grudging suggestion that a superior intellect must have been responsible for the atomic structure of carbon, could conceivably support the contrary proposition that no such intellect exists. Dawkins' startling claim that "God is the ultimate Boeing 747" seems to be based on nothing more than his belief that the existence of a designer "has got to be" at least as unlikely as that of any entity, however statistically improbable. No statistical demonstration as to the non-existence of God is ever provided, and one is left to assume that he actually believes this conclusion can be derived from Hoyle's analysis. The trick would seem to involve taking Hoyle's calculations that the likelihood of life emerging on earth spontaneously was infinitesimally small, adding Dawkins' oracular pronouncement that the existence of God must be even more unlikely, and concluding, therefore, that the statistical improbability of life arising without the involvement of a super intellect somehow demonstrates the absence of a super intellect. If I were one of Dawkins' many acolytes I would like to imagine that he may have had a more sensible argument in mind that he had merely been unable to articulate, but that would require a considerable leap of faith.

A PLEA FOR CONSCIOUSNESS RAISING

In the next section of the chapter Dawkins actually calls for 'consciousness raising', a concept he borrows from feminism and seeks to apply to natural selection. This is not an entirely reassuring exercise. In feminism, the call for consciousness raising has been a form of political and social activism intended to highlight issues such as sexual assault and domestic violence and evoke empathy and support. Dawkins invokes the concept as an argumentative device, repeatedly suggesting that those who disagree with him about what the evidence reveals concerning the existence of God "have not had their consciousness raised by natural selection."[15] There may be many

15. See, for example, Dawkins, *The God Delusion* at 175.

people who fail to understand the potential for natural selection to explain apparently unlikely developments and I do not begrudge him the odd lapse into hyperbole, but one is entitled to be wary of his claim that those who seek the suggested heightened consciousness will come to agree with him. Propositions of this kind are found more often in religious or new age literature than in scientific or philosophical debates. I am sure that Dawkins would have instantly recognized this danger had he read a suggestion by a popular guru that those doubting some tenet of his/her teaching could not have had their consciousness raised by theological study or meditation. Amused skeptics may respond to pleas of this kind by suggesting that their consciousness is sufficiently elevated; it is the quality of analysis that has not risen to the necessary level.

THE NEED FOR AN 'ABRACADABRA!' MOMENT OF CREATION

Dawkins goes on to suggest that one must logically choose between natural selection and creation. This assumption underlies many of his subsequent arguments. He expresses continuing astonishment at those theists who have failed to heed the call and actually see natural selection as a means by which God may have chosen to achieve an unfolding creation. This is surprisingly naive.

It is true that many fundamentalist and evangelical Christians share his view that the theory of natural selection is incompatible with the belief in divine creation, if only because they see the necessary time scale as contrary to Biblical teaching. Most adopt a literal interpretation of the first chapter of Genesis and assume that the reference to six days must be taken to mean six periods of 24 hours.[16] This approach was also taken by some early church leaders such as St Victorinus[17] and St Basil the Great,[18] but even then it was not a universal Christian view.[19] Some cited Psalm 90 as

---

16. See, for example, Gish, Duane , *Creation Scientists Answer Their Critics* (1993) Dallas: Institute for Creation Research, 1993; Sarfati, Jonathan, *Refuting Evolution* (5th ed) Powder Springs: Creation Book Publishers, 2012; and Johnson, Phillip, *Darwin on Trial*, Washington: Regnery Publishing, 2015.

17. St Victorinus, *On the Creation of the World,* Translated by Robert Ernest Wallis, Ante-Nicene Fathers, Vol. 7. Edited by Alexander Roberts, James Donaldson, and A. Cleveland Coxe. (Buffalo, NY: Christian Literature Publishing Co., 1886.

18. St Basil, *Hexaemeron*, homily 2, paragraph 8. Translated by B.l. Jackson, St Basil the Great Resources Online and in Print, Elpenor, https://www.elpenor.org/basil/hexaemeron.asp.

19. Ku, John Baptist, "Interpreting Genesis 1 with the Fathers of the Church."

evidence that a thousand years were like a day in the eyes of the Lord and this led St Cyprian to conclude that the world was created in 7,000 years.[20] Others, including Clement of Alexandria[21] Origen of Alexandria[22] and St Augustine of Hippo,[23] thought that time itself was formed with the physical universe and considered the story of the creation being completed in six days to be allegorical. A literal interpretation is difficult to sustain since the sun is said not to have been created until the fourth "day." This point was made by Origen, writing in the 3rd century:

> *Now who is there, pray, possessed of understanding, that will regard the statement as appropriate, that the first day, and the second, and the third, in which also both evening and morning are mentioned, existed without sun, and moon, and stars — the first day even without a sky? And who is found so ignorant as to suppose that God, as if He had been a husbandman, planted trees in paradise, in Eden towards the east, and a tree of life in it, i.e., a visible and palpable tree of wood, so that anyone eating of it with bodily teeth should obtain life, and, eating again of another tree, should come to the knowledge of good and evil? No one, I think, can doubt that the statement that God walked in the afternoon in paradise, and that Adam lay hid under a tree, is related figuratively in Scripture, that some mystical meaning may be indicated by it.*[24]

Many modern Christians accept natural selection[25] and tend to see the early chapters of Genesis, not as a divinely inspired explanation of cosmology and other branches of science, but as prophetic or allegorical literature concerning humanity's intended relationship with God and perhaps as a refutation of earlier pagan beliefs.[26] As Terence Fretheim, puts it, the primary concerns

---

20. St Cyprian referred to "the first seven days in the divine arrangement containing seven thousand of years," *Treatises*, treatise 11 paragraph 11.

21. Clement, *Miscellanies*, 6:16.

22. Origen, *De Principiis*, book IV, 16.

23. Augustine, Saint "On Genesis: A refutation of the Manichees," I.23.35–41 and I.25.43; and Augustine, Saint "Excursus on Time," *The Confessions*, Book 11.

24. Origen, *De Principiis*, book IV, 16.

25. A survey of Americans carried out in April 2013 revealed that, whilst 64% of white evangelical Protestants believe that that humans have existed in their present form since the beginning of time, most Catholics and white mainline Protestants believe that humans and other living things evolved over time. Pew Research Center, *Public's Views on Human Evolution*.

26. See, for example, the discussion in Frye, *Is God a Creationist? The Religious Case Against Creation-Science*.

of Genesis are theological and kerygmatic.[27] Some maintain that a misconceived insistence that the world was literally created in six days merely creates an distraction from the essential message that God not only created the cosmos and all it contains, but that he also calls people to maintain an appropriate relationship with him and his creation. Maimonides (1138–1204) went further, actually arguing that the belief that fidelity to the Bible required literal interpretation was a stumbling block to love of God and led to a material conception of God, which he suggested amounted to idolatry.[28] I will leave the theological debate to others more qualified; I merely wish to emphasize the point, made by Kenneth Miller in *Finding Darwin's God*[29], that there is nothing inherently incompatible between evolutionary theory and belief in God.

One can only surmise that Dawkins' raised eyebrows must have been locked in place for a long time. In a letter written in May 1879, less than 3 years before his death, Darwin himself said that: "It seems to me absurd to doubt that a man may be an ardent Theist and an evolutionist."[30] On the Sunday after his funeral at Westminster Abbey in 1882 the Bishop of Carlisle expressly disclaimed the notion "that there is a necessary conflict between a knowledge of Nature and a belief in God..."[31] The Islamic scholar, Jamal al-Din al-Afghani (1838–1897), insisted that God made human souls but accepted the Darwinian theory of evolution and claimed that the principle of natural selection was known in pre-Islamic and Islamic cultures.[32] The Jesuit priest, Teilhard de Chardin accepted the concept of natural selection as early as 1940,[33] though he dismissed the 'quasi philosophical' suggestions that this had made God superfluous and reduced reality to matter.[34] Pope Pius XII agreed that evolution was a legitimate subject of research in 1950[35] and it was accepted by his successor, John Paul, in 1996.[36] In 1999 Stephen Jay Gould said that almost all religious leaders had taken the same side as scientists in relation to evolution.[37] And in 2006 Rowan Williams,

27. Fretheim, Terence, *The New Interpreter's Bible*, 326.
28. Seeskin, *Maimonides*.
29. Miller, *Finding Darwin's God*.
30. Darwin, "Letter 12041 Darwin C. R. To Fordyce, John 7 May 1879."
31. Westminster Abbey, "Charles Darwin."
32. Glick, *The Comparative Reception of Darwinism* Chicago, 384.
33. Teilhard, *The Phenomenon of Man*, 219.
34. Delfgaauw, Bernard, *Evolution: The Theory of Teilhard de Chardin*, 59.
35. Pope Pius XII, *Humani Generis*, 1950.
36. Gould, *Rock of Ages*, 75–82.
37. Gould, *Rock of Ages*, 148.

then Archbishop of Canterbury, observed that for "most of the history of Christianity there's been an awareness that a belief that everything depends on the creative act of God, is quite compatible with a degree of uncertainty or latitude about how precisely that unfolds in creative time."[38] Whilst some still maintain Bishop Ussher's view that the world was created on Sunday 23 October 4004 BC,[39] there has been ample time for Dawkins and other atheists to realize that natural selection has been widely accepted within mainstream religions.[40]

Of course, all life is evolutionary, even the development of our own bodies, and despite our human limitations we have consciously used evolutionary processes to produce desired outcomes. We have created a multiplicity of animal breeds, flowers and vegetables by selective breeding over successive generations. Why should a god who created natural laws and processes not have used them? Yet, whilst there is no logical reason to imagine that the concept of evolution is inconsistent with intention or design, Dawkins insists that God would not have have created the universe by evolutionary processes. Why? Well, this would have been lazy. No, I am not making this up; this is the argument he advances in "The God Delusion."[41] Dawkins was ranked the world's leading intellectual in a poll conducted by Prospect Magazine in 2013,[42] yet this amusingly naive response was apparently the best he could offer. He presumably felt competent to judge whether a more direct act of creation, perhaps prefaced by some magic words or a thunderclap, would have proven more physically taxing for a cosmic creator, and confident that, if God really existed, he would have moved with greater alacrity. Of course, no one has any experience that could support rational expectations as to how a supernatural being might go about formulating physical laws and establishing a universe, and I hope Dawkins will understand that I intend no offense in suggesting that even he may not be qualified to set performance standards for deities.

Of course, he is not the only person to have mounted an argument based upon his presuppositions about how he would have expected God to behave. Atheism has always been able to muster a few brave souls who seem convinced that if there were a God they should be able to deduce his or her purpose in life, the universe and everything. This is an intriguing

---

38. Rusbridger, "Interview with Rowan Williams."

39. Ussher, *The Annals of the World*, 17.

40. For a further discussion see Peters, and Hewlett, *Evolution from Creation to New Creation: Conflict, Conversation, and Convergence*.

41. Dawkins, *The God Delusion*, 144.

42. Wolf, "World Thinkers 2013."

proposition, if only because it washes onto the shores of common ground shared by the fundamentalists of various religions who sometimes seem convinced they fully understand God's will. Other theists are less presumptuous. St Paul famously proclaimed that "now we see through a glass darkly"[43] and, as one writer said recently, "an apophatic thread, a belief that the only way to conceive of God is through conceding that he is ineffable, runs throughout Christian history."[44] Undeterred by such concepts, some atheists seem to reason that any being who created the cosmos would have to be pretty intelligent—you know, someone who would think much like them. Hence, if he had a grand design they should be able to understand it. If they cannot see why he would have done something in a particular way, he cannot exist. This is a mode of argument by which an intelligent eight year old could logically exclude the possibility of sex.

In any event, it seems there was an abracadabra moment; standard cosmological theory suggests that the Big Bang was a single explosive act of creation that gave birth to the universe and ultimately to all it contains. Our understanding of the manner in which the universe unfolded is still limited. Our finest scientists devote their lives to unravelling its mysteries, but there may be things we never know even about our own lives and consciousness. The proposition that God created the universe cannot sensibly be dismissed by speculation that he should have made everything in a fully-formed static condition and prevented further creation from unfolding by means of evolutionary processes.

IRREDUCIBLE COMPLEXITY

Dawkins then moves on to discuss the issue of irreducible complexity, that is the suggestion that some biological features, such as eyes, could not have evolved by successive variations in earlier features through processes of natural selection. He finds some common ground with theists in accepting that the world and its currently diverse life forms did not occur by chance, but insists that the true explanation is natural selection and not the creation of a designer.[45] He concedes that the discovery of any genuine example of irreducible complexity would undermine Darwin's theory, but argues that none have been found. In fact, this concession may have been more broadly stated than necessary. The discovery of a single irreducibly complex entity would obviously undermine the contention that natural selection wholly ex-

---

43. I Corinthians 13:12.
44. Bryant, "God is unknowable—stop looking for him and you will find faith."
45. Dawkins, *The God Delusion*, 144–151.

plains all life forms, but it would not provide any reason to doubt that it was of widespread, if not of universal, application. The cyanobacteria that build stromatolites in Australia are similar to life forms found on Earth up to 3.5 billion years ago[46] but, whilst they have failed to evolve into more complex life forms over that period, the evolution of other species has proceeded in leaps and bounds. In any event, Dawkins maintains that suggested instances of irreducible complexity, such as wings and eyes, can be explained in terms compatible with natural selection.

There have been many arguments to the contrary,[47] and an array of responses, including the suggestion that apparent examples of irreducible complexity could be attributable to random mutations.[48] Despite the legal case in which arguments for irreducible complexity were rejected,[49] I suspect that the debate will continue unabated and that neither further evidence nor rhetoric about the competing possibilities are likely to persuade many people to abandon their existing beliefs. But even if the validity of Dawkins' contentions were to be assumed, they could at best provide some argumentative sandbags to shore up his defense of natural selection against attacks that most theists have no interest in making. Many believe that God initiated the entire evolutionary process.

In fact, if one were to follow Dawkins in stepping onto the thin ice of speculation about the likely approach of a divine creator, that is the approach one might expect. Imagine, if you will, that you were endowed with all attributes of God and that you were mulling over the idea of creating a universe. How would you go about it? Would you cause everything to come into existence in one stupendous act of creation, so that, whilst plants and animals might reproduce and die, the cosmos and all it contains would otherwise remain fixed for all eternity? Or would this be an ongoing project that you would permit to develop and evolve, an unfolding process of creation that could be maintained over countless aeons? Of course, no mortal has ever wrestled with such stupendous options, and angels, if not Dawkins, might baulk at rushing in to pontificate about the choices a supernatural creator might make. Perhaps all one can say with confidence is that God

---

46. Monroe, "Stromatolites".

47. See, for example, Behe, *Darwin's Black Box*, and Dembski, *No Free Lunch: Why Specified Complexity Cannot Be Purchased without Intelligence*; but see also Miller, *Only a Theory: Evolution and the Battle for America's Soul*.

48 Shanks and Joplin, "Redundant Complexity: A Critical Analysis of Intelligent Design in Biochemistry"; Bridgham, Carroll & Thornton,. "Evolution of hormone-receptor complexity by molecular exploitation."

49. United States District Court , Kitzmiller,, et al. v. Dover Area School District, et al..

would have been unlikely to have been moved by fear of being accused of laziness a few billion years down the track.

GAPS

In a somewhat similar vein, Dawkins debunks the tendency to treat every apparent gap in the evolutionary process as evidence of divine creation.[50] He argues that it is unreasonable to expect evidence of every step and points out that only a tiny fraction of animal corpses fossilize. He answers some of the objections that have been raised to natural selection and attacks the approach of some creationists as ill-informed and irrational. In contrast, he applauds the work of scientists who seek out gaps in current knowledge as opportunities for further research. Much of this is well reasoned and informative, though it glosses over the implicit invitation to take a leap of faith that all the gaps in current evolutionary theory will one day be filled. But, taken at its highest, the argument merely provides another defensive sandbag to fortify natural selection against another anticipated attack on the concept of natural selection that most believers have no wish to launch.

FINE TUNING AND ANTHROPIC PRINCIPLES

Dawkins then moves on to what he calls "the anthropic principle" which, he suggests, provides an alternative explanation for the extraordinary combination of apparently finely-tuned circumstances necessary for stars and planets to form and conditions hospitable to life to emerge. If any of the basic building blocks, like the strength of gravity, the speed of light, the mass of an electron or even the amount of dark energy, had been even slightly different, the universe could not have formed planets that permitted the evolution of life as we know it. Life would also have been impossible without water, energy, a benign and reasonably stable temperature range and an abundance of chemical elements including oxygen, hydrogen, nitrogen, sulphur, phosphorus and, of course, carbon. And the environment permitted by this combination of fortuitous circumstances had to be maintained reasonably consistently throughout the aeons that passed whilst life emerged and then evolved from its most primitive form to produce the current crop of humanity. Paul Davies calls this the 'Goldilocks enigma'; things had to be just right.

---

50. Dawkins, *The God Delusion*, 151–161.

In other contexts, a combination of apparently improbable circumstances could perhaps be explained on the basis that even the most extraordinary things are bound to occur sooner or later somewhere in a vast universe that has developed over billions of years. But these basic building blocks are the stuff from which the entire universe was created. The 'Big Bang' that gave birth to our universe was not an explosion of the usual kind, even on a titanic scale, but rather an stupendously rapid expansion of space.[51] Particles that coalesced into stars, planets and entire galaxies moved away from each other, like raisins progressively move apart as a loaf of raisin bread is baked and the dough rises.[52] All this occurred at unimaginable velocities that, according to the cosmic inflation theory, actually exceeded the speed of light.[53] Many scientists also now accept that time itself also began with the Big Bang,[54] a view broadly consistent with Plato's belief that time was created when the creator set the heavens in order[55] and with those of Clement, Origen, Augustine and others. If, as atheists suggest, the Big Bang was unplanned, then it was spectacularly unlikely that this explosion of matter could have produced a well-ordered universe hospitable to life.

The theoretical physicist, Freeman Dyson, said that: 'The more I examine the universe and study the details of its architecture, the more evidence I find that the universe in some sense knew we were coming.'[56] Hoyle suggested that the conditions under which life could emerge were so stringent that what has been described as a bio-friendly universe looks like a 'put up job'. He added that it looked as if a super-intellect had been 'monkeying' with the laws of physics.[57] Stephen Hawking has explained that 'The laws of science, as we know them at present, contain many fundamental numbers, like the size of the electric charge of the electron and the ratio of the masses of the proton and the electron. . .and the remarkable fact is that the values of these numbers seem to have been very finely adjusted to make possible

51. See, for example, Strassler, Matt, "Big Bang: Expansion, Not Explosion."

52. Heckert, *Was the Big Bang an Explosion?* See also Silk, *The Big Bang*.

53. Peebles, *Principles of Physical Cosmology*, chapter 17. Astrophysicists have recently found indirect evidence for the existence of gravitational waves which, if verified, may confirm the theory of cosmic inflation proposed by Alan Guth in 1980. Overbye, "Detection of Waves in Space Buttresses Landmark Theory of Big Bang." See also Sample, "Gravitational waves discovery: 'We have a first tantalising glimpse of the cosmic birth pangs.'"

54. For a discussion of this issue see Frampton, *Did Time Begin? Will Time End?*

55. Zeyl, and Sattler, "Plato's Timaeus," 1 Overview of the Dialogue.

56. Dyson, Freeman, 'Disturbing the Universe', 250—in Barrow & Tipler, *The Anthropic Cosmological Principle* (1988) Oxford: Clarendon. at 318. The observation is cited in Dennett, *Darwin's Dangerous Idea: Evolution and the Meaning of Life*.

57. Hoyle, Fred, "The Universe past and present reflections," 16.

the development of life.'⁵⁸ Paul Davies has put it even more directly:' On the face of it, the universe *does* look as if it has been designed by an intelligent creator expressly for the purpose of spawning sentient beings.'⁵⁹ (emphasis in the original)

Dawkins effectively concedes this, acknowledging that, "physicists have calculated that, if the laws and constants of physics had been even slightly different, the universe would have developed in such a way that life would have been impossible." He refers to Martin Rees' list of six fundamental constants,⁶⁰ each of which is finely tuned in the sense that if they were slightly different the universe would be "comprehensively different and presumably unfriendly to life." He even cites as an example Rees' observation concerning the magnitude of the 'strong force' that binds the components of an atomic nucleus and had to be very close to its actual value in order for any chemistry to exist.⁶¹ And he does not suggest that any of this can be explained by natural selection. The building blocks of the universe did not evolve from earlier organisms; they are constants.

But, whilst identifying the "problem" that "we live in a life friendly place", he says, "What the religious mind then fails to grasp is that two candidate solutions are offered to the problem. God is one. The anthropic principle is the other. They are *alternatives*' (emphasis in the original).⁶² The implicit sneer at 'the religious mind' again seems to reflect his view that anyone with any religious beliefs must be stupid, but it offers no logical support for his argument. Nor is it warranted by the context. There is nothing inherently irrational in suggesting that things may appear to be fine-tuned because they have been finely tuned.

In fact, there are at least two versions of the anthropic principle and neither are incompatible with the possibility of a sentient tuner. The strong version of the anthropic principle ('SAP') states that the universe must have those properties which allow life to develop within it at some stage in its history."⁶³ Few atheists are keen to embrace this version because it may seem to support an inference that the universe was designed to permit intelligent life to emerge and develop.

The version most commonly cited is the weak anthropic principle ('WAP') which states that the 'conditions that are observed in the Universe

58. Hawking, *A Brief History of Time*, 125.
59. Davies, Paul, *The Goldilocks Enigma*, 3.
60. Rees, Martin, *Just Six Numbers*.
61. Dawkins, *The God Delusion*, 169–170.
62. Dawkins, *The God Delusion*, 164.
63. Barrow and Tipler, *The Anthropic Cosmological Principle*, 21.

must allow the observer to exist'.[64] Well, few people would argue with that! It may be difficult to see this tautological truism as an atheistic bulwark, but some seemingly well-educated and intelligent atheists have sought shelter behind it. The 'argument', to use the word somewhat loosely, runs along these lines: it is true that we could not have evolved had it not been for a combination of circumstances, each highly improbable, but "we should expect that our universe has features compatible with our existence, since, after all, we exist."[65] Despite the breadth of their analysis, even Barrow and Tipler have embraced this argument, insisting that 'the enormous improbability of the evolution of intelligent life in general and *Homo sapiens* in particular does *not* mean we should be amazed we exist at all.' They compare the evolution of intelligent species with the fact that Elizabeth II is Queen of England and suggest that both are examples of 'WAP self-selection in action'.[66] The obvious problem with this type of reasoning is that it simply misses the point. The issue raised by the 'Goldilocks enigma' is not the improbability of intelligent life evolving from the physical circumstances that exist within our universe, but the extraordinary improbability that such a combination of 'life-friendly' circumstances could have come into existence.

William Lane Craig has attempted to illustrate the point by the following scenario: "Suppose you are dragged before a firing squad of 100 trained marksmen, all of them with rifles aimed at your heart, to be executed. The command is given; you hear the deafening sound of the guns. *And you observe that you are still alive*, that all of the 100 marksmen missed!"[67] In such an event, Barrow and Tipler and others could argue that you should not be amazed you still exist, because the conditions you observe when you nervously open your eyes must be such as to permit your continued existence. Or, to put it in concrete terms, you should not be surprised to be alive because you were obviously not struck by the bullets. But it would still be amazing that all 100 marksmen, firing from point blank range missed. A skeptic might reasonably assume that there must have been a common cause, such as the entire squad having been bribed to miss. It would be a brave marksman who would tell the outraged captain there was no reason to be surprised.

64. Merriam Webster Dictionary, "anthropic principle." See also Barrow and Tipler, *The Anthropic Cosmological Principle*, 16.

65. Kelly, Kyle, "Is the Weak Anthropic Principle Compatible With Divine Design?" See also Barrow and Tipler, *The Anthropic Cosmological Principle*, 566.

66. Barrow and Tipler, *The Anthropic Cosmological Principle*, 566.

67. Craig, William Lane, 'Barrow and Tipler on the Anthropic Principle vs. Divine Design'. *British Journal for the Philosophy of Science* 38 (1988): 389–395.

The combination of extremely unlikely circumstances that permit our life is at least equally amazing. The astonishing improbability of this occurring cannot be dispelled by the observation that, once it happened, the emergence of life was not surprising. And an observer wielding Occam's razor might equally suggest that there must be a common cause. One does not need a religious mind to see that, merely an open one.

Of course, the concept of selection bias should not be wholly discounted. Dawkins relies upon it in suggesting a 'planetary' version of the anthropic principle.[68] He argues that, given the profusion of planets in the universe, life was bound to emerge somewhere, even if the odds of it occurring on any given planet had been only one in a billion. This is again somewhat simplistic. Had the necessary physical laws and constants not been as they are, the odds would have been zero. There is no obvious basis for an assumption that the odds of life emerging on earth, even given those laws and constants, were as high as one in a billion. More fundamentally, this sort of analysis seems to presuppose a degree of knowledge about the emergence of life that is still currently unavailable.[69]

It is true that, if life did emerge as a result of combination of factors unguided by an intelligent hand, then the odds of recurrence, however small, might be improved by an assumed prevalence of potentially life friendly planets in the universe. But none of this really explains the fact that it is not simply our planet but the entire universe that appears to have been fine tuned. The extraordinary combination of improbable cosmological constants obviously governs the conditions existing on all planets in the universe and it cannot be explained by the issues raised by Dawkins in his planetary version of the weak anthropic principle.

Hence, when he moves from planetary considerations to those affecting the universe, he is obliged to change tack. He mentions the suggestion by some "hard-nosed" physicists that the long anticipated "theory of everything" will eventually reveal that the appearance of fine tuning can be explained by some factors being dependent upon others or "something else as yet unknown in ways, that we today cannot imagine" and that we will discover that this is 'the only way for a universe to be'.[70] This suggestion must be one of the vaguest formulations in the history of science. Dawkins rightly rejects it, because he regards it as implausible that the "only way for a universe to be" would just happen to be "such a set up" for our evolution. Instead, he defends the weak anthropic principle, citing an earlier

---

68. Dawkins, *The God Delusion*, 162 et seq.
69. See the discussion in chapter 6.
70. Dawkins, *The God Delusion*, 173.

version of the firing squad scenario before suggesting that the answer to this "objection" is that there are many universes, co-existing "like bubbles of foam" in a multiverse.[71] The suggested implication is that a multitude of universes permitted the dice to be rolled so many times that one was bound to be just right. Sooner or later, all 100 marksman would all do their best but just happen to miss. This is too simplistic.

HOW MANY UNIVERSES CAN DANCE ON THE HEAD OF A PIN?

Multiverses are a captivating concept and there is clearly no reason to imagine that there may not be realities that lie beyond our present perceptions. This is one proposition about which theists and atheists should be able to find some common ground. But the musings of modern theoretical physicists and cosmologists now seem far more adventurous than those of the theologians. A cosmologist, Max Tegmark, speculates that there may be an infinite number of inhabited universes with dopplegangers, or copies, of people with the same appearance, name and memories as you and me, who play out every possible permutation of our life choices'.[72] This suggestion obviously surpasses the imaginative musing of theologians like poor Giordano Bruni who was accused of heresy for, among other things, advocating an infinite universe, and was burnt at the stake.[73] Perhaps countless versions of him still live on, with some maintaining the same view and others conceding that the priests with matches may have a point.

Tegmark has identified different types of possible multiverses and categorized them in "levels":

- A Level I multiverse would consist of an infinite number of galaxies, stars and planets that lie beyond the 'cosmic horizon' of our observable universe.

- A level II multiverse would be like an infinite set of level I multiverses in bubbles of space, some perhaps involving different spatial dimensions and physical constants.

- A level III multiverse would consist of multiple copies of our universe, each on another branch of infinite dimensional space, that may exist,

---

71. Dawkins, *The God Delusion*, 173.

72. Tegmark, "Parallel Universes." See also Cox, 'Parallel universes are real, say physicists'; and Greene, *The Hidden Reality*. For a brief account of the concepts see Fabry,"Welcome to the Multiverse!"

73. Gatti, Hilary (2002). *Giordano Bruno and Renaissance Science*. 18–19.

unseen, all around us. This is said to follow from a theory of quantum mechanics involving the proposition that random processes cause the universe to branch into multiple copies—one for every possible outcome.

- A level IV multiverse would not be bound by the laws of physics as we understand them but would consist of 'mathematical structures' existing outside space and time.[74]

Those disconcerted by such speculative departures from conventional concepts of reality might be even more alarmed by the alternative formulations offered by the theoretical physicist, Brian Greene, who has suggested nine different types of multiverse.[75] I will not burden you with a discussion of all these concepts, but a few points can be made.

First, these are all hypotheses, not established facts. Tegmark has explicitly conceded this. On a website, still current at the time of writing, he urges reviewers to note that his "book does *not* claim that parallel universes exist" (emphasis in original). He also explains that "that parallel universes are not a scientific theory, but prediction of certain scientific theories."[76] Greene has sounded a similar note of caution, warning that "the subject of parallel universes is highly speculative" and adding that "no experiment or observation has established that any version of the idea is realized in nature." He has also said: "I'm not convinced — and speaking generally, no one should be convinced — of anything not supported by hard data."[77]

The hypotheses are largely based upon mathematics. As Tegmark explains, modern theoretical physicists tend to be Platonists in that they suspect that the universe is inherently mathematical.[78] He has developed a "Mathematical Universe Hypothesis" that implies that our physical world is actually an abstract mathematical structure. He suggests that "complete mathematical democracy" holds that mathematical existence and physical existence are "equivalent."[79] Hence, he explains, "mathematical existence equals physical existence. . . ..This means that all structures that exist mathematically exist physically as well . . ."[80] Tegmark also suggests that, if this theory is correct, then "all properties of all parallel universes, including the

74. Tegmark, "Parallel Universes." See also Vilenkin, Alexander & Max Tegmark. 'The Case for Parallel Universes."
75. Brian Greene, *The Hidden Reality*.
76. Tegmark, Max, "Critique."
77. Greene, *The Hidden Reality*, 9.
78. Tegmark, "Parallel Universes," 49.
79. Tegmark, *The Mathematical Universe* (2007), 17.
80. Tegmark, *Our Mathematical Universe*, (2014) 357.

subjective perceptions of (self-aware beings) could in principle be derived by an infinitely intelligent mathematician."[81] Of course, the concept of an infinitely intelligent mathematician able to understand the perceptions of all sentient beings in an infinity of universes would obviously suggest God, but that does not seem to be intended.

These are wonderful flights of imagination that soar not only beyond the musings of theologians but also beyond the soaring conceptions of most science fiction writers. String theorists insist that there are other dimensions and maintain that their theoretical equations actually correspond to existing universes. There are differing "many-worlds" interpretations of quantum theory.[82] Some theorists suggest that every time a subatomic action occurs the universe splits into multiple, slightly different, copies of itself.[83] It has also been suggested that this may permit time travel by shifting between different branches of reality.[84] Hugh Everett, who is generally acknowledged as the pioneer of the many worlds interpretation of quantum physics, apparently believed that his theory even guaranteed his own immortality, because at each split his consciousness would follow whatever path did not lead to death. At least so far as this universe is concerned, he died in 1982 at the age of 51 and there was a sad footnote to his theory; his daughter subsequently left a suicide note in which she said she was going to another universe to be with him.[85]

Whilst the divine foot may still be kept from the door, other religious concepts are not merely embraced but surpassed. The gamut of universes would presumably encompass heavens in which everything went well and hells where everything went wrong, and there may be countless others offering varying degrees of happiness for particular denizens. Physicists now claim even to have calculated the number of universes in a multiverse. I had hoped it would turn out to be 42, the number 'The Hitchhiker's Guide to the Galaxy', suggested was the meaning of life. Alas, they found it may exceed $10^{10^{10^{7}}}$' which they described, reasonably enough, as a 'humongous' number.[86]

Margaret Wertheim has poured some well-needed cold water on these fancies, noting that "the equations are taken to be the fundamental reality.

---

81. Tegmark, *Our Mathematical Universe*, (2014) 17.

82. Vaidman, Lev, "Many-Worlds Interpretation of Quantum Mechanics" (2014), *Stanford Encyclopedia of Philosophy*.

83. See, for example, Morgan,' We came from your Future', 108–109.

84. David Deutsch quoted by Highfield, "Parallel universe proof boosts time travel hopes."

85. Shikhovtsev, *Biographical Sketch of Hugh Everett, III*.

86. Linde and Vanchurin, "How many universes are in the multiverse?"

The fact that the mathematics *allows* for gazillions of variations is seen to be evidence for gazillions of *actual* worlds. This kind of reification of equations is precisely what strikes some humanities scholars as childishly naive."[87] In fact, it is not only humanities scholars who have rung alarm bells. Some eminent physicists have also rushed to their nearest belfries to express their concerns.[88] Almost anything is theoretically possible and the possibility of other universes, perhaps generated by other ' Big Bangs' cannot be wholly excluded, but the faith some seem to invest in such theoretical edifices would leave many devout religious believers hanging their heads in shame. Of course, even within the relevant scientific communities, such theories have been criticized as not "testable" or "falsifiable."[89] It has been argued that the lack of any causal connection between any of the suggested multiverses places them "beyond any scientific support"[90] and that even the basic theory of inflationary cosmology is not scientific because it is so flexible that it can accommodate any observational result.[91]

Some devotees have responded by suggesting that the very conception of science should be modified to defuse the criticism. It has been seriously argued that if a theory is sufficiently elegant and explanatory, it need not be tested experimentally. In other words, verification is unnecessary.[92] The theoretical physicist, Sean Carroll, has actually suggested that the falsifiability criterion is a "blunt instrument that should be jettisoned in the interests of "subtlety and precision." In his view, scientific theories should be judged by whether they are "definite" and "empirical." Whilst that may create a reassuring impression, he explains that, by "definite," he means only that the theories say something clear and unambiguous about how reality functions and, by "empirical," he means that they should be judged by their ability to explain the data.[93] Others have supported their theories by reference to their perceived "elegance".[94]

---

87. Wertheim,"Physics Pangolin."

88. See, for example, Smolin, Lee, *The Trouble with Physics*; and Woit, *Not Even Wrong*.

89. See, for example, Stoeger, Ellis and Kirchner, "Multiverses and Cosmology: Philosophical Issues"; Woit, P. *Not Even Wrong*; Smolin, L. *The Trouble with Physics*; and Baggott, *Farewell to Reality*.

90. Ellis, "83 years of general relativity and cosmology: Progress and problems."

91. Steinhardt,"Inflation Debate: Is the theory at the heart of modern cosmology deeply flawed? See also Steinhardt,"Big Bang blunder bursts the multiverse bubble."

92. Ellis, Silk, 'Scientific method: Defend the integrity of physics'.

93. Carroll, "Falsifiability."

94. See, for example, Greene, *The Elegant Universe*.

The dangers of such an approach should be obvious to any skeptic. The requirements, that the theory say something definite about how reality functions and explain the data, could be fulfilled by many theories that few would regard as scientific. Almost any of the religious creation myths could arguably satisfy the "definite" and "empirical" criteria as defined in this manner and so could some of the more fanciful conspiracy theories that abound on the internet. Whilst "elegance" is obviously not used in an aesthetic sense, it does suggest that the test should consist of a purely subjective judgment about some quality of the theory, rather than an enquiry about whether the theory is adequately supported by evidence. Such approaches have led to concern that "theoretical physics risks becoming a no-man's-land between mathematics, physics and philosophy that does not truly meet the requirements of any."[95]

Others, perhaps conscious of such criticism, concede the need for verification but propose almost illusory standards. Tegmark has suggested that "...a fundamental physical theory can be testable and falsifiable even if it contains certain entities that you cannot observe. To be testable and falsifiable, it merely needs to predict at least one thing that we *can* observe."[96] Really? If a creation myth predicts that the sun will rise every morning, may we assume it is objectively valid? If the need for theories to be adequately tested by evidence is to be effectively discarded then the status and authority of science will be seriously eroded.

A few researchers have actually claimed that there is some evidence for the existence of other universes. In 2010 astrophysicists reported what they regarded as "tentative evidence" of "bruises" in circular patterns in the cosmic microwave background of our universe. They suggest that this might imply that our universe must have smashed into other "bubbles" of universes. It has been suggested that this is "the first evidence of universes beyond our own." It was acknowledged that the effects they reported could easily be a trick of the eye and that "it is rather easy to find all sorts of statistically unlikely properties in a large dataset like the CMB (cosmic microwave background)."[97]

In May 2013 a theoretical physicist announced that her multiverse hypothesis had been "proven" by studying a map of the universe prepared from data gathered by the Planck spacecraft. This revealed that cosmic microwave radiation from the Big Bang was not evenly distributed as earlier predicted but concentrated more strongly in the southern half of the sky

---

95. Ellis and Silk, "Scientific method: Defend the integrity of physics."
96. Tegmark, "The Universes of Max Tegmark."
97. MIT, "Astronomers Find First Evidence of Other Universes."

with a "cold spot" that could not be explained by the then current understanding of physics. It was suggested that this provided "hard evidence" for the existence of other universes that would have been pulling on our own.[98] Then in March 2014 scientists announced direct evidence of primordial gravitational waves which, if confirmed, would suggest that space-time expanded at many times the speed of light just after the Big Bang. These findings are said to support the existence of a multiverse by showing that when the universe grew exponentially in the first tiny fraction of a second after the Big Bang some parts of space-time expanded more quickly than others. It is thought that this could have created bubbles of space-time that developed into other universes.[99]

All this may be theoretically possible, but there is much enthusiasm for multiverse theories amongst the current generation of theoretical scientists and a skeptic might reasonably fear that these suggestions have been tainted by wishful thinking. Or, to revisit a note of caution sounded earlier, "the temperament, the imagination and the feelings" may have misled some of our physicist friends in the chase. We humans have long drawn inferences from our observations of the sky, ranging from early beliefs that stars were holes in the sky made by the fingers of God exposing light from Heaven to more contemporary assumptions that moving lights in the sky must be attributable to alien spacecraft. The quest for compelling evidence of multiverses must surely loom as one of the most alluring of scientific holy grails. I wish them well. But as a skeptical lawyer, I can only say that if they really believe that these observations are hard evidence for their theories, I would hate to be tried for a serious offense by a jury of theoretical physicists.

As Pedro Ferreira has observed, all this is "a wonderful setting for speculation, a vast blank canvas for storytelling."[100] Some theoretical physicists are also skeptical. Lee Smolin has suggested that whilst speculation about extra dimensions, exotic particles, multiple universes, and string theories have captured the imagination of some of his peers, these ideas have not been tested experimentally and some seem untestable. Yet these speculations dominate the field, attract many able young physicists and deter others from pursuing other areas of research. He believes that this situation threatens to impede the very progress of science.[101] Perhaps the most balanced assessment has been offered by George Ellis:

98. Taylor, "Is our universe merely one of billions?"
99. Kramer, "Our Universe may Exist in a Multiverse, Cosmic Inflation Discovery Suggests."
100. Ferreira, *The Perfect Theory*, at 232.
101. Lee Smolin, *The Trouble With Physics*.

Parallel universes may or may not exist; the case is unproved. We are going to have to live with that uncertainty. Nothing is wrong with scientifically based philosophical speculation, which is what multiverse proposals are. But we should name it for what it is.[102]

Second, even if some or all of these hypotheses were verified, the existence of other universes would obviously not be inconsistent with the existence of a sentient creator. The concept of multiverses is invoked by atheists as a means of countering the strong prima facie inference that arises from the apparent fine tuning of the universe. As one cosmologist apparently put it, 'If you don't want God, you'd better have a multiverse.'[103] But, despite the confidence with which this is propounded and the scientific aura in which it is bathed, the argument is less than compelling. There is no rational reason to suppose that, whilst Henry Ford produced millions of T model cars, God's production schedule would have been limited to one universe.

Third, multiverse concepts do not explain the creation of this or any other universe. As Paul Davies has pointed out, all of the multiverse theories are dependent upon about ten different basic assumptions, such as pre-existing space and time, the normal notion of causality and sufficient principles of quantum physics, to create the necessary spontaneity of formation. Davies adds: "Where did they all come from? What about these meta-laws that generate universes and impose effective local by-laws, as Martin Rees would call it, upon these universes? What is this distribution mechanism? How does that work? Where do those rules come from? So all you've done is shift the problem of existence up from the level of universe to the level of multiverse. But you haven't explained it."[104]

Fourth, we really do not know that even a countless number of 'Big Bangs' would produce the infinite profusion of differences suggested. As Brian Cox puts it, "the idea is that there is some overarching framework, out of which our laws and the constants of nature are selected randomly."[105] Whilst that may be the prevailing theory, it is as unverifiable as Plato's forms, Aristotle's eternal universe and other ideas once widely held by the contemporary intelligentsia. And how could that theory be reconciled with other aspects of multiverse theory?

---

102. Ellis, George, "Scientific American, Does the Multiverse Really Exist?" 43.

103. Polis, *God, Science and Mind*, 88.

104. The comments were made during an interview on *Closer to Truth* on August 23, 2014 and are cited at Kuhn, "Physicist Paul Davies' Killer Argument Against The Multiverse."

105. Cox, Brian, *The Human Universe*, 225.

Tegmark actually maintains that the fundamental laws that govern nature would remain the same in level I, II or III multiverses, though with different initial conditions and physical constants,[106] whilst his level IV multiverses would exist outside space and time. Not all of Greene's theories would fill the atheist bill either. He suggests that the simplest type of multiverse would consist of "islands" lying beyond our visual horizon within "the cosmic sea" of a "quilted multiverse."[107] Since such island universes would have been created by the same Big Bang they would presumably share the same fundamental physical laws.

What about the dopplegangers? If the other universes are replete with identical copies of us, then there would have to be similar physical laws and constants to permit their existence. Isn't that evident from the weak anthropic principle? And, of course, if there are similar laws and constants, then the phenomenon of fine-tuning could not be explained by their repetition.

Of course, the great attraction of speculation about an infinite number of possibilities is that it permits one to to ignore improbability. Even a one chance in a trillion long shot would have to pay off on infinite occasions if the bet could be infinitely repeated. Alan Guth, one of the pioneers of inflation theory and a supporter of multiverse concepts, points out that in a single universe, cows with two heads would relatively rare, but in an infinitely branching multiverse there would be an infinite number of two-headed cows as well as an infinite number of single-headed cows. He asks, "What happens to the ratio?"[108] With infinite throws of the dice almost anything is conceivable. Orbiting teapots, giant green lobsters, flying spaghetti monsters and other fantasies might all be plausible under this type of rationalization. In an infinite number of universes they would be bound to exist somewhere, so why not here?

Almost everything is theoretically possible. There might be one or more multiverses. Some might be of a type that permits laws and the constants of nature to occur randomly. There might be an abundance of universes, all with different laws and physical constants such as the speed of light and the gravitational constant, Planck's constant, the electrical constant and the elementary charge. The diversity of laws and constants might support an argument that human and animal life were bound to occur somewhere. Hence, the apparent fine tuning of our universe might be seen as nothing more than a fortuitous outcome that just happened to allow us hit a cosmic

---

106. Tegmark, "Parallel Universes," 49.
107. Brian Greene, *The Hidden Reality*, chapter 8.
108. Quoted by Wolchover and Byrne, "In a Multiverse, What Are the Odds?."

jackpot. But how much weight should be placed on such theoretical possibilities? Apparent indications of fine-tuning most obviously suggest a tuner, not an infinite panoply of other universes with infinite forms and laws.

In any other context, this would be self-evident. Suppose Neil Armstrong and his team had found a monolith on the moon like that described in Arthur C Clarke's book, "2001 A Space Odyssey" and its sequels; a black, perfectly flat, non-reflective rectangular block with dimensions in the precise ratio of 1:4:9 (the squares of the first three positive integers). It could be argued that there may be billions of moons in our universe and one of them was bound to have a monolith like this. But would you really believe that it occurred by chance? The laws and constants of our universe seem to provide even more compelling evidence of design than this hypothetical obelisk and reluctance to draw the obvious conclusion may be more attributable to contrary presuppositions than to logical analysis.

KINDLY EXPLAIN THE EXISTENCE OF GOD.

One common argument is that the existence of a creator cannot be accepted unless one can explain how he was created. This argument is not new and it has not improved with the passage of time or the accumulation of new scientific knowledge. In its crudest, and perhaps most commonly cited, form it is predicated upon the assumption that if something cannot be adequately explained it cannot provide an explanation for something else. This is clearly invalid. Our ancestors could not explain the existence of lightning but they could see the flash of light in the darkened skies and knew it explained why trees could suddenly burst into flames during storms. They could not provide even the most tentative explanation for what we now describe as gravity but they could see that apples fell from trees and deduce that this must be attributable to some, albeit inexplicable, force.

Of course, there may be circumstances in which the absence of an explanation may be of crucial, perhaps decisive importance. For example, any report of an elephant on an ice floe, could readily be dismissed unless there was some rational explanation, such as the recent sinking of a ship carrying a circus. Dawkins and other atheists suggest that the existence of a creator is also very unlikely but, whilst there is ample evidence that elephants do not live in arctic regions, there is no comparable body of evidence that would support their view. Furthermore, whilst the report of the elephant on the ice floe could easily be attributed to a prank or fervid imagination, the evidence provided by the apparent fine tuning of our laws and constants cannot be similarly dismissed.

As Paul Davies observes, the traditional monotheistic view, that the universe was designed by God and intended to be suitable for life, has the advantage of being a simple explanation for "the cosmic fine tuning and bio-friendliness" as well as being a natural explanation for those who already believe in God. He adds that "It also attributes the design-like qualities of the universe to a designer, which seems reasonable enough."[109] But Davies goes on to say that this is a "conversation stopper" and he not only raises the question of who designed the designer but also suggests that the proposition that God created the universe explains nothing unless one can say how and why he did.

This objection is difficult to understand. The absence of an explanation for something normally provides no reason for doubting its existence unless there is some reason to assume that, if it did exist, such an explanation would be available. There is no sensible reason to imagine that any mortal should be able to explain the existence of God.

The methodologies of a sentient creator would obviously remain largely impermeable to human analysis and, whilst theologians may debate his purposes, our inability to define them would not mean that sentient creation lacked significance. Countless generations of religious believers have accepted that God has revealed certain truths, but accept that he is otherwise beyond human knowledge or, as the Old Testament prophet, Isaiah, put it, 'his understanding no one can fathom'.[110] That may be frustrating for those of us who might like to cross-examine him about the various things that trouble us, but there is no reason to suppose that a conclusion that he created the universe would be meaningless. For Christians and other religious believers, recognition of the existence of a divine creator is a starting point that has implications for them and for the lives they live.

THE FIRST CAUSE AND SIMPLICITY

Dawkins takes a different view from Davies. He argues that any god capable of creating the universe and fine tuning all of the physical constants necessary to sustain life would have to be a supremely complex entity. Consequently, his existence would need an "even bigger" explanation that the one it supposedly provides.[111] He wisely accepts the proposition that there must have been a first cause of the processes that gave rise to the universe as we know it and declares that, "It is not just scientists who revolt at the

---

109. Davies, *The Goldilocks Enigma*, 299.
110. Isaiah 40:28.
111. Dawkins, *The God Delusion*, 176.

acceptance of such improbability arising spontaneously; common sense baulks too."[112] But, he insists, the first cause must have been simple, some mechanism that could be described as a "crane," rather than a "skyhook" and therefore could not be a "god" as that term is commonly understood. He dismisses any suggestion that the first cause may have been a being capable of creating the universe and speaking to many people simultaneously as "a dreadful exhibition of self-indulgent, thought-denying, skyhookery."[113]

Unfortunately, this remarkable use of emotive language is accompanied by an almost equally remarkable failure of reasoning. The fundamental problem with Dawkins' argument is that it confuses the simplicity of an explanation with the simplicity of the entity whose actions provide the explanation. Suppose, for example, that a book is found face up in the centre of a reading desk in a library. One possible explanation is that it had been left upright on one of the shelves and that a sudden gust of wind through an open window caused it to topple off a shelf and land, coincidentally, right way up on the desk. Another is that someone had been reading it and had left it there. The latter is the simpler explanation, even though the reader would have been a more complex entity than the air moving through the window. And of course, the real question is not which is explanation is simpler but which is more plausible.

It is true that the first cause of the universe set in train chains of events in which complex things emerged from simpler ones, but this does not mean that whoever or whatever started this process must have been simple. Since this seemingly obvious point seems to have eluded Dawkins and others anxious to adopt his argument, perhaps you will bear with me whilst I illustrate the point. If someone detonates a homemade bomb, the physical consequences of the resulting explosion may progress from the relatively simple, an initial eruption causing a loud bang and a cloud of smoke, to the more complex, as previously condensed matter strikes objects and creates chains of indirect reactions. But that does not means that the person who struck the match or pressed the button was more simple than the sticks of gelignite, the initial eruption or the ensuing effects.

Of course, the Big Bang that spawned the universe some 13.8 billion years ago involved a rapid expansion of space that was vastly more spectacular than any simple explosion a terrestrial terrorist could have produced, but there is no logical reason to imagine that whoever or whatever caused the Big Bang must have been a simple entity. Imagine a much older civilization in another time and place. War and sickness have been overcome

---

112. Dawkins, *The God Delusion*, 185.
113. Dawkins, *The God Delusion*, 185.

and accidents virtually eliminated from a world in which unimaginably sophisticated technology protects its citizens from harm and provides for all their physical needs. Anthropology has long since given way to the study of behavior by androids and other forms of artificial intelligence, but one question remains unanswered: what would happen if new artificially created lifeforms were to permitted to evolve afresh in circumstances that could be subtly influenced and covertly studied? And so the greatest minds of an advanced race spend centuries devising a stupendous experiment. A new universe is meticulously created; not a real one of course, but one in which the simulation will be sufficient to deceive the planned sentient beings, at least until they achieve highly advanced levels of knowledge. The apparent time scale is condensed so that the experiment can actually be completed within several millennia though it will seem much longer to the inhabitants. As they progress from hunter-gathering to farming and form larger communities, philosophers emerge and in time scientists who not only study the world in which they find themselves but also seek to plumb the evolutionary processes from which their race apparently emerged. They correctly deduce that there must have been a first cause for these processes, but an ongoing debate rages about whether it was an act of God, an idea derided by atheists who insist that sentient design would be extremely unlikely, or whether it was a spontaneous phenomenon occurring perhaps in one of an unknown multiplicity of universes. Then one of their leading intellectuals proclaims, "You know, it is obvious that whatever started all this must have been very simple." And the directors of the experiment dissolve into laughter.

This is not an entirely fanciful scenario. It has been seriously argued that our own universe may be a vast computer simulation,[114] and that, in principle at least, it may even be possible for we, the simulated, to discover the simulators.[115] Two types of simulation have been suggested. In one theory, we live in a real universe, but one created by a super-intelligent being who lives in another universe. In the other, our universe and all it contains are merely strings of information and our lives are subject to manipulation like the characters in a computer game. It has even been suggested that the universe could be a gigantic hologram.[116] In either scenario we would

---

114. Bostrom, 'Are you living in a computer simulation?'; Campbell, "Elon Musk Thinks That Our Existence Is Someone Else's Video Game"; and Ball, "We might live in a computer program, but it may not matter,."

115. Beane, Davoudi and Savage, *Constraints on the Universe as a Numerical Simulation*.

116. Stone, "There Is Growing Evidence that Our Universe Is a Giant Hologram"; Beall, "Theory claims to offer the first 'evidence' our Universe is a hologram"; Bagchi, Arjun, Rudranil Basu, Daniel Grumiller, Max Riegler. Entanglement Entropy in

be artificially created laboratory rats unknowingly conscripted into a vast anthropological experiment. There is no real evidence to support either of these hypotheses, which obviously depend upon the existence of other universes, and they stand as further examples of the need to distinguish between science and speculative philosophy. Nonetheless, it is interesting to note that some people who baulk at the idea that the universe might be the product of an intelligent designer, would be relaxed about that proposition if the designer were a super-intelligent being from another universe.

This must make many atheists very nervous. From a human perspective, such a super-intelligent being, who designed and created the universe and presumably stands out side at least our conception of time, would be god-like. So why cavil at the traditional conception? Perhaps one explanation is that atheists tend to think of God as a vaguely humanoid, if supernatural, figure, like that revealed in Michelangelo's depiction of the creation on the ceiling of the Sistine Chapel. In contrast, classic Christian theology insists that God is not only omnipotent, but also immanent and omnipresent; a super-intelligent being pervading the universe.

In any event, Dawkins' conviction that the first cause must itself have been simple is hopelessly misconceived. As Ward, Swinburne and others have pointed out, one logically seeks simplicity of explanation and there can be no more simple explanation for the fact that the universe appears to have been designed than that it was designed. The theologian, Richard Swinburne puts the argument in these terms:

> *Theism claims that every other object which exists is caused to exist and kept in its existence by just one substance, God. And it claims that every property which every substance has is due to God causing or permitting it to exist. It is a hallmark of a simple explanation to postulate few causes. There could in this respect be no simpler explanation than one which postulated only one cause.*[117]

It may be noted that Swinburne addresses the simplicity of explanation rather than the simplicity of God. Keith Ward, a philosopher turned priest, has taken a similar line, explaining that:

> *The theist would claim that God is a very elegant, economical and fruitful explanation for the existence of the universe. It is simple because it attributes the existence and nature of absolutely everything in the universe to just one being, an ultimate cause which*

Galilean Conformal Field Theories and Flat Holography.

117. Swinburne, *Is there a God?* 43.

assigns a reason for the existence of everything, including itself. It is elegant, because from one key idea—the whole of the most perfect being possible—the whole nature of God and the existence of the universe can be intelligibly explicated.[118]

Dawkins attacks these approaches, again on the basis that God would not be simple. Indeed, after quoting the last passage, he says that he is "not clear whether Ward really thinks God is simple, or whether [the passage] represents a temporary 'for the sake of argument' exercise." This clearly reveals that he has misunderstood the point both are making. Neither are suggesting that God is simple; they are suggesting that divine creation is a simple explanation.

It is conceivable that there may be some infinite but unknown process of inflation by which an infinite number of universes are somehow formed and that this one proved to be just right. It is also conceivable that further explanations will emerge for the unresolved questions, such as why a spontaneously created universe was so well ordered at its beginning and why there is more matter than antimatter. There may be a myriad of explanations for a myriad of mysteries, but Swinburne and Ward would suggest that there is one simple explanation: God created it all.

SUFFERING

Whilst not raised in the chapter, "Why there almost certainly is no God," Dawkins and others have also relied upon the so called 'Epicurean paradox' which suggests that, if God existed, he would intervene to prevent human suffering. I am not a stranger to tragedy and would not suggest that this is an argument that can be lightly dismissed. In a long legal career I have seen many people overcome by suffering, whether due to violence, accidents causing horrific disabilities, physical or mental illnesses or the heart wrenching grief of losing children or others they love. My wife and I lost our first born daughter when she was still a toddler and, no matter what you may think you believe, the first question that bursts from your lips when such a catastrophic incident occurs is 'why?'

Such questions trouble religious believers as well as atheists and, whilst some explanations have been offered for why a loving and compassionate god would permit such things to occur,[119] there have been none that I have found adequate. Most approaches involve chipping away at the edges the

---

118. Ward, *God, Chance and Necessity*, 98–99. See also Ward, *The Evidence for God*.
119. See Lewis, C.S., *The Problem of Pain*; Kushner, *When Bad Things Happen to Good People*; and Yancey, *Where Is God When It Hurts?*.

problem. It is argued that that pain is sometimes necessary to protect us from injury and illness, that some is caused by our own foolish behavior and some by the actions of others that God permits as the price we must all pay for free will. Some fundamentalists suggest that misfortune is inflicted as punishment for sins or that we would be relieved from much of our pain and distress if we had sufficient faith. It has also been argued that the existence of pain enhances pleasure and even that suffering may be redemptive.[120] Then when these rationalizations have all been exhausted, we are assured that God is a loving father who shares in our suffering. Christians believe that this love impelled God to send his son, Jesus, to suffer and die so that death may be overcome and we may pass on to a life in which there will be no more pain.

None of the arguments explain the existence of predators. Why is the natural order of life so dependent upon some creatures meeting violent deaths at the jaws or talons of others? Nor do they explain natural disasters like the tsunami that swept across the coast of Sumatra in December 2004 killing more than 230,000 people. Whilst some may find consolation in the belief that God weeps with them in their pain, I agree with Dawkins' view that this does not provide a wholly satisfying answer. If one of my children were in pain and it was within my power to alleviate it, I would do more than express sympathy, tell them that I share their suffering and assure them that they will enjoy life later.

The Epicurean paradox raises questions to which we have no wholly adequate answers. Are God's hands tied in some way? Is he not wholly omnipotent? Did he initiate a vast creative process that rolls on inexorably? Is he unable to intervene without compromising some vast unknowable plan? Does he not care? Or, worse, does he want us to suffer? Is there a titanic struggle between good and evil, not merely in the hearts and minds of people but in the entire cosmos? Is there really a devil who is able to frustrate God's attempts to protect us? Why would an omnipotent god not destroy or disempower such a malign being? Is evil allowed to flourish so that, like Job, we may be tested? Is there some other way of reconciling the existence of God, divine love and the more harsh realities of life?

There are several possible responses: one may embrace some explanation requiring one or more faith-based assumptions; one may focus on the consolations offered by one's faith, such as an expectation of being reunited in an afterlife; one may reject the existence of God altogether; or one may simply move on, perhaps with the acknowledgement that there are limits

---

120. Waters, *When Suffering Is Redemptive: Stories of How Anguish and Pain Accomplish God's Mission.*

to human understanding. Propositions like the last of these alternatives are often criticized as a 'cop out' by people who seem to believe that if there is a god there would be an obvious theological rationale for everything. This is an unrealistic expectation. There is so much in the world we cannot understand. Yet ordinary religious believers are apparently challenged to fully explain the mind of a god they believe created time, space and all of reality.

This expectation may not be wholly reasonable, but the atheistic argument is not easily dismissed. Craig argues that the existence of evil is not inconsistent with the existence of God and that one has to consider the whole of the evidence rather than focus on a single issue.[121] It is also true that religion may provide consolation that is denied atheists. No one can walk away from a child's grave without weeping, but some leave bearing the pitiless grief of an eternal loss and others a sadness mitigated by expectation of an ultimate reunion in another life. Nonetheless, skeptics are entitled to weigh the absence of an adequate explanation in the balance.

SO HAVE YOU SEEN THE LIGHT YET?

Well there you go. You too may be inducted into the ranks of the intelligentsia. All you need to do is to renounce 'skyhookery', hope (though surely not pray) for natural selection to raise your consciousness and ignore your misgivings about the validity of the arguments. Then your eyes may be opened, your doubts dispelled and you may perhaps rejoice in calling yourself a 'bright'.

On the other hand, you may find all this unpersuasive. The essential problems with the analyses offered by Dawkins and others is not that the facts are inaccurately stated, but that that they are largely used as springboards for leaps of logic they cannot rationally support. Atheists are clearly right to insist upon the importance of evidence and reason, right to decry unquestioned superstition and right to rail against evil committed in the name of religion. Yet their own claims cannot be immune from rational scrutiny and, as I have sought to demonstrate, a decision to embrace atheism does not make one immune from the effects of presupposition and emotion. Indeed, those naively confident of their own objectivity may be especially vulnerable to them. In reality, many of the arguments that are often advanced with smug confidence are of dubious, if any, validity.

As the next chapter may demonstrate, this can also be said about many of the arguments that are often raised by Christians and other religious believers. This chapter has been intended to raise questions, to suggest that

---

121. Craig,, "The Problem of Evil."

cliches about science and other other simplistic answers should not be permitted to foreclose rational debate and to advocate a skeptical approach to all of the arguments. Those, like the horsemen of the non-apocalypse, who claim to ride under the banner of reason should at least agree with this approach, even if they bridle at the suggestion that much of the rhetoric uttered in their quest to purge the world of religious belief cannot withstand logical analysis.

5

The Classic Arguments for God

Whilst the arguments advanced by Dawkins may provide shields from some of the argumentative volleys loosed by theists, there appear to be few real arrows in atheistic quivers. As Sagan suggested, God could have chosen to reveal himself in some undeniable manner, but his failure to comply with this expectation does not establish that no one is at the helm of heaven. A more fruitful question is whether there are actually any valid grounds for an affirmative belief that God does exist. In discussing this question, I will again engage in my penchant for skipping from one intellectual lily pad to another. There is an obvious need to avoid oversimplification, but these lily pads float on the surface of a broad, deep and murky pond. This observation might pique the odd philosopher who has made it this far into the book without succumbing to Hume's admonition to consign it to the flames, but humanity has struggled with questions about the existence and nature of God since we first acquired the capacity for wonder and there is a vast bulk of literature that could be explored, including some that is remarkably turgid. I will try to avoid losing anyone to terminal boredom, by mentioning only the major or most cited arguments and leave some references in the footnotes for those who wish to dive further into the Stygian depths.

One should perhaps begin by shedding any unreasonable expectations. As previously mentioned, proof in the sense of mathematical certainty is rarely possible outside the world's laboratories. Whilst this is well understood as a general proposition, some people still suggest that it should be possible to conclusively prove the existence or non-existence of God. How? This is not an issue that one could reasonably address by some arcane scientific procedure and, in the absence of any eye-witnesses, we are inevitably reliant upon what we know about the cosmos, life, human experience and our capacity for reasoning.

Of course, some of the arguments for the existence of God are very old. This may comfort those convinced that wisdom and insight evaporated at the end of some special dispensation or golden age in antiquity; it is unlikely to impress those convinced that human intelligence sprang unexpectedly into existence at the start of a new age of enlightenment that reached its apotheosis with the advent of arguments founded upon a hypothetical teapot. Those unimpressed by either assumption might simply consider the arguments on their merits, though in the light of all we now know in a modern scientific age rather than in the context of the world views within which they were formulated.

Whilst a plethora of scientific discoveries have been unveiled over the centuries, none have had a greater impact upon debates about the existence of God than the theory of natural selection. It does not provide the killer blow to religious belief that fundamentalists seem to fear and some atheists seem to imagine, but it is nonetheless significant, if only because it undermines some, though not all, of the traditional arguments based on apparent design. But there have been other revelations about the nature of the universe that might lead a fair minded atheist to ruefully reflect on the capacity of science to give with one hand and take with the other. Arguments of creation have been substantially strengthened by evidence that the universe has not always existed and that the odds of it emerging spontaneously were infinitesimal. It is true that new explanations have been suggested, but they do not have the obvious force of the now largely abandoned argument that there was no need to explain the origin of an eternal universe. Furthermore, the materialist insistence that everything is reducible to elementary particles of matter has faced further challenge in the light of quantum theory.[1] Other recent discoveries have helped bridge what some may have seen as a credibility gap. We now know that space is permeated by invisible but omnipresent quantum fields and waves of various kinds. In this context, the suggestion of an unseen but omnipresent intelligence presence may seem less challenging than it did in earlier years.

For some reason, the ranks of those who have attempted to establish the existence of God include many theologians and philosophers whose names began with the letter 'A'. It is unclear whether this was a coincidence or whether their mothers thought that the roll outside the pearly gates might be called in alphabetical order and wanted to give their boys a chance to jump the queue. What is clear is that the musings of people like Aristotle,

1. Campbell, *The Metaphysics of Emergence*, especially chapter 9.

Avicenna, Augustine, Anselm and Aquinas spanned some 15 centuries and that they approached this crucial question in a number of interesting ways.

INNATE KNOWLEDGE

The big three of Greek philosophers were undoubtedly Socrates, Plato and Aristotle. Nothing written by Socrates has survived to the modern age, but he is renowned for his 'dialectic' method of asking probing questions and, perhaps fortunately, he believed that God arranges everything for the best.[2] Plato took up the Socratic approach in his 'dialogues', writings in which various characters, including Socrates, are cast as debaters arguing about various topics. Plato's god was not the god of the Bible or the Qur'an, but the "demiurge," a supernatural artisan who, though not wholly omnipotent, made the universe by shaping disordered but pre-existing elemental materials to reflect ideal or eternal forms.[3] The first theory of innate ideas and knowledge emerges in Plato's dialogues. He argued that some things such as mathematical truths are not simply learnt but are embedded in the soul. One gains understanding gradually over time by, for example, learning to add, subtract or multiply, but this is really a process of coming to "remember" what one already knows rather than learning things afresh.[4]

If Plato was outshone by anyone in the Greek world it was Aristotle, who left a vast legacy of literature[5] and was revered by medieval Muslim intellectuals as "the First Teacher" and by Christian theologians as "the Philosopher."[6] His philosophy was described by Ayn Rand as "the intellect's Declaration of Independence."[7] Of course, with all this deference, there had to be at least some scandal and an early tradition suggests that he may have been involved in the death of Alexander the Great. There is little evidence to support this suggestion,[8] but justice may have been done; Dante consigned him to the first circle of hell.[9] Aristotle believed the universe was

2. Janko, "Socrates the Freethinker," 59.
3. Ross, *Plato's Theory of Ideas*.
4. See Plato's dialogues, *Meno* and *Phaedo*. Plato, *The Dialogues of Plato*.
5. See Aristotle, *The Works of Aristotle*.
6. For those who wish to know more of his life without departing from the ranks of authors whose names start with 'A' see: Ackrill, *Aristotle the Philosopher* and/or Adler, *Aristotle for Everybody*.
7. Ayn Rand, *For the New Intellectual*, 22.
8. Green, *Alexander of Macedon 356–323 B.C*, 379 and 459.
9. Alighier, *Dante's Inferno (The Divine Comedy: Volume I, Hell*, Canto IV. Lines 131–135.

eternal.[10] God was not the creator but the primary source of movement who imbues all things with order and purpose. He rejected Plato's conceptions of eternal forms and innate ideas and taught that, whilst concepts have an eternal essence, knowledge is gained by cognitive processes applied to sensory information. He also developed the first system of logic and syllogistic deduction.[11]

Aristotle's view that all knowledge is learned generally prevailed and nearly two millennia passed before Plato's theory of innate ideas was revived by Descartes, who suggested that knowledge of God is innate in everybody as a product of the faculty of faith.[12] Many of his philosophical colleagues remained unimpressed. John Locke argued that the mind of new born infants was a 'tabula rasa' (a blank slate) and that all knowledge was acquired by experience and learning. He also warned that the concept of innate ideas or knowledge might open a floodgate to dogmatic claims.[13] Liebniz sought a middle path, arguing that there are some innate ideas, such as mathematical truisms, but that they remain latent until actuated by experience.[14] Kant struck out in yet another direction, suggesting that the mind operates through pre-existing categories, but that these are not innate ideas or implanted knowledge, but merely means by which information that has been derived by experience is processed.[15] More recently, Noam Chomsky has joined the debate, arguing that innate knowledge may explain certain types of abilities, such as the extraordinary capacity young children display in learning complex concepts and language.[16]

In fact, modern evolutionary psychologists now believe that the suggestion of a mental blank slate is implausible, since any newborn animal devoid of at least some basic knowledge and ability would not survive in the wild. They also point to practical studies in which numerous species have displayed knowledge and competences they could not have acquired from experience, or at least by experience alone.[17] Another recent study has found that some primitive initial concepts are present even in the youngest

---

10. Aristotle *Physics*, book 1, 7.
11. Shields, "Aristotle." 4.1.
12. Descartes, *Meditations on First Philosophy*, Meditation 3.
13. Locke, *An Essay Concerning Human Understanding*, book I.
14. Leibniz, *New Essays on Human Understanding*, book 1.
15. Kant Immanuel, *Critique of Pure Reason*.
16. Chomsky, *Aspects of the Theory of Syntax*.

17 Tooby, Cosmides, and Bennett, "Resolving the Debate on Innate Ideas," 309–310; Carruthers, *Human Knowledge and Human Nature: A New Introduction to an Ancient Debate*s; and Carruthers, Laurence and Stich, *The Innate Mind: Structure and Contents*.

children able to be tested.[18] Such innate knowledge is obviously extended and refined through learning and experience[19] and its significance should not be overstated. It has been suggested that what innate knowledge exists may be attributable to natural selection.[20] The concept clearly does not validate every conception of God.

Some years ago I was involved in a case concerning a man charged with arson. The police officers who interviewed him obtained his name and address and, emboldened by this success, they asked for his date of birth. "Oh," he said cheerfully, "I've always existed." Their attempts to obtain an explanation produced nothing but an enigmatic smile and they decided to move on and ask about his occupation. "I create things," he said in response. "What sort of things?" they asked. "Oh you know, just the usual," he replied modestly, "trees, lakes, mountains, people." Sadly, I was unable to see him create any of these things and a forensic psychiatrist who assessed him predictably concluded that he was delusional rather than divine. At the risk of betraying what I am sure he would have regarded as a lamentable lack of faith, I concluded that this diagnosis was a more likely explanation for his belief than innate knowledge.

Unfortunately, delusional states are not as uncommon as we might like to imagine and he was not the first man I had met who thought he was God. Years earlier a mentally deranged legal colleague of mine had attempted to blow up a cathedral because he thought he had been misrepresented by the sermon. I understand the explosion made quite an impression on a lady in the confessional.

Pascal suggested that God may have "imparted religion" to some people by intuition, but thought it could be given to others only by reasoning and waiting for God to give them spiritual insight.[21] It is obviously possible that some intuitively grasp the truth, but how can others know whether they have had a genuine insight or merely been moved by subconscious psychological influences? Concerns of this nature generally lead skeptics to insist that belief alone is rarely, if ever, an adequate substitute for evidence. Those who already believe in God may find some genuine reassurance in their conviction that their belief has been divinely implanted,[22] but atheists are unlikely to accept that we all know the truth and that they are merely too perverse to acknowledge it.

18. Hespos, and van Marle, "Physics for infants.".
19. Hespos, and van Marle, "Physics for infants."
20. Tooby, Cosmides, and Bennett, "Resolving the Debate on Innate Ideas," 309.
21. Pascal, Blaise, *Thoughts*, section IV paragraph 282, 69.
22. Romans 1:18–19.

ARGUMENTS FROM IMAGINATION AND REASON

Ontological arguments offer the intriguing, if credulity straining, prospect of proving the existence of God by imagination and logic. The most famous was offered by St Anselm (1033–1109). Despite the passage of nine centuries, there is still some debate about the precise nature of his argument, but the conventional interpretation involves a number of propositions:

- God is a being than which no greater can be thought;
- existing in both the mind and also in reality would be greater than existing solely in the mind;
- hence, if existing in the mind alone, God would not be a being than which no greater could be conceived;
- therefore, he must also exist in reality.[23]

The argument, as traditionally understood, was soon challenged by a skeptical monk, Gaunilo, who suggested that similar reasoning could be applied to 'prove' the existence of many things that do not exist, and offered the example of a perfect island or, in Anslem's terms, an island "than which no greater can be conceived."[24] Whilst Anselm's reply failed to silence critics,[25] Gaunilo's objection has been dismissed as "incoherent" on the ground that an island cannot have "conceptually maximal" qualities. For example, no matter how much fruit an island produces, it will always be possible to imagine one that produces more.[26] But not all maximal qualities are quantitative. A perfect circle need not be large, let alone of infinite size. And some qualities, like beauty, lie in the eye of the beholder. For many, the perfect island would not be large, have a large population or produce large quantities of fruit or anything else. Its attraction would lie in its scenery, location and climate. Had anyone asked Gaunilo to explain his own concept of a perfect island, he might have described a small but beautiful atoll in a convenient location free of squabbling prelates.

Of course, an island is not a sentient being and, had Gaunilo not been a monk, he might have suggested that Anselm's line of reasoning could be used to prove the existence of a perfect husband or wife. Since my own conceptions have to be formed within a male brain, I am inclined to embrace the latter as my theoretical yardstick, but what would a perfect wife be

23. Anselm, *St. Anselm: Basic Writings*. See also Logan, *Reading Anselm's Proslogion*.
24. Gaunilo. "Reply on Behalf of the Fool." In *Proslogion, with the Replies of Gaunilo and Anselm*. Translated by Thomas Williams, 27–33. Indianapolis: Hackett, 2001.
25. Wolterstorff, "In Defense of Gaunilo's Defense of the Fool."
26. Himma, Kenneth Einar, "Anselm: Ontological Argument for God's Existence"

like? Whilst any attempt to answer such a question would involve stepping onto very dangerous ground, I think I can safely say that she would not be the biggest or strongest woman in the world or the one likely to produce the most children. She might differ from my real wife, who is only almost perfect, by having a small fortune to lavish on my more expensive whims, but unlimited wealth would not be required. Apart from an engaging personality and some other attributes that I dare not mention lest I make some latter day Montaigne blush, the maximal qualities that would characterize a perfect wife would include those my real wife would suggest have always been required: infinite patience and forbearance. There is no obvious reason to doubt that such non-physical things may be conceptually maximal qualities. Hence, Anselm's argument might be applied to the conception of a wife greater (that is more perfect) than which cannot be conceived. Such a wife does not exist. Nor, I am told, does a perfect husband.

Aquinas rejected Anselm's argument on different grounds, arguing that not everyone understood the word "God" to mean "a being than which none greater can be imagined." He also argued that even those who accept that formulation may not understand that "what the word signifies exists actually, but only that it exists mentally."[27] It may be true that not everyone has the same conception of God as a perfect being. In reality, some may see God as an elderly, though all-powerful patriarch, whilst others see him as an omnipresent spirit permeating the cosmos. But Anselm's argument was not founded upon an assumption that everyone would share his own understanding of God. His premise was simply that God was a being so great than no greater could be conceived. Kant raised another objection, insisting that "being" is not a real predicate or, in other words, it is not an attribute that can be added to the concept of something.[28] It has been contended that, whilst this may also be true, it offers no real answer to Anselm's argument.[29] Hence, it has been dismissed as just a 'red herring',[30] though there has been a recent attempt to counter this criticism.[31]

---

27. Aquinas, St Thomas *Summa Theologica*, Volume 1, Treatise on the One God, Question 2, Article 1. See also this discussion in Matthews, "The ontological argument."

28. Kant, *Critique of Pure Reason*, Section IV. Of the Impossibility of an Ontological Proof of the Existence of God.

29. Plantinga, "Kant's objection to the ontological argument"; Matthews, "The ontological argument"; Millican, "The one fatal flaw in Anselm's argument"; Davies, "Anselm and the ontological argument"; and, Lowe, E. J.,'The ontological argument.'

30. Lowe, 337.

31. Heathwood, "The relevance of Kant's objection to Anselm's ontological argument."

A more fundamental objection is that the argument is based entirely upon what Anselm supposed might be thought. One may postulate the existence of something than which no greater can be thought and go on to postulate that such a being exists in reality and not in the mind alone. But that would still be a postulation. The thought would still be a thought. The reality would still be a postulated reality, And there would be no logical basis for an assumption that there is an actual reality that corresponds with the postulated reality. One can neither think something into existence nor, in the absence of evidence, prove that something exists by thinking alone.

Nonetheless, Anselm's argument has had some noted supporters, including Leibniz, who agreed that it was valid, though he was troubled by the fact that perfection was impossible to analyze.[32] Perhaps the strongest defense has recently been mounted by Richard Campbell who suggests that Anselm's argument has been misunderstood, largely because of an assumption that the gist of it was encapsulated in the second chapter of the "Proslogion" when Anselm does not actually reach his conclusion until the end of chapter 3.[33] Properly understood, the argument has three stages. In the first, he argues that "that than which a greater cannot be thought" cannot be only in the understanding. If it were, it could be thought to also exist in reality and that would be greater. In the second, he argues that "that than which a greater cannot be thought" so truly exists that it could not be thought not to exist. It is in the third stage that he concludes: "And this is You, Lord our God. Therefore, You so truly exist that You could not be thought not to exist." He offers two reasons for this conclusion. The first, if something greater than God could be thought, the creature would rise above the creator. As Campbell observes, this argument is unlikely to impress those who do not already believe in God. The second is the subject of Campbell's interesting gloss on the argument. Even Anselm's hypothetical 'fool' must recognize that "something-than-which-a-greater-cannot-be-thought" cannot be thought not to exist. Yet Anselm contended that whatever is other than God can be thought not to exist.[34] Campbell maintains that we know know that this is true because the universe did not exist prior to the Big Bang. Hence, if God does not exist, everything can be thought not to exist. But, since "something-than-which-a-greater-cannot-be-thought" cannot be thought not to exist, it is not true that everything can be thought not to exist. It follows, therefore,

---

32. Oppy, Graham, "Ontological Arguments." (revised 15 July 2011) *Stanford Encyclopedia of Philosophy*.

33. Campbell, *From Belief to Understanding*. See also Campbell, *Rethinking Anselm's Argument*.

34. According to a translation by Logan, *Reading Anselm's Proslogion: The History and Anselm's Argument and its Significance Today*.

that God does exist. The same reasoning would not apply to Gaunilo's hypothetical island because, unlike God, some island, than which a greater island cannot be thought, could be thought not to exist. Campbell also suggests that Anselm was not concerned with absolute proof, such as that provided by mathematical theorems. He recognized that belief in God is not dependent upon abstract reasoning alone and his argument was intended to provide confirmation of God's existence for believers and assure unbelievers that no-one who understands what God is, can think or say that He does not exist.[35]

Other ontological arguments have been developed by the Islamic philosopher, Mulla Sadra,[36] and more recently by Kurt Godel.[37] All seem vulnerable to the fundamental objection that one cannot prove the existence of someone or something without evidence of adequate factual premises or, as Hume put it, by *a priori* reasoning alone.[38] Descartes famously protested: "But, if the mere fact that I can produce from my thought the idea of something entails that everything which I clearly and distinctly perceive to belong to that thing really does belong to it, is not this a possible basis for another argument to prove the existence of God?"[39] The answer, in my opinion, is surely "no." In the absence of proven factual premises, neither the clarity nor the rational coherence of an idea can establish that there is an objective reality that coincides with it. Only Campbell seems to have addressed this issue, though you may think his citation of the non-existence of the universe prior to the Big Bang is not, of itself, sufficient to support Anselm's entire argument.

MORALITY AND CONSCIENCE

It is not only atheists who claim the high moral ground. There have always been religious believers who have seemed remarkably proud of their virtue. A striking example can be found in Psalm 26 where the author confidently assures God that he has led a blameless life. If correctly attributed to David, this was a bold claim to be made by a man who had taken over the wives of his former king to add to his existing collection, had a famous affair with Bathsheba and then arranged for the death of her husband.[40] Even those

35. Campbell, *That Anselm's God Exists but Gaunilo's Island is Lost Forever.*
36. Rizvi, "Mulla Sadra."
37. Maydole, *The Blackwell Companion to Natural Theology,* 574.
38. Russell, and Kraal, "Hume on Religion."
39. Descartes. *Meditations on First Philosophy,* "Meditation V: On the Essence of Material Objects and More on God's Existence."
40. 2 Samuel 11 and 12.

of us with less interesting domestic arrangements might baulk at making such a claim, especially to an omniscient being. Contemporary attempts to invoke the morality of believers as evidence for the existence of God are likely to be greeted with derision, especially in the light of recent scandals concerning the abuse of children by members of the clergy. But the philosophical arguments based on morality and conscience do not depend upon any claims that believers are morally superior people.

Thomas Aquinas (1225 – 1274) believed that the existence of God was self-evident, but suggested 'five ways' of proving that this was true.[41] The fourth was an argument based upon the gradation of things. Some beings are more or less good, true, or noble than others, but such a gradation ultimately involves a comparison with some absolute standard, "so that there is something which is truest, something best, something noblest and, consequently, something which is uttermost being; for those things that are greatest in truth are greatest in being." He went on to explain that:

> . . . the maximum in any genus is the cause of all in that genus; as fire, which is the maximum heat, is the cause of all hot things. Therefore there must also be something which is to all beings the cause of their being, goodness, and every other perfection; and this we call God.[42]

Aquinas is revered as a great theologian who forged a new '*modus vivendi*' between faith and philosophy,[43] gave rise to the philosophical school dubbed, somewhat unimaginatively, as 'Thomism' and generally made an enormous contribution to Western thought. Furthermore, this argument was merely one of his 'five ways' and, even if it seems insufficient in itself, one may ask whether it might nonetheless lend some weight to the cumulative effect of the others. But does it have any validity at all?

The argument seems to have two parts and they use the word 'cause' in different ways. In writing of the 'cause' of all in the genus, Aquinas presumably means a formal cause, that is the pattern or form which explains what something is, rather than the efficient cause, which explains what caused it to come into existence. Understood in this manner, the first part of the argument suggests that, if the beings we know have varying degrees of goodness and perfection, then another being must exist that is maximally good and perfect. The 'cause' referred to in the latter part of his formulation

---

41. Aquinas, *Summa Theologica*, First part, a, Question 2, Article 3.
42. Aquinas, *Summa Theologica*, Part I, Question 2, Article 3.
43. McInerny and O'Callaghan, "Saint Thomas Aquinas."

is an efficient cause.[44] Hence, the second part of the argument suggests that, since we possess these qualities in varying degrees, they are not intrinsic to us, but derived from some source that is the exemplar of such qualities, and that exemplar is God.

Neither proposition seems compelling. It is certainly true that people have good qualities in varying degrees. For example, some are more generous than others. But does this really justify a conclusion that there must be a being who is perfectly generous? Would the converse also be true? Does the fact that we also vary in degrees of stinginess demonstrate that there must be a perfect Scrooge? One may also question the assumption that our imperfect goodness must be derived from a God of perfect goodness. Positive character traits, such as concern for others, are fostered by familial and cultural conditioning, emotional factors, experiences, the decisions we make and the kind of people we aspire to be, though it might be conceded that many people do seem to display a bedrock of compassion that is difficult to explain by these factors alone.

Half a millennium passed before Kant proposed another argument, insisting that the morality of an action be judged, not by the likely consequences, but by its conformity to the principle on which it is based. The principle should be one capable of satisfying 'the categorical imperative', that is the maxim that you could wish to become a universal law. He acknowledged that all actions are intended to produce results and suggested that the ultimate goal of reason is the highest good, (*summum bonum* in Latin) which consists of a combination of virtue and happiness. Since it is our duty to promote the highest good, we should assume it is possible and, since that would be true only if God existed, 'it is morally necessary to assume the existence of God.' Reason would otherwise impose an unattainable goal.[45] Some have objected that morality does not require us to seek the highest good, merely that good which is humanly achievable.[46] However, the argument is surely open to the more fundamental objection that perceptions of moral necessity do not prove existence.

John Henry Newman advanced an argument founded upon human conscience, pointing out that people are driven to act morally even when this is not in their best interests. He thought that this suggested the existence of objective moral truths and argued that God must exist to give authority

---

44. Elders, *The Philosophical Theology of St. Thomas Aquinas*, 116; and Feser, *Aquinas : a beginner's guide*, 99–109.
45. Kant, *Critique of Practical Reason*, book 2, 1–2 para 35.
46. Adams, R.,"Moral Arguments for Theism," 152.

to them.[47] C. S. Lewis took up Newman's theme, arguing that our sense of right and wrong is evidence of a moral law that can only be explained by a divine lawmaker.[48] Arguments of this kind have been opposed on various grounds. John Stuart Mill remained unpersuaded, insisting that the "feeling of obligation" arises from "something that the internal conscience bears witness to in its own nature" and not from a source external to the mind.[49] Some, including John Locke, have protested that differences in people's consciences suggest contradictory moral rules.[50] Others have observed that conscience is influenced by various factors such as education, culture and the opinions of others.[51] Despite the oft repeated mantra that "we all know right from wrong," it is obviously true that the world abounds with different moral codes and standards. A Quaker may be a committed pacifist, whilst a soldier may feel compelled to fight, but both may be following the dictates of conscience.

However, the extent to which different moral standards lead to different actions should not be exaggerated. Lewis supports his view of the universality of what he described as the "Law of Nature" by reference to moral precepts drawn from Jewish, Christian, Hindu, Babylonian Old Norse, Egyptian, Chinese, Greek and Roman sources,[52] and the atheist philosopher, Peter Singer, has also noted a striking convergence of views about how we should live even amongst those who embrace quite different ethical traditions.[53] Lewis insists that there is a "Law of Nature" running through all cultures and all times and that standards of morality are invariably measured, even if subconsciously, against some "Real Morality."[54] This is not wholly convincing. There may well be common threads of moral belief, but it is difficult to see how that could demonstrate the existence of a transcendent source. One may also find common threads of upbringing, experience and aspiration that may shape our moral standards.

A further argument has been founded on the proposition that God is the only rational explanation for our awareness of moral truth.[55] Of course,

---

47. Newman, *An Essay in Aid of a Grammar of Assent.*
48. Lewis, *Mere Christianity*, book one.
49. Mill, *Nature, The Utility of Religion, and Theism*, 164–165.
50. Parkinson, *An Encyclopedia of Philosophy*, 344–345.
51. Singer, "Afterword," 543.
52. Lewis, *The Abolition of Man*, 95–121.
53. Singer, "Afterword," 543.
54. Lewis, *Mere Christianity*, 22–24.
55. Swinburne, *The Existence of God*. See also Ritchie, *From Morality to Metaphysics: The Theistic Implications of our Ethical Commitments.*

Pontius Pilate was probably not the first to cynically ask "what is truth?" But, whilst human conceptions of moral truths are not wholly aligned, we do seem to share a common moral sense that some things are right and some things are wrong. What is the source of this moral sensibility? Is God the only reasonable answer? Richard Swinburne insists that there is "no great probability that moral awareness will occur in a Godless universe."[56] But is this true? One might, perhaps, argue that the evolutionary concept of survival of the fittest should have meant that ruthlessness was an essential attribute of any emergent species, but humanity did not remain an emergent species. We developed interpersonal skills, founded communities and, in time, societies that gave rise to cultural expectations. There are also many psychological factors from which perceptions of moral truths could have emerged, even if not divinely inspired.[57]

A related argument draws upon the concept of human dignity or worth. It is suggested that the best explanation for this intrinsic value is that we are created by God in his own image.[58] This may seem obvious to some who already believe in a benevolent God and it may resonate with humanitarian sentiments, but does the value of our human lives really prove the existence of a divine creator? Some may protest that the turbulent history of our species is punctuated by enough atrocities to dispel any romantic notion of universal worth or dignity. Others may see brutality and depravity as aberrations from the norm and insist that the argument does not refute belief in the innate goodness of all humanity. But even if that view is accepted, one must surely make some allowance for human responsibility. Is human value any more than a reflection of human character? And is character something bestowed like a blessing or developed by one's responses to the moral choices and challenges of life? Of course, some who acknowledge the validity of these questions may nonetheless suggest that we have been touched by the spirit of God[59] or even made in his image.[60]

It has also been suggested that, irrespective of such arguments, knowledge of God may be derived from 'moral experience,'[61] a concept said to encompass "a person's sense that the values that he or she deems important

---

56. Swinburne, *The Existence of God*, 281.

57. Wright, *The Moral Animal—Why We Are the Way We Are: The New Science of Evolutionary Psychology*, See also FitzPatrick, "Morality and Evolutionary Biology" y.

58. Evans, "Moral Arguments for the Existence of God."

59. Qur'an, 15:29.

60. Genesis 1:27.

61. See, for example, the discussion in Plantinga, *Warranted Christian Belief*; and Rizzieri, *Pragmatic Encroachment, Religious Belief and Practice*.

are being realized or thwarted in everyday life."[62] It is true that experiences which evoke strong emotions such as a burning sense of injustice may create a heightened moral awareness, but does that offer a logical springboard for knowledge of God? One thing does seem relatively clear: we all seem to have an innate feeling that there must be justice. We may conceive of it differently. Some may even try to dismiss the feeling as a chink in their materialistic armor. Yet, as a lawyer, I saw even atheist clients recoil from warnings that they might lose their cases with exclamations like, "Don't you believe in justice?" It is a deeply engrained expectation that is expressed by people of all ages and cultures. Is it merely the product of self interest and cultural conditioning? Or does it reflect something more?

THE FIRST CAUSE

Whilst there have been some recent challenges to the Big Bang theory,[63] it is now generally accepted that there must have been a first cause of the known universe. This has not always been the prevailing view. The early Greek philosopher, Parmenides had famously said that 'nothing comes from nothing', a proposition endorsed by Maria, the singing nun in *The Sound of Music*. Both Plato and Aristotle accepted this dictum but they responded to it in different ways. Plato argued that all movement was 'imparted motion' that must have been initiated by a 'self-originated motion.'[64] Hence, he concluded that there must have been a first cause of the universe and this he attributed to the demiurge. On the other hand, whilst Aristotle accepted the concept of a 'prime mover', he rejected the suggestion of a first cause, maintaining that the universe had always existed. The Islamic philosopher, Avicenna, (c. 980–1037) followed Aristotle in accepting that the universe was eternal. He thought it was a natural product of God, but that it succeeded him only in logical order and in existence. He argued that our experience of the world confirms that things exist but, since things come and go, it is obvious that their existence is not necessary. Such contingent existence cannot emerge unless made necessary by some cause. But there cannot be an infinite regression of causes. A causal chain must lead back to one cause that was not itself caused by anything else. Hence, things that have come into existence

---

62 Hunt and Carnevale. "Moral Experience: A framework for Bioethics Research."

63. See for example, Noble,"Novel Theory Challenges The Big Bang"; Quach, "Domain structures in quantum graphity"; and, Zyga, "No Big Bang? Quantum equation predicts universe has no beginning."

64. Plato, *The Laws of Plato*, book X.

must be attributable to a single necessary being, who he insisted, must be the God of religion.[65]

The steady state theory of cosmology, which maintained that whilst the universe was expanding it had neither a beginning nor an end, retained considerable support even in the mid-20th century.[66] But the discovery of cosmic microwave background radiation in 1964[67] provided strong evidence for the 'Big Bang' theory and the issue was substantially resolved by an analysis of data gathered from an experiment aboard NASA's Cosmic Background Explorer (COBE) satellite which earned George Smoot and John Mather a Nobel prize. Issues are still being raised. For example, a recent paper has presented a Big Bang model without an initial singularity.[68] But few reputable scientists now dispute the essential theory or doubt that the universe came into existence at a time now thought to have been some 13.8 billion years ago. The crucial question is what caused it?

Gnostics embraced the concept of the demiurge as a being, separate from God, who created the physical world they regarded as flawed, if not evil, in contrast with the spiritual world of God.[69] Other theists insist that the first cause must have been God. As the writer of the New Testament letter to the Hebrews put it, 'for every house is built by someone, but the builder of all things is God.'[70] And, if I may leap ahead a dozen centuries, three of Aquinas' five ways of proving the existence of God were essentially first cause arguments.

The first, which he thought was the 'more manifest' way, was another argument from motion. In this context, the concept of 'motion' extends to real change. It is obvious that some things are in motion and. he insisted, it is impossible for a thing to be in the same respects both mover and moved; it cannot move itself. Yes, I am sure he understood that the bird and animal kingdoms were replete with beings that moved of their own volition. His point was that since all movement has to have a cause, there had have been

---

65. Rizvi, "Avicenna (Ibn Sina) (c. 980–1037)."

66. Kragh, Helge. *Cosmology and Controversy: The Historical Development of Two Theories of the Universe.* See also Hoyle, "A New Model for the Expanding Universe."

67. Penzias, and Wilson, "A Measurement of Excess Antenna Temperature at 4080 Mc/s."

68. Ali and Das. "Cosmology from quantum potential."

69. Meyer (ed), *The Gnostic Gospels*, esp 67 et seq. See also Gflhus, "The Gnostic Demiurge—An Agnostic Trickster"; Jonas, *The Gnostic Religion: The Message of the Alien God*; Filoramo, *A History of Gnosticism*; and, Petrement, *A Separate God: The Christian Origins of Gnosticism.*

70. Hebrews 3:4.

a chain of events or "movements" leading back to "a first mover" and "this everyone understands to be God."[71]

His second way involved a similar process of reasoning relating to efficient causes. Nothing can be the efficient cause of itself. Whatever causes something must itself have been caused by something else and that must in turn have had another cause. Hence there must have been a chain of causes emanating from a first efficient cause "to which everyone gives the name of God."[72]

The third way was an argument based upon possibility and necessity. It is possible for some things to exist or not to exist but, if this were true of everything, then at one time there could have been nothing in existence. If nothing existed, nothing could have begun to exist, because there would have been nothing to bring anything into being. Hence, there must be something whose existence is necessary. But the necessity of one thing can only be caused by something else and there must therefore be chain of necessary things leading back to a being that does not derive its necessity from anything else, but rather causes necessity in others. "This all men speak of as God."[73]

Of course, Aquinas advanced these arguments in the 13th century, before people like Copernicus, Kepler and Galileo arrived to rock the cosmological boat and well before Darwin had launched his challenge to orthodox views of the natural order. It may now be argued that there is no need to posit a benevolent supernatural giant to stir the tides, blow the wind into being or to spin the celestial spheres like so many children's tops. But that is not the logical end of the process of enquiry. A better understanding of the arcane mysteries of computers does not refute the proposition that they must have been designed and made. Similarly, acceptance of evolutionary processes does not negate Aquinas' argument that something must have made the universe and set these processes in motion.[74] Indeed, the theory of natural selection points inexorably back to a first cause.

Whilst that may have seemed self-evident, it has recently been challenged by the rather startling claim that the entire cosmos may have sprung into existence from nothing. The noted atheist, Lawrence Krauss, begins his attempt to support this contention with the observation that particles of matter correspond to certain configurations of quantum fields. In a vacuum

---

71. Aquinas, *Summa Theologica*, First part, a, Question 2, Article 3.
72. Aquinas, *Summa Theologica*, First part, a, Question 2, Article 3.
73. Aquinas, *Summa Theologica*, First part, a, Question 2, Article 3.
74. For an account of the history of the cosmological argument see Craig, *The Cosmological Argument from Plato to Leibniz*.

state there may be no particles but it is possible for particles to come into existence. Hence, he argues, matter can emerge from a space in which there is no matter.[75] These propositions may be defensible by reference to contemporary quantum field theory,[76] but he then moves on to more speculative suggestions: the universe as a whole might have zero net energy, space and time might emerge from a state without space and time, and the laws of nature might be "stochastic and random." And, if these "mights" were all linked together in a speculative chain, they might lead to a speculative conclusion: you might be able to imagine a universe, replete with hundreds of billions of galaxies, spontaneously winking into existence from a state with no matter, no particles, no space and no time. See? Something can come from nothing.

Dawkins wrote an afterword in which he said that the argument looked to him to be "the knockout blow" for theism but, despite this optimistic endorsement, the book has not been greeted with universal acclaim. In a scathing review,[77] David Albert, a fellow atheist, asked where the laws of quantum mechanics themselves were supposed to have come from? He said that Krauss had not suggested an answer and quoted Krauss' comment that he did not know "if this notion can be usefully dispensed with." But this was only Albert's opening salvo. He went on to explain that the fundamental laws of nature generally take the form of rules concerning arrangements of the elementary stuff (particles and fields) from which the universe is made; they do not address questions about where such elementary stuff may have come from. This is also true of the laws of relativistic quantum field theories upon which Krauss based his argument. According to the standard presentation of such theories, the elementary physical stuff consists of relativistic quantum fields. The universe is made from them. The fundamental laws of these theories concern arrangements of the fields; not their origins.

Whilst earlier physical theories assumed that the elementary physical stuff of the world consisted of material particles, relativistic quantum field theories insist that particles should be understood as specific arrangements of the fields. Those accustomed to imagining particles as microscopic but solid lumps of matter, like tiny marbles or grains of sand, might find this concept both disconcerting and difficult to grasp, but it does reflect

---

75. Krauss, *A Universe from Nothing*.

76. Ray, *Time, space and philosophy*, 205; Dittrich, Walter and Holger Gies, *Probing the quantum vacuum: perturbative effective action approach*. Berlin: Springer, 2000; and Lambrecht, "Observing mechanical dissipation in the quantum vacuum; an experimental challenge" 197.

77. Albert, "Sunday Book Review: On the Origin of Everything, 'A Universe From Nothing,' by Lawrence M. Krauss."

current scientific understanding. As Richard Campbell has put it, a particle is "a quantized excitation of a field."[78] Hence, both the fields and the laws of quantum mechanics that seem to govern their behavior may be seen as the fundamental bases from which all things have been formed.

In his assault on Krauss' approach, Albert explained that different arrangements of quantum fields may involve different numbers of particles or even no particles at all. An arrangement in which there are no particles is called a 'vacuum state'. Particles may emerge from such a state, but this does not mean that something can come from nothing. As Albert insisted, vacuum states, "no less than giraffes or refrigerators or solar systems," are arrangements of elementary physical stuff; they are not nothing. And, he concluded, "the fact that particles can pop in and out of existence, over time, as those fields rearrange themselves, is not a whit more mysterious than the fact that fists can pop in and out of existence, over time, as my fingers rearrange themselves."

Krauss' argument seems have been predicated upon an assumption that the word "nothing" merely means a quantum field arrangement involving a perhaps momentary absence of particles. Of course, quantum fields continue to exist at such times. Krauss himself concedes that empty space is "complicated" and describes it as "a boiling brew of virtual particles that pop in and out of existence . . ." It has also been suggested that other required ingredients would include: "symmetry and asymmetry, a small amount of matter to remain after almost equal amounts of matter and antimatter annihilate each other, the inequality driven by some random initial condition; underlying laws to allow quantum processes to drive the universe away from a featureless state; space, time, energy and its storage, general relativity, all possibilities allowed by the laws of nature as occurring, and inflationary dynamics."[79] A lot of things seem to be involved in his conception of nothing.

Krauss had sought to forestall criticism of this kind by deriding the "nothing" of his apparently anticipated critics as a "vague and ill-defined" and even an "intellectually bankrupt" notion of "nonbeing."[80] The compilers of the world's dictionaries presumably stand condemned. He responded to Albert's criticism by referring to him as "a moronic philosopher" who had said that "having particles and no particles is the same thing."[81] This was not

78. Campbell, *The Metaphysics of Emergence*, 65.

79. Boyer, "Did the Universe Emerge from Nothing? Reductive vs. Holistic Cosmology," 432.

80. Krauss, *A Universe From Nothing*, at xiii—xiv.

81. Andersen, "Has Physics Made Philosophy and Religion Obsolete?."

reassuring. Albert has a doctorate in theoretical physics, has written widely on quantum mechanics[82] and does not seem to have made the comment attributed to him. Furthermore, his criticism has been substantially echoed by others. Another atheist, Jerry Coyne, who is a professor of biology, also rejected Krauss' argument. He complained that Krauss had defined "nothing" as a "quantum vacuum," without explaining why that would have been the initial default state of the universe and asked, rhetorically, whether that was a sensible definition of "nothing"[83] Luke Barnes said he would like to defend a fellow cosmologist but concluded: "I'm with Albert and my reasons mirror his." Barnes explained that: "Particles can appear from no-particles, not from nothing. The underlying field is always there. A state with zero energy is not nothing."[84]

But if the cosmos did not spontaneously emerge from nothing, one must return to the question: what caused it? St Augustine and other Christian theologians believed that God created the universe *ex nihilo*, first creating formless matter and then using that to create the world and the heavens.[85] Other theories have been floated from time to time and there is now a minor epidemic of them. Stephen Hawking maintains that at the point of the Big Bang the universe was "scrunched up into a single point of infinite density."[86] Inflation theory holds that repulsive gravity then caused the scrunched material to expand at great speed, perhaps exceeding the speed of light, a phenomenon thought to have been possible because space itself was expanding. In doing so, it produced the entire cosmos, including light, cosmic waves, the visible objects like suns, planets and galaxies but also dark matter and dark energy.[87] Some cosmologists suggest that it is eternal inflation that leads to an infinity of universes,[88] a suggestion said to be a natural extension of standard inflationary cosmology.[89] However, it has recently been suggested that whilst, once begun, inflation may continue

---

82. Albert, *Quantum Mechanics and Experience*, 1994.

83. Coyne, "David Albert pans Lawrence Krauss's new book."

84. Barnes, Luke, 'A universe from nothing? Putting the Krauss-Craig debate into perspective'.

85. Augustine, *De Genesi Contra Manichaeos*, I: 5: 9. 'Two Books On Genesis Against the Manichees' in *The Fathers of the Church: A New Translation*, Vol. 84.

86. Hawking, *The Universe in a Nutshell*.

87. Guth, Alan H. *The Inflationary Universe: The Quest for a New Theory of Cosmic Origins*; and Guth, "Eternal inflation and its implications.." See also Singh, *Big Bang: The Origin of the Universe*; and Silk, *Horizons of Cosmology*.

88. Guth, "Eternal inflation and its implications"; and Tegmark, *Our Mathematical Universe*.

89. Cox and Cohen, *Human Universe*, 224.

indefinitely, that does not mean that it did not start at some point.[90] Nobody knows how or why it might have started and Paul Steinhardt has observed that "we think the conditions under which inflation could begin are very, very rare," an observation that led one writer to complain that "unless you believe in a Creator, that's not a good place to be."[91]

Other concerns have also been raised about the adequacy of cosmic inflationary theories.[92] Sir Roger Penrose has argued that the thermalization process proposed in common formulations of inflationary theory would be incompatible with the 2nd Law of Thermodynamics. Hence, he says: "If we want to know why the universe was initially so very special, in its extraordinary uniformity, we must appeal to completely different arguments from those upon which inflationary cosmology depends."[93] Steinhardt has raised other issues, observing that the energy values initially suggested for inflation were in an extremely narrow range and the flat and smooth universe now recognized by astronomers and cosmologists is much more likely to have occurred in some other manner. He explains that an apparently striking correlation between cosmic microwave background radiation (CMB) and initial predictions derived from inflationary theory in 1983 must now be discounted because the initial model was incorrect. He also observes that, since the concept of eternal inflation would suggest that all things will happen, the theory may be untestable.[94]

Alternatives to inflationary theory have been proposed, including a "technicolor" force mediated by "techniquarks" (almost unimaginably tiny particles that some scientists believe may bind together to form the Higgs boson),[95] accelerating expansion models with no cosmological constant, some involving "quintessence" (a hypothetical scalar field),[96] and models that reject dark matter and dark energy in favor of other explanations for the relevant phenomena, such as the suggestion that antimatter collecting

---

90. Linde, Andrei, *Inflationary Cosmology after Planck 2013*,19; and Cox and Cohen, *Human Universe*, 226.

91. Lemonick, "New model of the cosmos: a Universe that begins again."

92. Lemonick, "New model of the cosmos: a Universe that begins again."

93. Penrose, *The Road to Reality: A Complete Guide to the Laws of the Universe*, 754–757.

94. Steinhardt,"The inflation debate: Is the theory at the heart of modern cosmology deeply flawed?"

95. Smith,"The large hadron collider: The edge of physics"; Dubrow, "Testing Technicolor Physics."

96. Zlatev, Wang and Steinhardt, "Quintessence, Cosmic Coincidence, and the Cosmological Constant."

in empty areas of space may have been the repulsive gravitational force.[97] There are also cyclical models, including one that draws upon string theory and deems our universe to be a "*D-brane*," a type of mathematical object that collides with and bounces from other similar objects and every trillion years or so causes a contraction followed by another expansion.[98] Another cyclic model, dubbed "Conformal Cyclic Cosmology," suggests a pattern in which the universe emerges repeatedly from one Big Bang to another, each followed by an infinite future expansion.[99]

The profusion of ideas may remind one of the axiom offered by at least one exasperated forensic scientist in a case in which I once acted as counsel: "for every opinion there is an equal and opposite opinion." But this is not the place for an analysis of this smorgasbord of theories. Even in the unlikely event that one of them ultimately proved verifiable, it would still be necessary to ask what was the first cause of the inflationary or cyclical process. For present purposes, I am concerned only with the first cause of the universe we currently inhabit and, despite these imaginative conceptions, the origin remains unknown to science. More than two decades ago, a skeptical astronomer protested: "First there was nothing, then there was something. And the cosmologists try to bridge the two with a quantum flutter, a tremor of uncertainty that sparks it all... and before you know it, they have pulled a hundred billion galaxies out of their quantum hats..."[100]

Francis Collins, former Director of the National Human Genome Research Institute, has made the same point: there is something instead of nothing, when there is no obvious reason why there should be anything at all. He mentions the view of Eugene Wigner, a Nobel laureate in physics, that the amazing thing about the whole study of physics is that mathematics makes sense; it can describe the properties of matter and energy in simple, even beautiful, laws. Collins asks, "Why should that be? Why should gravity follow an inverse square law? Why should Maxwell's five equations describe electromagnetism in very simple terms, and they actually turn out to be true?"[101]

---

97. Zyga, Lisa, "Repulsive gravity as an alternative to dark energy (Part 1: In voids)"; and Zyga, Lisa, "Repulsive gravity as an alternative to dark energy" (Part 2: In the quantum vacuum). See also Villata,"The matter-antimatter interpretation of Kerr spacetime."

98. Steinhardt, and Turok. *Endless Universe.*

99. Penrose, *Cycles of Time: An Extraordinary New View of the Universe.*

100. Darling,"On creating something out of nothing," 49.

101. Collins, Francis, "Dr Francis S. Collins and Barbara Bradley Hagerty at the May 2009 Faith Angle Forum"

And no, everything is not explained by the Big Bang. As the string theorist, Brian Greene observes: "The big bang is a theory...that delineates cosmic evolution from a split second after whatever happened to bring the universe into existence, but it says nothing at all about time zero itself... The big bang leaves out the bang. It tells us nothing about what banged, why it banged, how it banged, or, frankly whether it ever really banged at all."[102] In fact, whilst there appears to be strong evidence for inflation at the time that atoms first formed, a time now believed to be about 380,000 years after the Big Bang began, the evidence for anything that may have happened earlier has been dismissed as "not in the least reliable."[103] Martin Rees, the Astronomer Royal, has gone further, suggesting that the goal of understanding the beginning of the universe may be unattainable. He explains that "there could be no 'final' theory; or, if there is, it could be beyond our mental powers to grasp it."[104]

So where does all that leave the 'first cause' debate? It may be fashionable to dismiss the great thinkers of earlier ages as people fumbling for answers in pre-scientific darkness but, perhaps ironically, their arguments remain undiminished and perhaps even strengthened by modern science. Throughout most of recorded history, the view that the world must have been created by a sentient being or beings remained largely unchallenged, save by those who, like Aristotle, maintained that the universe was eternal. That long sustained challenge to Plato's concept of a created world has now been repulsed. The arguments Aquinas advanced about motion, efficient cause and necessity have also emerged unscathed from the scientific advances of more recent centuries and been strengthened by evidence that the universe came into existence at a finite time. Indeed, if his saintliness had been able to recognize the existence of quantum fields and the physical laws that have since been identified by modern cosmology, he would almost certainly have added them to his list of things for which only God could be a likely explanation.

Many of those who seem sure that there must be an obvious alternative to creation theories may be surprised to find that the best science seems able to offer is speculation about an unknowable, unverifiable and non-sentient state of an unspecified something called inflation, mindlessly churning out infinite numbers of new universes throughout eternity. Of course, God is also said to be eternal, infinite and, at least so far as accepted scientific

---

102. Greene, Brian *The Fabric of the Cosmos: Space, Time, and the Texture of Reality*, 272.

103. Strassler, Matt, "Which Parts of the Big Bang Theory are Reliable, and Why?"

104. Rees, Martin, *Just Six Numbers*, 176.

methodology is concerned, unknowable and unverifiable. Indeed, despite widespread presuppositions that scientific and religious explanations for the universe must surely be 'chalk and cheese', there are striking similarities. But which is right? Attitudes have changed since the days of Aquinas. In earlier generations the great scientific thinkers like Copernicus, Kepler, Galileo, Newton, Faraday and Planck all believed in God. It is now fashionable to exclude even the possibility of God from scientific discourse and to approach this issue with a perhaps subconscious *a priori* commitment to finding an answer devoid of religious implications. Perhaps the most striking example of this commitment is the apparent acceptance of simulation theories, involving, the proposition that the universe was designed and created by a super-intelligent being, but continued insistence that this being must not be God.

Of course, the musings of theists and atheists alike are inevitably influenced by their presuppositions and biases but, if you could shrug off such psychological influences, what inference would you draw? And is there any other evidence that might cast some light on the likelihood of sentient involvement?

SIGNS OF DESIGN

The latter question leads, of course, to a discussion about indications of design. I am not, of course, concerned with arguments against the concept of natural selection that are sometimes promoted as "creation science" and "intelligent design." As Stephen Barr has observed, such arguments may have convinced many people that the concept of an intelligent designer involves rejection of mainstream science.[105] That is unfortunate because scientific issues require objective analysis, not peremptory dismissal.

Throughout the centuries there have been people who have seen evidence for God in the beauty of the world. Some 3,000 years ago David found time away from his domestic responsibilities to write: "The heavens declare the glory of God; The skies proclaim the work of His hands."[106] A millennium later St Paul said: "For since the creation of the world His invisible attributes, His eternal power and divine nature, have been clearly seen, being understood through what has been made."[107] In the fifth century St Augustine asked: "Who made these beautiful changeable things, if not one who

---

105. Farrell, "A Physicist Talks God And The Quantum."
106. Psalm 19:1.
107. Romans 1:18–20.

is beautiful and unchangeable?"[108] Isaac Newton (1642–1727) also believed that the existence of God was evident from the grandeur of his creation.[109] Countless people have looked at natural wonders such as the panoply of stars on a moonless night and been moved by awe to acknowledge the works of a sentient creator.

Others regard impressions of a supernatural artist as naive assumptions that may have been understandable in pre-scientific ages but are no longer tenable. Newton is included in virtually every list of the greatest scientific geniuses in history, but even he was born before Darwin formulated his theory of natural selection and modern cosmology revealed crucial facts about the universe. Our senses of beauty and wonderment may have emerged from the evolutionary processes that formed us and from our experiences of the world in which we have spent our lives. Yet neither an appreciation of beauty nor a sense of what might be described as the numinous seem readily attributable to notions of the survival of the fittest, and many people still see our capacity to appreciate beauty as evidence of the existence of God.[110]

Others see evidence of design in order and direction. Aquinas' fifth way was based on the apparent governance of the world. Inanimate bodies act consistently and in ways that suggest design. As Aquinas puts it: "whatever lacks intelligence cannot move towards an end, unless it be directed by some being endowed with knowledge and intelligence; as the arrow is shot to its mark by the archer."[111] Hume initially accepted that issues of causality pointed to a designer,[112] though he presented competing arguments in a dialogue.[113] However, it was the analogy of a watch, famously articulated by William Paley, that for most people seemed to encapsulate the argument based on design. Haley presented his version of the analogy in 1802, arguing, in essence, that complexity and utility akin to that evident in a watch can be discerned in the natural world and this suggests that it was designed and constructed by God.[114]

---

108. Augustine, "The beauty of the unchangeable creator is to be inferred from the beauty of the changeable creation."

109. Webb, "The emergence of Rational Dissent," 19.

110. Swinburne, *The Existence of God*.

111. Aquinas, *Summa Theologicae*, First part, a, Question 2, Article 3.

112. Wright, "The Treatise: Reception, Composition, and Response," 12.

113. Hume, *Dialogues Concerning Natural Religion*.

114. Paley, *Natural Theology: or, Evidences of the Existence and Attributes of the Deity*, chapter 1. See also McGrath, A. E., *Darwinism and the Divine: Evolutionary Thought and Natural Theology*, 94.

This was an entirely reasonable inference, given the prevailing knowledge, and Darwin initially found it compelling, though he later rejected it in the light of his theory of natural selection. Whilst a Christian in his younger years, Darwin later became an agnostic,[115] though, as previously mentioned, he continued to accepted that theism and evolution were compatible. A potentially more important controversy arises in relation to the apparent fine-tuning of the universe that makes it hospitable to life. The universe does not present as especially attuned to human life as distinct from animal and bird life, but the apparent fine tuning is nonetheless remarkable. There are so many cosmic bowls of porridge that had to be just right and the ranges of tolerance were extremely tight. As discussed earlier, the odds of all this coming together in a manner hospitable to life were astronomical. Even the conventional wisdom that order gradually emerged from chaos[116] has now been challenged. Greene has suggested that, whatever its origins, the universe did not begin in a thoroughly disordered, high-entropy state. He maintains that, if that had occurred, further cosmic evolution would have maintained the initial disorder. "Even though particular symmetries have been lost through cosmic phase transitions, the overall entropy of the universe has steadily increased. In the beginning, therefore, the universe must have been highly ordered."[117] How could this have occurred?

Of course, we could have just won a statistical jackpot, but all this obviously raises at least a strong prima facie case in favor of a designer. There is a cacophony of learned and strident voices anxious to answer this by reference to the cosmological theories already mentioned. But whilst striking indications of fine tuning logically suggests the existence of a fine tuner, they do not logically suggest the existence of an infinity of other universes. Some writers seem to treat multiverses, not as mere hypotheses, but as established facts and they suggest, explicitly or implicitly, that in the light of these unverified theories we should now accept that science has shown there was no sentient hand in the creation of the universe. This is not an expression of skepticism; it is a fanciful distortion of the evidence.

As previously mentioned, another possible explanation is that the universe is a simulation of some kind, but the simulator would presumably have lived in another universe whilst creating this one and the very concept of a simulation would also suggest that it would have had similar laws and properties. Furthermore, that universe would also have had a first cause.

115. Darwin, "Letter 12041—Darwin, C. R. to Fordyce, John, 7 May 1879."

116. See, for example, Stroglatz, *Sync: How Order Emerges from Chaos in the Universe*.

117. B. Greene, *The Fabric of the Cosmos: Space, Time, and the Texture of Reality*, 271.

Whilst Dawkins and others antipathetic to religious belief insist on a sharp distinction between natural processes and creation by an "abracadabra" exclamation, this is simply naive. Of course, it is a naivety shared by some religious believers whose image of God seems to involve a comforting blend of judge, magician and Santa Claus, But Carl Sagan was right: any sensible conception of God must take into account the magnificent grandeur of the universe and all it contains. It may be a universe of almost unimaginable complexity, but it is clearly subject to universal physical laws without which we could not exist. Theists insist that they were set in place by God. The crucial question is whether that is the true explanation or whether, despite the speculative nature of the alternative theories, there may be some other explanation.

In other contexts, people routinely draw inferences from established facts whilst remaining mindful of the possibility that there may be other possibilities. For example, juries are routinely asked to convict defendants on the basis of circumstantial evidence. In almost every case, even those in which there is apparently damning DNA evidence, alternative explanations might be conceivable. Evidence could have been planted, DNA samples contaminated, or the tests incompetently conducted, even though there is no evidence that any of these things actually happened. So how would you decide such a case? I suspect that most jurors would begin by considering the strength of the inferences that could otherwise be drawn from the facts actually established by the evidence and then consider whether unverified speculation about things that might have happened was sufficient to raise a reasonable doubt. A similar approach may be adopted when considering evidence of the apparent fine tuning of the universe. Is this a reasonable approach?

OTHER ARGUMENTS

There are many other arguments.[118] Some, including arguments from life, consciousness and religious experience, will be discussed in the next two chapters. Others I will pass over in the interests of brevity. This should not be seen as an indication that none of them are worth examining. On the contrary, I would encourage any skeptic to read and consider all of the arguments for and against the existence of God. But for present purposes it is again time to move on.

---

118. For a brief summation see Kreeft, *Twenty Arguments For God's Existence*.

6

Are We Just Meat?

What of us? Can our own lives and our capacity to experience things and make choices offer any insight into our nature and destiny? What do we know about the nature of life? And consciousness? Are our minds merely phenomena produced by our physical brains or something more? Souls perhaps? What of our feelings and other experiences? Do they provide us with reliable information? Can they cast any light on the existence of God or other spiritual phenomena? Do our beliefs about these things really matter? Are we free to make our own decisions or is free will an illusion? Are our beliefs and attitudes predetermined by unrecognized but nonetheless inexorable forces beyond our control? And, despite our achievements and even occasional flights of seeming transcendence, are we really just concatenations of meat and bone, animated by fortuitous evolutionary quirks but subject to remorseless fate?

LIFE

Any wholly satisfactory theory of everything would not only need to provide a plausible explanation for the origin of the universe and its extraordinary hospitality to life but also explain life itself. It is one thing to account for an hospitable environment and another to account for the living beings that populate it. Natural selection may explain the evolution of successive life forms from earlier ones but it does not explain either the nature of life or its origin. Of course, the world is teeming with different life forms and we homo sapiens may now be able to trace our emergence back through *Homo heidelbergensis*, the species that may be the common ancestor we share with

Neanderthals, to other primates and beyond to the earliest life forms. But things are either alive or they are not. So one must ask how and why did life pop into existence and, perhaps even more fundamentally, what is it?

Life is an enigma that enchants mystics and philosophers and affects whole branches of biology, biochemistry, genetics, and even the search for life elsewhere in the universe. Throughout human history men and women have accepted that life was not merely an artifact of the body but some animating force separate from the flesh that sustained it. Even those who reject the prospect of immortality have often stressed the difference between life and the body. In *Phaedro* Plato considered a suggestion that the relationship of soul and body might be like that of a musical harmony with the strings of a lyre producing the notes. Such a harmony is different from the instrument, but unable to survive its destruction. He rejected that suggestion and instead embraced the view that the soul is immortal. Whilst human knowledge has increased exponentially in the centuries that have elapsed since Plato's concepts first dazzled the intellectual community of ancient Greece, this remains a common view. But is it right?

The distinction between life and body has been challenged, though often on dubious grounds. Johnjoe McFadden suggests that the theory that life consisted of animation by a soul or spirit, once called "vitality," was discredited by the discovery that living organisms are made from the same physical particles as inanimate matter. Nineteenth century scientists are said to have suggested that life was just a chemical reaction based on the same principles as those governing steam trains or blast furnaces, though somewhat more complicated.[1] This was somewhat presumptuous. Decades later, Erwin Schrödinger conceded "the obvious inability" of then contemporary physics and chemistry to explain the events that occur within living organisms, though he thought this offered no reason to doubt that they could ultimately be accounted for by those sciences.[2] More recently, scientists have suggested that the biological compasses birds use to detect the earth's magnetic field actually involve quantum entanglement, a phenomenon Einstein famously described as "spooky action at a distance." This has led McFadden to suggest that life does have a "vital spark" but that it consists of quantum mechanics rather than magic.

We are constantly learning more about living organisms and the manner in which they function, but neither sub-atomic theories nor quantum mechanics actually contain anything capable of logically dispelling the

---

[1] McFadden, Johnjoe, "It seems life really does have a vital spark: quantum mechanics."

[2]. Schrödinger, *What is Life?*, 4.

impression that life is not a purely physical phenomenon. Assertions to the contrary often seem to miss the real point. Imagine, if you will, the sudden appearance of an opaque and seemingly alien space craft which remains enigmatically in orbit around the earth. The world is baffled by its appearance and debate rages about whether it is a drone or contains life forms. Then a scientist announces that it cannot contain any life form apart from the craft itself because it is made of subatomic particles, just like a steam train or blast furnace. Another announces that the craft is equipped with a navigation system using quantum entanglement. There is much wise nodding until some irritating skeptic asks, "but how does that prove no-one is inside?" Arguments about life and consciousness often seem to founder on similar objections. Materialists assume that the physical body is all that exists, but there is no real evidence that this is true. The science may be clear, but it does not support the leap of logic that follows.

But if life is not simply some by-product of our flesh, what is it? Dictionary definitions suggest it is the condition that distinguishes animals and plants from inorganic matter,[3] but this really avoids the issue. Within science there is no broadly accepted definition and interminable controversy seems inescapable.[4] Whilst J. B. S. Haldane[5] and others have wisely declined to answer this question, Brig Klyce has suggested a simple formulation: 'life is cells'.[6] This has the virtue of brevity, though it glosses over suggestions that at least some large DNA viruses should be recognized as non-cellular life forms. It also contains an element of truth; cells are alive.[7] Unfortunately, it misses the essential point.

Frank Sinatra's song, "My Way," is played at countless funerals. In the absence of any necessary feminist revisionism, it invites the mourners to ponder the question, "for what is a man?" Is the only real answer that he is a conglomeration of cells? Is that all life is? What if he dies like the hapless person whose demise has prompted yet another rendition of the song? It is routinely said that such a person "has gone." This may not be a scientifically verifiable concept, but there is a sense that some intangible but nonetheless real thing has left the body that once contained a person with a character and personality. The corpse still has cells. So what could have gone?

---

3. See, for example, *Oxford English Reference Dictionary* and *Webster's Comprehension Dictionary*.

4. Cleland, Chyba, "Defining 'Life.'"

5. Haldane, *What Is Life?*, 53.

6. Klyce, "What is life?"

7. Desnues, Boyer, and Raoult, "Sputnik, a Virophage Infecting the Viral Domain of Life."

Lynn Margulis makes a somewhat similar claim: 'the units of life are cells.'[8] But what could the concept of a 'unit of life' actually mean? Is life nothing more than an accumulation of biological Lego blocks? Are some bodies or organisms more alive than others because they have more units of life? And, conversely, if you lose an arm or otherwise lose cells, are you less alive than you were before? Should nurses who spend their lives taking blood samples, and hence depleting the number of cells in patients, be prosecuted for genocide?

Perhaps recognizing that his succinct definition is too simplistic, Klyce has suggested other properties of life: living things reproduce themselves, they use processes to convert materials and energy to sustain them, and life evolves.[9] He explains that when these processes, collectively described as 'metabolism', cease and there is no prospect of them starting again, 'we call it death'. This suggests that the intangible thing that seems to have gone is mere functionality. If there is any doubt about the mechanistic nature of this conception, it is candidly dispelled by his statement that machines "also convert materials and energy for their needs, create waste, and could be said to die."[10] One may speak metaphorically of engines dying or coming to life, but the implication that machines are alive in some real sense suggests that the essence of life may not be found in cells, but in functionality alone. But is there really no essential difference between life and the usefulness of a pair of pliers?

Campbell argues that life forms can be distinguished from inanimate objects by "recursive self-maintenance," that is by their capacity to maintain themselves and adapt to changing circumstances.[11] That is also true, but can any distinguishing characteristics really distill the essence of life? Living things have cells, and they perform functions and reproduce themselves, but what is life itself? Is it some aspect of reality that is wholly separate from the body?

This suggestion might be anathema to a committed physicalist, but physicalism itself has recently been challenged. Physicalism has long held that all reality is ultimately reducible to elementary particles, that is particles that cannot be composed of other particles. It now seems clear that this long standing dogma cannot be sustained in the light of current knowledge of quantum mechanics, a conclusion that has led at least one former atheist to

---

8. Margulis, *Symbiotic Planet: A New Look at Evolution*, 69.
9. Klyce, "What is life?"
10. Klyce, "What is life?"
11. Campbell, *The Metaphysics of Emergence*, Chapter 6.

suggest that, "one must reject materialism, as there is no material."[12] Campbell argues that the fundamental elements of the universe are not particles but processes.[13] Whilst this may seem to be a startling proposition, there is much support for his contention that there are no particles that can properly be described as elementary and that everything is ultimately formed from quantum fields.[14] Campbell maintains that those things previously understood to be "particles" should now be seen as "particle-like" processes and interactions. He adapts the metaphor mentioned in *Phaedro,* in making the point that they are no more particles "than are the integer number of oscillatory waves in a guitar string."[15]

One may perhaps conceive of life as a succession of processes, but questions would still remain. If everything consists of processes, how can one account for the distinction between life and the physical body? Should the body be seen as the guitar string and life as the oscillatory waves it produces? Of course, the continued existence of sound waves cannot be discerned long after the strings have last been plucked. Was Plato wrong to reject the the proposition that life is equally incapable of continuing beyond physical death? Or, to change the metaphor, is life more akin to light that emanates from a physical source like a sun but can span the vast reaches of the universe and be seen billions of years after the demise of its source? And can this indefinable thing ever be grafted into a purely physical theory?

The theologies of most religions include conceptions of some form of afterlife, whether in another plane of existence or in reincarnation, and many people who would not describe themselves as "religious" instinctively feel that there must be something after death. Of course, most atheists dismiss such feelings as wishful thinking and even the most devout may find it difficult to imagine that all life is eternal. They may be confident of meeting other human souls in heaven, but doubt that cabbages have spirits capable of surviving their destined shredding into coleslaw. Some may be sure that their dearly beloved, but regrettably defunct, dogs will be waiting for them in some heavenly park full of strategically placed trees, but baulk at any

---

12. Henry, "A New Introductory Essay."

13. Campbell, *The Metaphysics of Emergence.* See also Kelly, *Beyond Physicalism: Toward Reconciliation of Science and Spirituality.*

14. Weinberg, "The Search for Unity—Notes for a History of Quantum Field Theory"; Davies, Paul, "Particles do not Exist"; Weinberg, *The Quantum Theory of Fields, Vol. I, Foundations*; Weinberg, *The Quantum Theory of Fields, Vol. 2, Modern Applications,* (1996) Cambridge; and Campbell, Bickhard, "Physicalism. Emergence and Downward Causation".

15. Campbell Bickhard, "Physicalism. Emergence and Downward Causation".

suggestion that the eternal future of their fleas and bacteria has been equally secured. But is the essential nature of human life really different?

Has the quest for knowledge of the origins of life provided any insight? Theories about the spontaneous generation of life actually date back to Aristotle whose more imaginative conceptions included propositions that aphids arise from the dew on plants and crocodiles might be formed from rotting logs.[16] But there is still no compelling evidence for abiogenesis, nor even a single theory enjoying universal support within the scientific community. In a letter written in 1871 Darwin tentatively ventured the possibility that life may have been conceived "in some warm little pond with all sorts of ammonia and phosphoric salts, light, heat, electricity etcetera present, that a protein compound was chemically formed, ready to undergo still more complex changes . . ."[17] He introduced this suggestion with the word "if" and stressed its tentative nature by adding in parentheses: "and Oh! what a big if!" He later confirmed his skepticism with the blunt statement: "It is mere rubbish thinking at present of the origin of life; one might as well think of the origin of matter."[18]

But Genesis refers to God brooding over the waters at the time of creation and scientists have continued to brood over this idea of watery conception. It was embraced by Alexander Oparin in 1924 and J. B. S. Haldane in the following year. The most recent form of the 'primordial soup' theory they formulated involves a number of propositions: the early Earth had a chemically reducing atmosphere and hotter oceans; exposure to energy produced monomers (simple organic compounds); more complex organic polymers (large or macro molecules) then formed; and, ultimately life developed in the soup.[19]

Whilst this recipe might seem a little light on details, an experiment conducted in 1952 suggested that organic molecules could have been formed from inorganic precursors under the conditions suggested in the soup hypothesis.[20] And in 1967 J. D. Bernal suggested that the emergence of life had involved three stages: the origin of biological monomers, the origin of biological polymers, and the evolution of cells. He thought that the third stage of his theory would be the most difficult to validate as it would be

16. Lennox, *Aristotle's Philosophy of Biology: Studies in the Origins of Life Science*, 229–258.

17. Darwin, letter to Joseph Hooker, 1 February 1871.

18. Quoted by Priscu, *Origin and Evolution of Life on a Frozen Earth*.

19. See the summary provided by Shapiro, *Origins: A Skeptic's Guide to the Creation of Life on Earth*.

20. Miller, "A Production of Amino Acids Under Possible Primitive Earth Conditions."

necessary to determine how the biological reactions became incorporated behind cell walls. Fred Hoyle remained unimpressed, declaiming that: "The notion that not only the biopolymer but the operating program of a living cell could be arrived at by chance in a primordial organic soup here on the Earth is evidently nonsense of a high order."[21] Research has continued. There have been some developments, including the discovery of evidence suggesting that molecules as well as organisms can evolve[22] and the creation of artificial cells.[23] A new theory has also raised the possibility that life may have begun in freezing or very cold conditions.[24] But the goals of explanation and verification have not been attained[25] and, whilst there is still optimism, at least one scientist has felt obliged to suggest that we may never know precisely how life began.[26]

So, whilst there is much that science has revealed about our lives, the origin of life itself remains a mystery. We know from our experience that it is life that begets life and theists will continue to argue that it is most likely a gift of God, albeit one initially bestowed in ways beyond our comprehension. Physicalists recoil from the suggestion of a divine creator, but despite extensive research, we have not yet discovered a viable alternative explanation of how life began. Would it matter if we did? Issues of causation do not always explain what has been caused.

What is clear is that even the most primitive life forms have an animating quality that we do not really understand. We live in a great scientific age and this may create expectations that all mysteries will one day be revealed, but some things may forever lie beyond our intellectual reach. Even if the origin of cells were to be established by those still testing the waters of Darwin's warm pool, that would not explain the nature of this thing we call life. Nor would it explain why the universe should be so structured that life could have emerged from apparently inanimate particles, laws and fields.

---

21. Hoyle, Fred, "The Big Bang in Astronomy."

22. Follmann and Brownson, "Darwin's warm little pond revisited: from molecules to the origin of life."

23. Statt, "Scientists create 'alien' life form with artificial genetic code."

24. Priscu, *Origin and Evolution of Life on a Frozen Earth*.

25. Russell, Michael, *Origins, Abiogenesis and the Search for Life*, Cambridge, Mass.: Cosmology Science, 2011.

26. Priscu, *Origin and Evolution of Life on a Frozen Earth*.

CONSCIOUSNESS

The fact that we have consciousness gives rise to further issues. Thoughts, ideas, concepts and even flashes of inspiration are obviously not encapsulated within our genes at birth and it is difficult to imagine that they can be understood as purely physical phenomena. Some maintain that it is a separate realm of reality—the mind or soul as distinct from the physical brain—and that it can only be explained as the gift of a divine creator. Others have insisted that mental processes must in some way emerge from the physical brain or that there must some other 'natural' explanation. Many are now openly derisive of 'dualism', the view famously promoted by Descartes[27] that there may be a non-physical mind as well as a physical brain. Yet the quest for evidence rationally capable of resolving this controversy has not met resounding success and consciousness has come to be regarded as "the hard problem" of science. Many would echo a rueful comment made by "Darwin's Bulldog," Thomas Huxley: "How it is that anything so remarkable as a state of consciousness comes about as a result of irritating nervous tissue, is just as unaccountable as the appearance of Djin when Aladdin rubbed his lamp."[28]

Some assume that the the mystery may eventually be solved whilst others fear that it may forever elude us due to our limited intellectual and cognitive ability.[29] Thomas Nagel explains that the subjective nature of conscious states makes them effectively impervious to scientific explanation and that this makes "the mind-body problem really intractable."[30] Joseph Levine has taken up a similar theme, arguing that there is an explanatory gap between consciousness and physical phenomena. He insists that a scientific explanation should "deductively entail" the matter under consideration by permitting it to be inferred from laws, mechanisms and initial conditions.[31] But, despite some extravagant claims about the implications of what has already been discovered and optimism of further revelations, we do not have such an explanation; we merely know that we have a rich mental life in which we experience, perceive, think, imagine and have emotions.

David Chalmers has argued that the issue of consciousness actually poses a series of problems. Some relate to cognitive abilities and functions

27. Rosemond, *Descartes's Dualism*.
28. Huxley, *Lessons in Elementary Physiology*, 193.
29. See, for example, McGinn, "Can we solve the Mind-Body Problem?"; Levine, "Materialism and Qualia: The Explanatory Gap"; and Stanciu, "The Explanatory Gap: 30 Years after."
30. Nagel, "What is it like to be a Bat?" at 435.
31. Levine, *Purple Haze: The Puzzle of Conscious Experience*, 74 76.

and he suggests that these are easily explained. How? Well, they are functionally definable; hence one need only explain the function. Campbell objects that this is "rather too easy" and suggests that the basic notion is not whether something has a function but whether it serves a function.[32] A further and perhaps more fundamental, objection is that concepts of functionality do not explain the nature of thoughts, feelings and other mental activity. One may say that a hand can write, clap, grip or strike but that does not cast much light on the nature of a hand or explain its existence. This is also true of mental states or processes. Even problems of consciousness that some see as less difficult require more than a dismissive reference to functionality.

In Chalmers' view, the hard problem is conscious experience. He explains that this is "almost unique" in that it it extends beyond cognitive and behavioral functions and raises the unanswered question: "why is the performance of these functions accompanied by experience?" The problem is intractable because experience is not reducible to physical phenomena and it cannot be functionally analyzed.[33] He illustrates the inadequacy of a purely physical explanation by comparing a living person with a hypothetical zombie which would presumably possess similar similar physical structure and functionality, but lack the capacity for conscious experience. And, in a rare departure from the calm if faintly amused detachment expected from philosophy professors, he has been prone to shattering the calm reflection of his colleagues by mounting podiums to sing, or more accurately shout, a song about this comparison. He has even formed a "Zombie Blues" band. The zombie's song includes the line: "I act like you act, I do what you do, but I don't know what it's like to be you."[34] His point is clear; conscious experience is not wholly explicable in terms of the physical body or functionality.

This contention has proved to be controversial, but the hard problem has been widely discussed and no solution has been found that commands universal acceptance.[35] Chalmers suggests that we may eventually have a theory that explains at least the fundamental principles of how physical processes may be connected to conscious experience.[36] The existence of such connections cannot be sensibly doubted. The effect of hallucinogenic drugs and other mood-altering substances has been recognized for millennia. But,

---

32. Campbell, *The Metaphysics of Emergence*, 275.

33. Chalmers, "Facing up to the Problem of Consciousness.": and Chalmers, *The Conscious Mind in Search of a Fundamental Theory*.

34. Kaminer, "Where Theory and Research Meet to Jam About the Mind."

35. See the discussion in Stubenberg, Review of *Consciousness and Its Place in Nature: Does Physicalism Entail Panpsychism?*

36. Chalmers, "How Can We Construct a Science of Consciousness?

despite frequent claims to the contrary, this does not mean that consciousness is essentially physical. An unexpected bill may affect my emotional state and change my thinking, but this does not prove that my emotions or awareness are part of the accounting section of Visa.

Attempts to man the barricades of physicalism have been less than persuasive. When Descartes delivered his famous axiom, 'I think, therefore I am', he was effectively claiming that his consciousness was the one undeniable reality. Yet some ardent physicalists, including Daniel Dennett, have actually claimed that consciousness does not exist.[37] Yes, I am serious. Some philosophers do claim that reality can be successfully rewritten and life reimagined without consciousness or at least without aspects of consciousness such as such as beliefs, desires and subjective sensations of pain.[38] Proponents of this seemingly nonsensical concept, dubbed 'eliminativism', have attempted to support it by a number of arguments.[39]

First, it is argued that the term "consciousness" may not define a single phenomenon but a series of mental states, processes and functions. One may reasonably ask, "so what?" One may conceive of consciousness as a collection of phenomena such as perception, cognition, judgment and appreciation, though their inter-relatedness would suggest that such a conceptual subdivision may be problematic, but this would leave the essential problem unanswered.

The "so what" question' is also raised by the second point. It is said that the term may not advance any scientific theory and have no place in a "scientifically-fixed ontology." But conscious experience is not a mere semantic construction and it is not dependent for its existence upon recognition by our white-coated friends, whether by advancing a theory or finding it a home in some hospitable ontology.

The third is more explicitly absurd. It is argued that, if science defines what exists and does not recognize intrinsic qualities with no obvious function, then "there is no consciousness, so defined." Yes, it does seem to be suggested that those pesky scientists have defined consciousness out of existence. Of course, the argument involves a chain of misconceptions: science does not define what exists, at least not in this sense; scientists do not refuse to recognize things due to doubts about their functionality; consciousness has many functions; and, even if it remained scientifically undefined, it would still exist. So far as I am aware, no scientist has ever defined me and

---

37. Rey, "A Reason for Doubting the Existence of Consciousness."

38. Rorty, "In Defence of Eliminative Materialism."

39. A summary can be found in Weisberg, "The Hard Problem of Consciousness," paragraph 3(a).

I am sure that my wife gave up on any attempt many years ago. Yet I stubbornly remain in existence.

The fourth shares the prize for pseudo-intellectual gobbledygook. It is argued that the term "consciousness" may derive its meaning from a falsifiable theory and if the theory is falsified then "the entities it posits do not exist." This is simply silly. The term does not derive its meaning from a theory, it merely denotes an aspect of human and animal life as fundamental as our arms and legs. Furthermore, it is consciousness itself, not the term that describes it, that matters and it is unlikely to wink out of existence merely because someone manages to falsify a theory about it.

A further and slightly less ambitious attempt to rewrite reality is called "strong reductionism." This again takes up the theme that that consciousness can be broken down into separate phenomena, but it goes on to suggest that each of the elements can be analyzed and hence the whole problem duly explained.[40] Proponents of this view insist that consciousness is not as it seems. You may think that your consciousness includes all your awareness, thoughts and feelings and that it is an intrinsic part of you that permits you, not only to face the challenges of life, but also to engage in flights of fancy uninhibited by purely pragmatic considerations. But you are asked to accept that you are wrong about all this. It is not suggested that your consciousness is merely an illusion, but rather that it is a much more stunted thing than you had hitherto imagined, a mere collection of functions cobbled together with enough cerebral activity to make it all work. Of course, it cannot be sensibly doubted that consciousness serves many functions and it may not be beyond human ingenuity to describe some of them and to explain how they are served by various processes in the brain. But there is a striking poverty of imagination in strong reductionist discussions of experience and functionality. The richness of our inner life seems to be notionally whittled down so that what is left can be notionally attributed to our physical brains.

There is a rich vein of dubious theories based upon conflations of questions about what consciousness is with questions about what functions it may serve. But there are few things that can be adequately explained solely in terms of functions. Imagine a latter day Robinson Crusoe who has crash-landed on another planet in a spaceship rather than being being washed up on an island. When a non-humanoid 'Man Friday' unexpectedly arrives to save him by topping up his oxygen tank and offering him supplies, he contacts mission control and excitedly asks who or what this apparently intelligent being could be? The duty officer, who is a strong reductionist, then provides a functional explanation: the alien is an oxygen and food

---

40. Weisberg, "The Hard Problem of Consciousness," paragraph 3(b).

supplier. "Oh I see," responds the astronaut, "thanks for clearing that up for me." The suggestion that the essence of consciousness can be wholly encapsulated with a theory about the functions it enables us to perform is equally unrealistic.

In fact, even experiences that clearly involve brain functions may not be adequately explicable by neural activity alone. Take knowledge. Our memories are drawn from neural activity in the hippocampus[41] and proponents of strong reductionism seem convinced that there is no knowledge that cannot be grasped theoretically.[42] If that were true, a full knowledge of color could presumably be obtained from a textbook. But is that credible? As Josh Weisberg has protested, the most studious blind person would surely still lack some knowledge of the experience of seeing a color like red.[43] Can you really imagine that if he or she were suddenly healed, the experience of watching a sunset for the first time would reveal nothing new? The same point could be made about other experiences: new love, one's first sexual experience or the birth of a longed-for child. We harbor grief, guilt and irrational fears. We are driven to find meaning in our lives.[44] We know moments of near transcendence with the soaring notes of a sonata and even a sense of awe in the deathly hush of some solemn and perhaps religiously charged moment. Such feelings may serve some function, but functionality alone seems a wholly inadequate explanation.

Weak reductionism flirts with realism by conceding that consciousness is a basic phenomenon that cannot be explained by being conceptually broken down into simple non-conscious elements. But the flirtation is not consummated by a rigorous application of reason. Weak reductionists insist that consciousness can be identified with physical properties of the body if such an identification is supported by "the most parsimonious and productive theory." Arguments like this need to be approached cautiously. Parsimony can, at best, offer a flimsy basis for tentative hypotheses and "productive" is a value-laden adjective that a cynic may suspect sometimes means supportive of some proposition the proponent would like to believe. In this instances, one is asked to accept that such an identification does not merely reveal that thoughts, feelings, aspirations and other mental activities are related to physical states; it reveals that they are physical states. How do

---

41. Rosen, Jill, "Hopkins neuroscientists pinpoint part of brain that taps into our memory banks."
42. Weisberg, "The Hard Problem of Consciousness."
43. Weisberg, "The Hard Problem of Consciousness."
44. See, for example, Frankel, Victor E., *Man's Search for Meaning*, Boston: Beacon, 2006.

we really know this? Well, we are assured, no further explanation is required because "a thing is just what it is."[45]

Of course, the fact that one thing can be identified with another does not justify a conclusion that it is the other. Whilst this distinction may seem self evident, it apparently eludes many scientists who are committed to a purely physical view of reality. Allan Hobson makes the unequivocal claim that: "All available evidence is that consciousness, including what we might call spirit or soul, is a brain function." In support of this claim, he cites his own research which he says shows that we sleep because the brain changes its state, and we dream when that change in state assumes certain physiological dimensions.[46] That may may be well true. Neurotransmitters such as serotonin and norepinephrine keep some parts of the brain active while we are awake and we apparently become sleepy when neutrons at the base of the brain "switch off" the signals that keep us awake. There is also evidence that a chemical called adenosine causes drowsiness as it builds up in our blood and gradually breaks down while we sleep.[47] But this does not establish Hobson's claim. No one who has had even a cursory glance at the evidence can rationally doubt that there are complex interrelationships between neurological processes and conscious states and that changes in one can cause changes in the other, but how can this demonstrate that they are the same thing? The only answer seems to be: "a thing is just what it is." Answers like this have long offered haven to astrologers, necromancers, cult leaders and others unable to rationally defend their claims, but they do not inspire confidence.

In fact, neurology has not unravelled the mystery of consciousness. We now know that the human brain contains about 100 billion neurons interconnected by trillions of synapses and that these connections transmit signals. But what does that reveal about consciousness? It has been suggested that "Somehow. . . that's producing thought."[48] This does not inspire confidence either. A telephone system transmits electronic impulses through numerous connections, but this does not mean that it somehow produces the conversations. Research on neutral activity may well yield further insights but that does not mean that we are on the threshold of an adequate explanation. Chalmers suggests that, like space and time, we may have to take consciousness for granted. This has not been received with en-

45. Weisberg, "The Hard Problem of Consciousness," paragraph 3.

46. Hobson, "Neuroscience and the Soul: The Dualism of John Carew Eccles."

47. National Institute of Neurological Disorders and Stroke, *Brain Basics: Understanding Sleep*.

48. Charles Jennings, director of neurotechnology at the MIT McGovern Institute for Brain Research. Quoted by Dougherty, *What are thoughts made of?*

thusiasm by committed physicalists, but neither speculation nor optimism about future discoveries do much to dispel the mystery.

Susan Greenfield believes that consciousness is an emergent property of the brain, similar to the 'wetness' of water or the 'transparency' of glass.[49] but she does not claim that this belief can be scientifically verified and, again, the comparison is not reassuring. Wetness and transparency are physical qualities of physical things and they are discernible by the physical senses. The baroness has also highlighted the fact that we do not even know what kind of explanation to expect: "If I said to you I'd solved the hard problem, you wouldn't be able to guess whether it would be a formula, a model, a sensation, or a drug."[50]

There are even further theories: there may be a more basic substance underlying all matter with both phenomenal and physical properties;[51] such a substance may be neither phenomenal nor physical but may underly both;[52] or all physical things may have an underlying phenomenal nature.[53] There may be no evidence to support any of these propositions, but some are enchanting. My own favorite is the proposition that consciousness might correlate with physical matter in this world but perhaps separate from it in a different world.[54] The implications of this theory are not clear. Would it mean that astronauts landing on some other planet might find themselves suddenly discorporated, leaving mindless bodies in their spacesuits? Or, if you prefer to put a more positive gloss on this hypothesis, would the path to immortality begin with the stairs leading up to a space ship and end when a conscious soul disengages from the body on some alien landing place? Would consciousness be reabsorbed during the return journey or hover in disembodied amusement whilst earnest psychologists try to debrief the mindless body it had abandoned? Only a spoilsport would wish to see such flights of fancy dashed on the rocks of reason, but a skeptic might wonder whether an *a priori* insistence that everything must be physically based has not led some theorists astray.

The impressions one forms on listening to an oratorio, watching a sunset, reading a novel or reflecting on one's life are obviously not comparable in any meaningful sense to parts of the body like a foot or an elbow

49. Than, Ker, "Why Great Minds Can't Grasp Consciousness."

50. Than, Ker, "Why Great Minds Can't Grasp Consciousness."

51. Spinoza, *Ethics*; Nagel, *The View from Nowhere*; and Strawson, *Individuals: An Essay in Descriptive Metaphysics*.

52. Russell, *The Analysis of Matter*; and Stoljar, "Physicalism and phenomenal concepts."

53. Leibniz, "Monadology"; and Skrbina, *Panpsychism in the West*.

54. Weisberg, "The Hard Problem of Consciousness."

or even to physical sensations like pain. And attempts to demonstrate that all thoughts, sensations and feelings are merely manifestations of the brain have not been wholly successful. Of course, mental and bodily states can be interdependent. For example, depression can cause pain and pain can cause depression.[55] But there is no compelling evidence that impressions of a complex interrelationship between interdependent but separate minds and brains are wholly misconceived.

The case for dualism has recently been revived by Edward Kelly and others who review the empirical evidence and challenge the assumption that mental properties will ultimately be fully explained by brain activities.[56] The authors cite numerous experiences, including some they claim are well established by the evidence despite being dubbed "paranormal." They concede that there are examples of states of mind being changed by neurophysiological changes, but say that some supporting examples can be found for almost any theory. Of course, the real test of whether a theory is valid is not merely whether it can be shown to be consistent with some experimental results, but whether it is capable of withstanding vigorous attempts to falsify it. Kelly et al suggest that this test has not been rigorously addressed because the focus of modern psychology has shifted from the mind to the body and there has been a reluctance to seriously consider experiences that might challenge accepted dogma. Those who bridle at this suggestion might pause to reflect on the long maintained insistence that anorexia was a purely physical problem. Others also argue that a strictly physicalist conception of consciousness fails to account for many common human experiences, not necessarily of a religious nature.[57]

Hobson seems unable to understand how scientists who support dualism, like John Eccles, could remain unmoved by his work on the causes of sleep and dreaming and he attributes their apparent obduracy to religious beliefs. He concludes an article about Eccles with the observation that "in the end, when facts contradict our cherished beliefs, each of us decides, with only intellectual honesty to guide us, whether our beliefs or the facts are dispensable." If this was directed at Eccles, it was unduly patronizing. Eccles was a distinguished neurophysiologist whose work on the biophysical properties of synaptic transmission within the brain led to the award of a Nobel Prize and, as Hobson fairly acknowledges, he espoused a philosophy that enabled him to "rejoice even in the falsification of a cherished theory,

---

55. Hall-Flavin, Daniel K., "Is there a link between pain and depression? Can depression cause physical pain?"

56. Kelly et al, *Irreducible Mind: Toward a Psychology for the 21st Century.*

57. Sheldrake, *The Sense of Being Stared at and other aspects of the Extended Mind.*

because even this is a scientific success."[58] A more plausible explanation for his failure to be persuaded by Hobson's research is that it had merely provided further confirmation for what he had already known: the mind is affected by the state of the brain. This should be evident to anyone who has ever seen someone become unconscious or dazed when struck in the head, but it does not support Hobson's assumption that "the facts" exclude dualism.

The existence of a separate mind or soul is suggested by all manner of religious or psychic experiences and it might explain the numerous accounts of 'out-of-body' experiences, such as astral travel and near death experiences, in which people have reported leaving their bodies and, in some cases, being able to look down on them from a higher vantage point. Of course, other explanations for these phenomena have been suggested (see chapter 8) and there is an alternative view that, whilst nonphysical, consciousness is either caused by or dependent upon the physical brain and hence unable to exist separately from the body.

The debate has most recently moved to the phenomena of quantum entanglement. According to standard quantum theory, particles have no definite states, only the potential to become one thing or another, until they are measured. Then they suddenly assume a particular formation. When two particles interact, they may become "entangled," in the sense that they seem to become components of what has been described as "a more complicated probability function that describes both particles together."[59] A pair of entangled photons are polarized in perpendicular directions, with some probability that photon A is vertically polarized and photon B is horizontally polarized, but also some chance of the opposite. The two photons may travel light-years apart, but they remain linked and if photon A is measured and found to be vertically polarized, then, as if by magic, photon B instantaneously becomes horizontally polarized. This occurs even though B's state was unspecified a moment earlier and no signal has had time to travel between them. A theoretical physicist has recently suggested an explanation: A and B might be controlled by something separate from the physical world: the human mind. Lucien Hardy has actually proposed an experiment in which 100 people, hooked up to EEG headsets, would be used to switch the settings on measuring devices for particles 100 kilometers apart. He suggests that if the correlation in results did not match other test results involving entangled particles, it would spark debate about the potential implications. He added, "What it could mean is this: that the human mind (consciousness) isn't made up of the same matter governed by physics. Fur-

---

58. Hobson, "Neuroscience and the Soul: The Dualism of John Carew Eccles."
59. Wolchover, "Experiment Reaffirms Quantum Weirdness."

thermore, it could suggest that the mind is capable of overcoming physics with free will."[60]

If the experiment is eventually conducted, the results will be interesting. But does any of this really matter? The most obvious answer is that the dualistic view, that consciousness is a distinct thing capable of existence independently of the body, naturally raises the issue of whether the soul might be capable of surviving physical death. Of course, not all religious believers are troubled by this question. Whilst most insist that we are immortal beings, Muslims and adherents of many other religions generally insist that the mind and body are one and look forward to bodily resurrection. But for many, hopes of an existence capable of continuing beyond this present life are inextricably related to the existence of a non-physical soul. On the other hand, those who baulk at prospects of any form of spiritual reality, let alone immortality, may find dualism disturbing. As mentioned earlier, belief in a purely physical universe has already been severely challenged by the discovery of quantum fields, but such fields are at least inanimate. It may be even more difficult to reconcile physicalist orthodoxy with a sentient mind separate from a physical body. If that were to be accepted, how could the possibility of purely sentient beings be rationally excluded? How could the divine foot be kept from the door?

Some writers also argue that consciousness provides strong evidence for their belief in God. There are several variants of the argument,[61] including some based on Bayesian style inferences and others based on deductive reasoning,[62] but most are based on two central propositions: no physical explanation will be found for consciousness and there can be no other explanation except divine creation.

The first proposition cannot be dismissed as fanciful. There has been a recent suggestion that an ancient virus may have injected humans with "alien genetic code" and human consciousness may be the result of a string of instructions making its way into our genome through an infection.[63] However, even if you embrace the interesting idea that consciousness may be contagious, it remains a mystery. No wholly adequate scientific explanation has emerged and, whilst many theorists insist that it is nothing more than a manifestation of brain activity, the supporting arguments are by no means compelling.

60. Norman, "Scientists Have an Experiment to See If the Human Mind Is Bound to the Physical World."
61. Adams, Robert, "Flavors, Colors and God"; and Swinburne, *The Existence of God*, Chapter 9.
62. Moreland, *Consciousness and the Existence of God: A Theistic Argument*.
63. Collins, Tim, "Could an ancient virus be responsible for human consciousness?"

The second proposition may seem too speculative to be sustainable, but it is difficult to identify any other non-physical explanation that seems plausible. Steven Conifer and others have protested that consciousness could be attributable to different gods, such as Vishnu or Thor, or to even multiple deities.[64] This oft-repeated proposition may raise an arguable point in debates about the validity of particular religions, but as a rejoinder to a suggestion that something can only be attributable to divine creation, it is a non sequitur, on the same logical plane as a contention that a pedestrian's injuries could not have been caused by a car because it might have been a Ford or a BMW.

Conifer also argues that any god who exists outside space and time could not have created consciousness within them.[65] This seems to suggest that, having finished the cosmos, God would have locked himself out of it. That does not seem to be self-evident. He then asks how God could have created consciousness. Whilst no mortal can answer such a question, our inability to suggest a divine *modus operandi* is neither surprising nor compelling. He completes his volley of arguments by insisting that "personal explanations of psychophysical correlations in terms of God's intentions" seem improbable because our own human intentions do not directly cause physical events.[66] Even if true, this proposition would obviously strain anthropomorphic protection to breaking point. As a more modest soul, I doubt that my inability to move salt shakers by psychokinesis reveals much about the powers of a god capable of creating the universe.

So, what do you think? Did the rapid expansion of particles thrown out by the single explosive event we know as the "Big Bang" eventually cause mindless particles to generate minds capable of self-awareness? Or is consciousness essentially a non-physical phenomenon? And, in either event, does it point to the existence of a sentient creator or suggest the possibility of life after physical death?

FREE WILL

The concept of human responsibility is usually accepted by religious believers and atheists alike, but there are various forms of determinism[67] that

---

64. See, for example, Conifer, "The Argument from Consciousness Refuted."
65. Conifer, "The Argument from Consciousness Refuted."
66. Conifer, "The Argument from Consciousness Refuted."
67. The most common forms are logical determinism, theological determinism, psychological determinism, and physical determinism. For a list of such theories see Doyle, *Free Will: The Scandal in Philosophy*, 145 – 146.

suggest we are not wholly masters or mistresses of own destinies. Of course, many things exert powerful, perhaps decisive, influences on our attitudes and decisions. That was discussed in chapter 2. I am here concerned with hard determinism, a view that human conduct is pre-determined and that free will is an illusion.[68] This somewhat startling contention is not based upon any view that we are subject to the will of God and it extends far beyond theological concepts of predestination such as those famously promoted by John Calvin. Whilst proponents of this view may seem to be at least first cousins of eliminativists, they do not necessarily join them in denying the existence of their own consciousness. Instead, we are asked to accept that we are thinking puppets, but that, unlike Pinocchio, we have no puppeteer. Our strings are said to be pulled by chemical processes occurring within our own brains. The potential implications are profound. Since we could never have chosen differently, we have no personal responsibility for our actions. Whether we are caught with our hands in the proverbial cookie jar or revealed as serial killers, we can simply plead "the neurons made me do it."

In most jurisdictions people may escape criminal liability if their free will has been overborne in some way. They may be acquitted on the ground of automatism if the relevant acts occurred without conscious volition (such as when someone is sleepwalking or in a profoundly dissociative state) or duress (if their will has been overborne by threats or violence). They may also be able to rely upon defenses of insanity or diminished responsibility due to mental illnesses. But hard determinists insist that all of us are devoid of free will, even if awake, reasonably sane and free from coercion. The courts are simply victimizing people who are not morally responsible for their actions. Of course, neither judges nor juries should be criticized for such bullying; they also lack free will.

Attempts have recently been made to defend this remarkable contention by reference to neurology. Our brains are composed of molecules arranged by our genes and environment. Our decisions are said to result from molecular-based electrical impulses and chemical substances transmitted from one brain cell to another. Jerry Coyne maintains that to claim we can freely make choices is to claim that we can "step outside the physical structure of our brain and change its workings." Since molecules must obey the laws of physics, we are told that our decisions are like the output of a computer; only one choice is possible.[69] This is quite a stretch of logic.

---

68. Harris, *Free Will*.
69. Coyne, "You Don't Have Free Will."

Our brains are vastly more complex than the most sophisticated computers and there is no reason to believe that consciousness is subject to the same kind of limitations as existing operating systems, even those capable of limited self programming.[70] One does not need to embrace dualism to recognize that, as living organisms have evolved into increasing complex forms, new abilities have emerged. Whilst invertebrates are limited to instinctive reflexes, primates are capable of reasoning and we homo sapiens possess creativity and self awareness.[71] We can perceive, learn, and reason. Why should our emergent abilities not extend to the freedom to make our own decisions? If we can consider the implications of alternative courses of actions, why can we not freely choose between them?

Sam Harris suggests that a person could not have free will unless he or she could have acted otherwise. This is a dubious proposition. Can a convict whose sentence has expired not leave prison freely even if he would not be permitted to remain? More controversially, Harris insists that a person could not have acted otherwise unless he or she might have taken a different course given such factors as beliefs, desires, character and psychology. This suggests that such things are not merely influential; they are coercive. Is this credible? Are thugs compelled to beat up their wives? Are those haunted by thoughts of pedophilia compelled to rape children? Should the very concept of people being responsible for their actions now be dismissed as an entirely obsolete notion?

Harris adds a further rationalization, protesting that to have free will you would have to be aware of all the factors that determine your thoughts and actions and to have complete control over them.[72] This seems to imply that only an omniscient being could make a free choice between alternatives. In reality, of course, all decisions are made within prevailing contexts. We choose what seems to be the best course available in the context of limited knowledge, limited means and limited options. Our freedom is also limited. We may not be held in a prison or detention centre, but we are confined by our physical, intellectual, emotional and financial limitations and also by our commitments and responsibilities. Our limited insight into our own psychology and perhaps subconscious biases may also influence the choices we make. But does this really mean that we lack free will? Of course, one could redefine the term "free will" to accord with the absolutist concept Harris advocates and use another term, such as "doing- the-best-

---

70. Merrett, Rebecca, "Self-programming machines next phase of computer science: Wozniak."

71. Cloninger, *Feeling Good: The Science of Well-Being*, table 3.1 at 96.

72. Harris, *Free Will*, 24.

we-can-ism," to describe our capacity to make decisions within the context of our human limitations. But would such a semantic change demonstrate that we have no responsibility for our actions?

Challenges to the concept of free will have not been purely semantic. There have also been claims that our brains may actually make our decisions some seconds before our conscious selves are even allowed to know what they are. Benjamin Libet asked subjects to spontaneously flex their wrists while watching a moving dot on a cathode ray tube and note the position of the dot when they first became aware of 'the urge to act'. They consistently reported that their inclination to move occurred 0.2 seconds before they acted upon it, but the use of an electroencephalogram (EEG) revealed a significant increase in what was described as "readiness potential" approximately 0.55 seconds before the wrist-flexing.[73] Brain scans have enabled neuroscientists to predict with 60% accuracy which of two buttons subjects would choose to push before they were conscious of having made those decisions.[74] Similar results were obtained from subjects asked to move their fingers whilst watching a clock with a dot circling it.[75] In another study by Itzhak Fried and others electrodes were implanted into the brains of twelve patients with pharmacologically intractable epilepsy (please do to try this at home, even if you have a few expendable friends). Subjects were instructed to wait for at least one complete clock revolution of the clock handle and then press a key whenever they "felt the urge." They were then asked to move the clock handle back to the spot where it had been when they first felt the urge and this was assumed to be "the onset time of conscious free will." He noted progressive neuronal "recruitment" a second and a half before this onset time and progressive increase or decrease in neuronal firing rate as the reported time of decision was approached.[76] This is apparently supposed to prove that at some point, "things that are predetermined are admitted into consciousness"[77]

Inferences like this have been taken seriously by many people whose enthusiasm seems to have stifled their skepticism, but they have been

---

73. Libet,"Theory and evidence relating cerebral processes to conscious will"; Ostrowick, "The Timing Experiments of Libet and Grey Walter."

74. Deecke, L., "The Bereitschaftspotential as an electrophysiological tool for studying the cortical organization of human voluntary action"; Soon et al, "Unconscious determinants of free decisions in the human brain."

75. Nelson, "Libet's dualism."

76. Fried, Mukamel, and Krieman, "Internally generated preactivation of single neurons in human medial frontal cortex predicts volition."

77. Smith, "Neuroscience vs philosophy: Taking aim at free will."

criticized on numerous grounds[78] and seem to require some optimistic assumptions. In the study conducted by Fried et al the subjects were instructed to move the handle back to where it had been "when they first felt the urge to move" and this was assumed to have been "the onset time of conscious free will." It seems to have been assumed that all of the subjects made the decisions instantaneously when they felt the urge and that the fingers responded instantly. That seems implausible, if only because it fails to make adequate allowance for human reaction times. It has been suggested that the average human reaction time is as short as 274 milliseconds,[79] though an Australian study found that the reaction times of Australian drivers varied from 1.26 to 3.6 seconds,[80] and there is evidence that people with epilepsy have slower reaction times than average.[81] The researchers also seem to have assumed that all subjects were able to retrospectively pinpoint the position of the handle when they felt the urge. All these assumptions are more courageous than prudent. More fundamentally, the researchers seem to have assumed that the neuronal activity indicated that a decision had been made. In reality, of course, neurology does not extend to a mind reading function. Neither the fMRI scans nor the electrodes picked up the sound of neutrons shouting "Push now!" All we know is that there was some cerebral activity and this was progressive rather than instantaneous.

If any inference can be drawn from studies so beset with potential for error, the most plausible would be that the increasing readiness potential or increasing neural activity reflected mental activity leading up to an imminent decision. Whilst we may occasionally make decisions almost instantly, such as when a child runs out from behind a parked van, most are the culmination of processes that may occur very rapidly, perhaps in a fraction of a second, but are not instantaneous. Brain scans or EEGs may be able to detect which way the volitional wind is blowing before the conscious mind confirms the decision, like my wife noticing my nose twitch when a pie comes out of the oven, but this does not mean that the decision has already been made. In any event, even a subconscious decision, like whether to swerve to the left or the right to miss the child, may not be wholly involuntary. And, unless immediately acted upon, initial inclinations are obviously provisional, As Libet observed, one remains free to change one's mind.[82]

78. See, for example, Klemm,"Free will debates: Simple experiments are not so simple."
79. Human Benchmark, Reaction Time Statistics
80. Tiggs and, *Reaction time of drivers to road stimuli.*
81. Jambaqué, Lassonde, and Dulac, *Neuropsychology of Childhood Epilepsy,* 166 et seq.
82. Ostrowick,"The Timing Experiments of Libet and Grey Walter."

The most recent study said to negate the existence of free will involved asking subjects to watch five white circles and predict which one would turn red. Since this change occurred randomly, one would have expected 20% of the predictions to prove correct. In fact, when the subjects only had a fraction of a second to make a prediction, they "were likely to report" a higher incidence of correct predictions but, when they had nearly a full second the reported number of accurate predictions dropped back to the expected 20% success rate. This is supposed to demonstrate that people subconsciously perceived the color red before they predicted it would appear, but consciously experienced these two things in the opposite order. Hence, the researchers suggest, "the conscious experience of choice may be constructed after we act."[83] The study evoked a series of dramatic headlines, including my favourite, "More evidence that you're a mindless robot with no free will."[84]

Whilst it seems churlish to throw cold water over such outpourings of enthusiasm, the study raised questions about memories of earlier predictions, albeit made only seconds earlier, not about free will. The subjects had been free to choose what predictions to make. The suggestion that they subconsciously perceived the color red before making their predictions was based upon mere supposition. The apparent disparity in claimed predictions was more likely a product of faulty recollection arising from the extremely limited time span. Human memory is not like that saved onto a computer chip. Our initial perceptions have to be encoded[85] and, whilst this can occur rapidly, it is not instantaneous. Nor are our decisions. A subject given only a fraction of a second to choose amongst 5 possibilities may not have made a concluded decision when the time expired and may subconsciously resolve the lingering uncertainty as the color changes. The phenomenon of "postdiction," or hindsight bias, is well established,[86] and we all have a tendency to subconsciously reconstruct events in a manner that reflects favorably upon us; hence, the T shirts that proclaim, "The older I get the better I was." On the other hand, those with almost a full second may have made a concluded decision within the time span and hence been uninfluenced by

---

83. Hathaway,"You may have already decided to read this article"; Bear and Bloom, "A Simple Task Uncovers a Postdictive Illusion of Choice."

84. Kurzweil Digest.

85. For a concise explanation see, Ricker, Jeffry, *Psy 101—Introduction to Psychology*; See also Baddely, Eysenck, and Anderson, *Memory*; and Schacter, *Searching for memory: The brain, the mind, and the past.*

86. Shimojo,"Postdiction: its implications on visual awareness, hindsight, and sense of agency."

the actual result. Whilst some have seen these studies as evidence that we lack free will,[87] others remain understandably skeptical.[88]

Are we really putty in the hands of a non-sentient fate, mindlessly governing our minds and determining all we choose to do or think? When I decide what to have for breakfast, am I predestined to choose scrambled eggs? Has my decision been foreordained by unfelt and unseen forces? What could they be? Compulsory menu choices implanted in my DNA? A melange of psychological forces that are not merely influential but coercive? Vibes transmitted by meditating egg producers? If I can think, then why can I not decide? If, as Fried suggests, decisions are predetermined, then one must surely ask, by whom or what? It would seem to require a dominating personality of some kind lurking within the brain, but does the subconscious self really fit that description?

Owen Jones insists that "science hasn't killed free will," but it has clarified some of the factors that constrain it.[89] That seems to be a fair reflection of the evidence. In fact, this is one area in which I agree with Richard Dawkins. His view is that we currently lack any theory of mind sufficiently mature for anyone to define, with certainty, the manner and extent to which human intentions cause human behavior, but that it is a totally unjustified leap to "assume them away."[90] Is he right? Or is that just something he was compelled to say by whatever unseen forces hold him in thrall?

So are we just meat? Or are we mind and/or soul as well as body? Both life and consciousness undoubtedly exist and neither are obviously meaty things. Those committed to a materialist paradigm insist that they are merely manifestations of physical things, but this seems to be an article of faith rather than a conclusion reached by an unbiased examination of the evidence. The neurological studies cited may be interesting, but they do not support the inferences physicalists attempt to draw from them. Of course, this does not prove that the opposite view is correct. From a purely scientific viewpoint, life and consciousness remain mysteries. But beliefs that we are more than flesh and blood, and that we have a separate mind or soul capable of surviving physical death, have been held for many millennia. Burial customs during the Neolithic Age, the Bronze Age, and the Iron Age consistently reflect the idea of a free soul passing on to next existence.[91]

87. Libet, Benjamin, "Do We Have Free Will?"; Wegner, *The Illusion of Conscious Will*; Soon, et al, "Unconscious Determinants of Free Decisions in the Human Brain."

88. See, for example, Mele, *Effective Intentions: The Power of Conscious Will*; and O'Connor, "Degrees of Freedom."

89. Jones, "The End of (Discussing) Free Will."

90. Dawkins, *Harris and Free Will*.

91. Gräslund, "Prehistoric Soul Beliefs in Northern Europe."

The validity of this widely-held belief cannot be proven scientifically but, despite persistent efforts to undermine it, it remains at least a reasonable hypothesis. This is also true of free will. The studies cited in support of the contention that free will is an illusion again fail to provide any convincing evidence for this proposition. So, are life, consciousness and free will merely unintended and inexplicable consequences of forces unleashed by the Big Bang, or are they gifts of a sentient creator?

7

What of Our Experiences?

Even before we land, slippery and squirming, into tthe hands of a midwife waiting to submit us to various indignities and dump us onto the breasts of our relieved if breathless mothers, our lives are pervaded by experience. We may not remember the sights, sounds and sensations we experienced whilst still in utero, the drama of birth or our earliest impressions of this bright new world into which we had been unceremoniously thrust, but even then we perceived things around us. As we grew our perceptions changed. Sounds of our mothers' heartbeats gave way to rattles, the squeaks of toys and the laughter of playmates. We learned to associate sensations with particular things or occurrences, and, in time, words enabled us to describe these associations. As our mobility improved and we began to express our emotions by more than gurgling or screaming, we discovered that certain actions had consequences. A capacity for reasoning began to emerge. We learned new things from what we saw and heard and this process continued as we grew older, began our education and eventually became adults. It continues still. Our lives are spent in worlds of experience and, in one sense or another, experience is the foundation of all we know, think or believe. Reason and imagination may be the qualities that have lifted us from the primitive lives our ancient forebears shared with other primates and thrust us into a world blessed by science, technology and culture, but even our most visionary insights are almost invariably dependent on knowledge gained from human experience.

Of course, human perceptions are not always reliable. Some people make up or recycle stories, embellish real events or add dubious interpretations. Some stories grow in dramatic content as as they are progressively retold. Courtroom dramas may feature stark incidents of perjury, but we are more often misled by honest mistakes, perhaps aggravated by the subconscious re-editing of events. Such difficulties of perception have long been recognized,[1] and the risk of error is compounded when people look back and try to remember events that occurred in earlier years.[2] Yet, as fallible as our perceptions may be, few of us take the view that what we see and hear is inherently unreliable. Human testimony is often all we have. Not all claims or suggestions are amenable to scientific verification or rebuttal; the reliability of the things we have been told can often be assessed only by imperfect criteria such as the apparent credibility of the person telling the story and the plausibility of what is described. This may cause us to proceed cautiously and make some allowance for the possibility of error, but few of us are inclined to brusquely dismiss information derived from human experience as inherently unreliable.

SPIRITUAL EXPERIENCES
—MORE THAN SENSORY PERCEPTIONS?

Whilst many of our experiences obviously involve one or more of our five senses—sight sound, touch, taste and smell—there are other sensations with which we are all familiar and which are nonetheless real. The most obvious are our emotions. The undeniable power of emotional responses like love or anger may sometimes overwhelm our much lauded objectivity and even blind us to things we would otherwise have perceived by our senses. And there are other feelings, like affection, uneasiness or curiosity that may lack such intensity but nonetheless form part of the warp and weft of our lives. Within this smorgasbord of human experience there are some that seem to suggest a reality beyond the physical. They may be relatively commonplace, such as the feeling that a house has a "good feel," but others may seem more ethereal. People may speak of a shiver running up their spines or, conversely, of moments of awe or transcendence. Some are overtly 'religious' or 'spiritual' and much of the discussion has related to experiences of that nature, though they do not occur only in explicitly religious contexts.

Whilst those who report such experiences often insist that they are beyond description, there have been some attempts to analyze and characterize them. A suggested starting point has been a perceived distinction between religious experiences and religious feelings. It has been argued that a feeling of elation in a religious context should not be regarded as a religious experience, even if the person who experienced this emotion had come to

1. Crane and French, "The Problem of Perception."
2. Balko, Radley, "Eyewitness Testimony on Trial."

believe it was caused by some objective reality of religious significance.[3] This note of caution is not wholly inappropriate, but spiritual experiences may be both intensely personal and emotionally moving and those affected by them may be unable to humor pedantic philosophers by subdividing them into subjective and objective elements, even if they could see some point to doing so.

More than a century ago William James suggested that religious experiences were characteristically:

- transient — though perhaps outside normal perceptions of space and time;
- ineffable — beyond description;
- noetic — providing knowledge or insight beyond normal understanding; and
- passive — beyond control, even if sought by prayer, meditation or some other activity.[4]

This spattering of adjectives may narrow the focus of enquiry, but it may not be very enlightening. Richard Swinburne has tried to provide a little more illumination by dividing such experiences into categories:[5]

- perceptions of seeing 'God's hand at work' in some natural phenomenon, such as a sunset, that could otherwise be explained by purely physical causes;
- unusual events that breach the normal laws of physics, such as someone walking on water;
- visions and other phenomena that can be described using normal language, such as Jacob's vision of a ladder;
- mystical experiences that cannot be described using normal language, such as the reported explanation, "white did not cease to be white, nor black cease to be black, but black became white and white became black"; and
- a general feeling of God working in one's life.

Experiences such as these may be sought in various ways—through prayer, praise, meditation, religious music, dance and even the use of drugs such as peyote—but they can also occur spontaneously, or at least without any

---

3. Webb, Mark, "Religious Experience."
4. James, *The Varieties of Religious Experience.*
5. Swinburne, *Faith and Reason.*

conscious initiative on the part of those affected. Christians insist that the Holy Spirit touches people and leads them into truth.

CONVERSION EXPERIENCES

Spiritual experiences sometimes lead people to embrace a lifelong commitment to a particular faith, though conversion experiences are also reported by some who are already adherents. The experiences may take many forms. John Wesley, the Anglican priest who became the founder of Methodism, simply felt "his heart strangely moved." Many conversions seem to occur gradually, perhaps over extended periods of time, and some involve more than one experience. On the other hand, some people are profoundly affected by a single life changing moment. John Wesley's brother, Charles, described his own conversion to Christianity in a famous hymn which he wrote in 1738:

> *Long my imprisoned spirit lay,*
> *Fast bound in sin and nature's night;*
> *Thine eye diffused a quickening ray—*
> *I woke, the dungeon flamed with light;*
> *My chains fell off, my heart was free,*
> *I rose, went forth, and followed Thee.*[6]

Even with due allowance for imagery and hyperbole, this clearly describes a dramatic experience characterized by a sudden, astonishing feeling of freedom. Subsequent verses of this hymn and the many others that he subsequently wrote suggest that this feeling of freedom was substantially sustained throughout his life.

Tim Costello has described a more recent experience of this nature that occurred when, as a 17 year old boy, he attended a youth camp and went for a walk at night. He suddenly found himself trembling uncontrollably and struggled to stay on his feet as he had an overwhelming feeling of God's presence and love. He later explained that he had felt lost in awe at the natural beauty around him, even though he had seen it many times before. He lost track of time but, when the experience finished, he felt a new person. The boundaries between physical and spiritual seemed to have collapsed and he felt he "had glimpsed a parallel universe." Barriers between him and others also seemed to have collapsed and he realized that God loved everyone without qualification.[7]

---

6. Wesley, *And can it be that I should gain?*
7. Costello, *Faith*, 161 – 162.

Others may attribute feelings of this kind to a catharsis, borne of naivety and psychological need and perhaps triggered by emotive aspects of religious services or even manipulation. But many look back on them, even many years later, as a time when they had felt confronted by the presence of God.

OTHER ENCOUNTERS WITH THE NUMINOUS

Another type of experience that burst into public prominence with the emergence of the Pentecostal and Charismatic movements is usually described as the baptism in the Holy Spirit. Whilst all Christian denominations and traditions accept the concept of the baptism of the Holy Spirit, views differ as to significance of this phenomenon, with some seeing it as an element of the sacraments of initiation into the church, some as being synonymous with the concept of regeneration and others as an empowerment for Christian life and service.[8] Many within the Pentecostal and Charismatic movements relate powerful experiences, sometimes involving an initial episode of "speaking in tongues." The experience is intensely personal and variable in nature, but many claim that the 'infilling' of the Holy Spirit in this way has brought them new faith and new gifts or abilities.[9] As St Paul explained:

> *to each one the manifestation of the Spirit is given for the common good. To one there is given through the Spirit a message of wisdom, to another a message of knowledge by means of the same Spirit, to another faith by the same Spirit, to another gifts of healing by that one Spirit, to another miraculous powers, to another prophecy, to another distinguishing between spirits, to another speaking in different kinds of tongues, and to still another the interpretation of tongues. All these are the work of one and the same Spirit, and he distributes them to each one, just as he determines.*[10]

Pentecostals and Charismatics expect to have spiritual experiences. Like other Christians, they insist that, whilst their faith is dependent upon certain beliefs, the Christian life requires more than acceptance of dogma or even hope of eternal salvation; it involves a present relationship with God.

---

8. Macchia, *Baptized in the Spirit: A Global Pentecostal Theology*, 64. See also Yun, *Baptism in the Holy Spirit: An Ecumenical Theology of Spirit Baptism*.

9. Bennett, *Nine o'Clock in the Morning*; Phillips, *An Essential Guide to Baptism in the Holy Spirit*; The Doctrinal Commission of International Catholic Charismatic Renewal Services, *Baptism in the Holy Spirit, Catholic Charismatic Renewal, Holy Spirit, Theology*.

10. 1 Corinthians 12: 7–11.

This relationship is not seen as one-sided. They accept that they are called to love and serve God and others, but they also expect him to play an active part in their lives and may see this as an ongoing reality. For some the most significant experience is simply a sense of God's presence and love. Hence, they may speak of being "touched" by the Spirit during worship. They also expect to obtain direction from God and may speak of being "led" to seek out some person or embark upon some ministry activity.

The Baptism of the Holy Spirit is meant to bring positive changes to personality and character. To quote Paul again, ". . . the fruit of the Spirit is love, joy, peace, forbearance, kindness, goodness, faithfulness, gentleness and self-control."[11] A cynic might suggest that such qualities are not always evident in arguments at church synods, but the early disciples seem to have been transformed by this experience. According to the *Acts of the Apostles*, this small group of frightened and disillusioned people had fled into hiding when Jesus was arrested, but they abruptly emerged to boldly proclaim their allegiance to this man who had recently been executed by the Romans as a potential challenger to the authority of the emperor. Few contemporary Christians face such challenges, but many speak of the reality of changes in their own lives.

Of course, Christians are not the only people who claim to have spiritual experiences. The Old Testament recounts the experiences of Jewish patriarchs, including Abraham's encounter with the burning bush, Moses' feat in dividing the Red Sea, and an assortment of dreams, visions and angelic visitations. Islam is said to owe its origin to Muhammad's experience in a cave on the mountain of Hira in Mecca when the angel, Gabriel, appeared to him in a dream and commanded him to read from a book the angel was carrying.[12] Contemporary believers report less dramatic but nonetheless moving experiences of a spiritual nature. For example, one woman writing of her battle with cancer explained that: "I had a real spiritual sense of an inner warrior, something I'd never felt before. There was a presence of love and something greater guiding me through it."[13] Whilst such experiences may be intensely personal, they are are not rare occurrences. And even those with no religious convictions may have sometimes have experiences they cannot explain. As Christopher Hitchens perhaps ruefully conceded, "everybody has had the experience at some point when they feel that there's more to life than just matter."[14]

11. Galatians 5:22–23.
12. Fatoohi, Louay, "One Night in a Cave that Changed History Forever."
13. Quoted by Mexted, Kathy, "The music of recovery," *Slow Living Magazine*, 39.
14. Sewell, "Was Christopher Hitchens Religious?"

IS ANY OF THIS REAL?

Attitudes to spiritual experiences span a broad spectrum, ranging from gullible assumptions that almost any unusual event must be of supernatural origin to the view that anyone claiming to have had such an experience must be either lying or delusional. Whilst the latter view may be seen to be skeptical, it also strains credulity. Fully 49% of respondents to a Pew survey conducted in 2009 said that they had had a religious or mystical experience, defined as a "moment of sudden religious insight or awakening."[15] Of course, the results of surveys based on imprecise criteria must be approached cautiously, especially when they involve subjective impressions, but it does seem unlikely that half of the population had embarked upon a conspiracy to deceive the other half or that they were all similarly delusional.

Within these extremes, many people try to make sense of their own experiences and those described by others. They may be cautious; unable to wholly reconcile their tentative beliefs with their scientific worldview and yet also unable to dismiss the feeling that what they and others have experienced cannot be adequately explained by physical factors alone. Or they may have taken a particular view about the existence of God, yet find themselves unable to wholly still their nagging doubts. And their levels of belief may fluctuate, with optimism sometimes giving way to pessimism and vice versa. Is there a logical way to assess accounts of spiritual experiences?

Swinburne suggests two principles, both of which are generally defensible, though I think they require some qualification. The first, which he describes as the 'principle of credulity', is that, in the absence of any reason to disbelieve it, one should accept what appears to be true. The second, which he describes the 'principle of testimony', is that, in the the absence of any reason to disbelieve them, one should accept that people are telling the truth when they testify about religious experiences. Both of these principles are generally reasonable, but questions about what appears to be true are not necessarily resolved by impressions about whether people involved in the relevant events are honestly trying to recount what really happened. Furthermore, there are grounds for special caution in dealing with claims of spiritual experiences.

First, they are subjective and often intensely personal. Hence, there is greater scope for misinterpretation than there is with perceptions arising from things we see or hear.

Second, they are emotionally laden. Religious convictions may bring forgiveness, meaning and emotional security to the lives of believers and

---

15. Heimlich, "Mystical Experiences."

they may hold out the promise of another perfect life beyond physical death. Many people feel at least a subconscious need to find validation for their beliefs in their experiences, but subconscious needs may also shape our perceptions of what has occurred. Our own sense of identity and self esteem may also have persuasive, if unrecognized, influences on what we believe.

Third, those who have had such experiences may be unable to adequately explain them. This may leave others uncertain about the reliability of the limited description given to them and unable to understand the significance of what has occurred.

Fourth, corroborative evidence is rarely available. There are cases in which prayers made in front of entire congregations appear to have been spectacularly answered, but few atheists are likely to find anecdotes of spiritual experiences wholly compelling. It is almost invariably possible to attribute such experiences to some transient psychological condition, such as an emotional response to religious exhortations or music, to simple naivety, or to an underlying pathology of some kind. And some are clearly the product of delusional disorders or other mental illness. This has led some people to conclude that spiritual experiences are of no evidentiary value. The point has been succinctly made by Keith Augustine: "while it is possible that some mystics experience an ultimate reality while others do not, in the absence of further evidence—evidence other than the experiences themselves—there is no way to distinguish 'genuine' mystical experiences from 'delusional' ones."[16]

That may sometimes be true. Few delusional people seem to have the insight of the young litigant who had lunch with the King of Siam. Old Testament scholars might also be interested to know that I once met the "Queen of the South" who consulted King Solomon and is to rise up at the judgment and condemn a faithless generation.[17] She seemed remarkably spry for a 3,000 years old lady, and I was later told that her longevity had been maintained when she later hurled herself from a cliff towering over a wild sea, but apparently landed on the crest of a freak wave that swept in at just the right time to save her from smashing onto the rocky shore beneath. She was dragged from the sea unconscious, but lived to assure her rescuers that the episode had only confirmed her immortality.

Of course, not all who report spiritual experiences are delusional, but the accounts of those who are more rational may still be be misleading. People make up stories to gain attention, misinterpret what occurred, exaggerate or subconsciously embellish their memories over time. Even the

16. Augustine, Keith, "Religious Experience."
17. Matthew 12:38–42.

most implausible beliefs may be formed or entrenched due to factors such as "groupthink." An extreme example has been provided by the account of a young North Korean defector who had been brought up to believe that the leader, Kim Jong-il, was "a god" who could read her thoughts.[18] Yet it is irrational to ignore human experience merely because reported incidents might be false, exaggerated or even delusional. We do not do that in other areas of our lives. Furthermore, since spiritual experiences tend to be intensely personal, they are often recounted by close friends and family members whose general reliability may be known to us. Consequently, we may be able to take into account the fact that Aunt Dorothy usually has her feet firmly planted on the ground or that Uncle Fred is prone to flights of fancy.

However, some experiences have a reality that cannot be adequately explained by recounting a series of events or sensations. William James acknowledged and defended this proposition more than a century ago:

> *Vague impressions of something indefinable have no place in the rationalistic system. . . . Nevertheless, if we look on man's whole mental life as it exists . . ., we have to confess that the part of it of which rationalism can give an account of is relatively superficial. It is the part that has the prestige undoubtedly, for it has the loquacity, it can challenge you for proofs, and chop logic, and put you down with words. . . . Your whole subconscious life, your impulses, your faiths, your needs, your divinations, have prepared the premises, of which your consciousness now feels the weight of the result; and something in you absolutely knows that that result must be truer than any logic-chopping rationalistic talk, however clever, that may contradict it.*[19]

The red lights that such a claim turns on might well outshine those on Santa's sleigh. Yet there are many circumstances in which conscious beliefs may be based on the subconscious processing of a huge range of experiences and information that may not be accessible to rational debate. Imagine asking someone in a long term relationship to justify the belief that her partner truly loves her. She would not be reliant upon isolated instances alone, but upon a myriad of experiences, some perhaps long forgotten at a conscious level, and a myriad of expressions, verbal intonations and other subtle clues that have together forged an overall impression perhaps strengthened over many years. Cynics might protest that she may have been misled by a seductive cocktail of naivety, romanticism and wishful thinking. They

---

18. Withnall, "North Korean defector says she believed Kim Jong-il was a god who could read her mind."

19. Quoted by Mounce, *The Two Pragmatisms: From Peirce to Rorty*, 106.

may be right. Love may change, perhaps even die, but is it non-existent or unrecognizable?

Religious believers may also draw upon a history of experiences and impressions, perhaps sustained over decades, that has given them a confidence in the reality and love of God. Some may try to describe them, but the reality of truly profound experiences can never be adequately transmitted to others. Words alone are too pedestrian for such a task. No matter how eloquently or forcefully expressed, they cannot equip others to stand in their shoes and share their perceptions of what occurred. Those who have never had spiritual experiences or who have rationalized them in some manner may attribute anecdotes of such experiences to the imaginings of suggestible people. How can people know whether experiences they have not shared were genuine?

NEUROTHEOLOGY, GOD HELMETS AND THE QUEST FOR THE UNHOLY GRAIL

Plausible arguments can be made that at least some spiritual experiences may be attributable to psychological or neurological disorders. The potential impact of psychological factors on belief is well established and there is no reason to doubt that many experiences people attribute to supernatural intervention might actually be due to nothing more mystical than their own states of mind. Psychosis and some other mental illnesses can produce delusions that may involve religious themes, but the prevalence of such conditions is not commensurate with the overall incidence of spiritual experiences and there has been a quest for a more reassuring medical explanation.

One current hypothesis is that phenomena such as visionary experiences and momentary lapses of consciousness are consistent with 'hyper-religiosity' associated with temporal lobe epilepsy and perhaps even Geschwind syndrome.[20] Craig Aaen-Stockdale has, somewhat charitably, observed that the evidence for a such an association is not "terribly compelling." He points out that studies with hundreds of patients have estimated the frequency of religious experience to be between 1 per cent and 2.3 per cent, which is actually much lower than the incidence of religious experience in the normal population. One study revealed that of 137 patients suffering from temporal lobe epilepsy, only three were found to have had religious experiences and in two of those cases the patients had been living

20. Devinsky, Julie and Steven Schachter,. "Norman Geschwind's contribution to the understanding of behavioral changes in temporal lobe epilepsy." See also Ramachandran and Blakeslee, *Phantoms in the Brain*.

in a what was described as a "religion-heavy environment."[21] Furthermore, most people with strong religious beliefs do not exhibit signs of a neurological or psychological disorder, and there is evidence that religion can actually help people cope with stress and, in many cases, reduce anxiety and depression.[22] In any event, it is difficult to see how any such association could provide a logical basis for an assumption that all spiritual experiences could be explained by epilepsy. What of other experiences? The fact that people with temporal lobe epilepsy have nightmares does not rationally suggest that all nightmares are caused by epilepsy.

Other hypotheses based on psychological or neurological conditions have also been suggested, but none seem to be wholly compatible with the events they are supposed to explain. This can be illustrated by some recent attempts to explain St Paul's life-changing experience on the road to Damascus. According the Acts of the Apostles, Saul, as Paul was known prior to his conversion, was approaching Damascus when a light from heaven suddenly flashed around him. He fell to the ground and heard a voice ask, "Saul, Saul, why do you persecute me?" "Who are you, Lord?" Saul responded. "I am Jesus, whom you are persecuting," the voice replied. "Now get up and go into the city, and you will be told what you must do." The men traveling with him were speechless; they had heard the sound but had not seen anyone. Saul got up again but had no vision and had to be led by the hand into Damascus. For three days he remained blind and did not eat or drink anything. Then a man named Ananias had a revelation that he was to visit Saul and restore his sight. Despite some initial reluctance, he complied with this direction and went to lay hands on Saul, who reported that "something like scales" immediately fell from his eyes and he could see again.[23]

In 1987 it was suggested that his experience of seeing a bright light, falling down, hearing a message from God and becoming blind might be explained by temporal lobe epilepsy, perhaps leading to a convulsion.[24] This suggestion was immediately challenged[25] on the ground that it failed to explain why his companions also heard a voice,[26] saw a light,[27] and fell to the ground.[28] And there are other reasons to doubt this retrospective diagnosis.

---

21. Aaen-Stockdale, "Neuroscience for the Soul."
22. Newberg, "Religion, Evolution and the Brain: What Caused What?"
23. Acts 9:1 – 19.
24. Landsborough, "St. Paul and Temporal Lobe Epilepsy."
25. Brorson and Brewer, "Matters arising: St Paul and temporal lobe epilepsy."
26. Acts 9:7.
27. Acts 22:9.
28. Acts 26:14.

The biblical accounts do not suggest that Paul suffered any loss of memory, his blindness vanished suddenly rather than fading gradually as typically occurs if due to epileptic seizures, and if he had suffered convulsions, they would probably have been considered demonic in origin and prevented Paul's acceptance as an apostle. Another explanation, suggested in 2012, was that a mood disorder and associated psychotic symptoms may have been responsible for what Paul saw and heard.[29] This seems to have reflected a similar willingness to focus on some of the reported circumstances and ignore others, such as Paul's subsequent blindness and the effects the incident had on his companions. Then in 2015 it was argued that the incident may have been caused by a fireball like the meteor that exploded over Chelyabinsk Oblast in 2013. It was suggested that this might have caused people to be knocked off their feet and perhaps suffer temporary blindness.[30] Whilst I remain open minded about most things, I suspect that talking fireballs are astronomical rarities and doubt that a meteor with delusions of divinity exploded in the sky near Paul on that fateful night. Of course, even if it did, that would not have explained other aspects of the story such as the arrival of Ananias and the instantaneous restoration of Paul's sight.

One may, of course, discount the story on other grounds, such as suspicion that the story was later embroidered by enthusiastic fans, though Paul himself spoke of Christ's appearance to him and others in a letter written in 53 or 54 AD.[31] But "rational, scientific explanations" that ignore crucial aspects of the scenarios they supposedly explain are neither rational nor scientific.

Some neurologists have speculated that even normal human brains may be 'hard-wired' in some way for religious belief. Such suggestions have led to the development of "neurotheology," a relatively new discipline concerning the relationship between the brain and religion that permits scientists and theologians to explore questions of mutual interest, such as whether science and religion can be integrated in some manner that preserves and perhaps enhances both.[32] But neurological experiments have not always produced compelling findings. During the 1980s Michael Persinger conducted experiments with a device, that became known as the

---

29. Murray, Cunningham, and Price, "The role of psychotic disorders in religious history considered."

30. Hartmann, "Chelyabinsk, Zond IV, and a possible first-century fireball of historical importance."

31. 1 Corinthians 15:3–8. Scholars insist that Paul was actually the author of this letter. See Wall, *New Interpreter's Bible*.

32. Newberg, "Neurotheology: This Is Your Brain On Religion" See also Newberg, *Principles of Neurotheology*.

"God helmet," which stimulated the temporal lobes of subjects by exposing their brains to a weak magnetic field. Many claimed to have experienced a "sensed presence."[33] This seemed to be an interesting phenomenon, though whilst portraits of the great saints of history have often shown them wearing haloes, it is not suggested that they wore God helmets and, whatever the perceived significance, other researchers remain skeptical.

A Swedish team led by Pehr Granqvist suggests that the results could have been influenced by the participation of graduate students who might have known what sort of results were expected and others who may have derived subconscious clues from questionnaires designed to test their suggestibility to paranormal experiences. The team carried out their own double blind trials and the results were starkly different. Three participants did report intense spiritual experiences, but two of them had not been exposed to the magnetic fields at the time and, whilst twenty-two reported more subtle experiences, the helmets had been turned off when eleven of them had occurred. The approach taken by the team was later criticized on various grounds, including suggestions that the magnetic fields had been maintained for only fifteen minutes and that the computer software they used may have altered the nature of the magnetic fields.[34] The team remained unimpressed and insisted that the magnetic fields generated by the God helmet had been far too weak to penetrate the cranium and influence neurons in the brains of those tested.[35] A subsequent experiment with a commercial version of the God helmet found no difference in response to graphic images when the device was on or off.[36] As Richard Wiseman has said, the idea of "electromagnetic spirits" may have caught the public imagination, but the scientific jury is unconvinced.[37]

Nonetheless, there does appear to be some association between spiritual experiences and brain activity. Of course, scientists cannot compare a specific prayer with some corresponding neurological response, as one might compare, say, a shoe with a footprint, but they can use brain-imaging

33. Persinger, "The Sensed Presence Within Experimental Settings: Implications for the Male and Female Concept of Self."

34. Persinger and Koren, "A response to Granqvist et al. "Sensed presence and mystical experiences are predicted by suggestibility, not by the application of transcranial weak magnetic fields." See also Murphy and Persinger, *Debate concerning the God Helmet*.

35. Aaen-Stockdale, "Neuroscience for the Soul."

36. Wiseman, "The Haunted Brain." See also French et al, "The 'Haunt' project: An attempt to build a 'haunted' room by manipulating complex electromagnetic fields and infrasound"; and Gendle, "Can the 8-coil shakti alter subjective emotional experience? A randomized, placebo-controlled study".

37. Wiseman, "The Haunted Brain."

technologies to explore the physiological changes associated with spiritual practices such as prayer or meditation. Positron emission tomography (PET), single photon emission computed tomography (SPECT) and functional magnetic resonance imaging (fMRI) can be used to measure various changes in the brain, including cerebral blood flow and electrical and neurotransmitter activity. Researchers may also evaluate other physiological responses such as blood pressure, body temperature, heart rate and galvanic skin response.

Andrew Newberg has scanned the brains of people undertaking various religious practices, including praying Franciscan nuns, meditating Tibetan Buddhists, and Pentecostal Christians speaking in tongues. The scans revealed changes in multiple areas of the brain, with increased activity in the frontal lobe, a region that is activated when we focus on a particular activity, and a significant decrease in activity of the parietal lobe, which is responsible for one's sense of place. Similar neurological activity was found in adherents of different religious practices and across traditions,[38] though there was one striking exception. The images obtained from the brains of five women while they spoke in tongues were quite different from those obtained from people otherwise praying or meditating. Their frontal lobes (through which we control thoughts and actions) and language centers were relatively inactive, whilst the regions involved in maintaining self-consciousness were active. The women were healthy churchgoers and they were not in trances. Newberg said that the women believed that God was talking though them and added that: "The amazing thing was how the images supported their interpretation of what was happening."[39]

As Newberg said in 2014, neuroscientific research into spiritual phenomena is still in its nascent stages and there are unique methodological challenges.[40] He suggested that, viewed overall, the brain scans already undertaken provide evidence that universal features of the human mind may make it easier for us to believe in a higher power. The research has also helped delineate the physiological correlates of religious experiences, but this does not explain the origin or nature of such experiences. Brain scans may show associated changes, but they do not establish whether these changes caused the experiences or were produced in response to some external stimulus.[41] Despite this note of caution, some believers see this research as proof of an innate, physical conduit between people and God

38. Newberg, *Principles Of Neurotheology*.
39. Quoted by Carey "A Neuroscientific Look at Speaking in Tongues."
40. See also Newberg, "The neuroscientific study of spiritual practices"
41. Newberg, "Religion, Evolution and the Brain: What Caused What?"

whilst, conversely, some atheists see it as proof that the emotions associated with religious belief are merely manifestations of brain circuitry.[42] Newberg himself says that the scans simply reveal what happens in the brain when people have the experience of being in God's presence; they do not prove whether or not that experience is real in the sense that God is really in the room, communicating through them or with them.[43]

Newberg is right to be cautious. In a book with the evocative, if not inflammatory, title, *Brainwashed: The Seductive Appeal of Mindless Neuroscience*, Sally Satel and Scott Lilienfeld argue that, whilst the science may be sound, many of the inferences drawn from it are often dubious. They cite a study conducted during the lead up to the American presidential election in 2008 in which neuroscientists from UCLA scanned the brains of undecided voters as they reacted to photographs of candidates seeking nomination and assessed their unspoken attitudes towards them by reference to the brain activity revealed by the scans. This led them to conclude that two candidates had utterly failed to "engage" with 'swing' voters: John McCain, who proceeded to win the Republican nomination and Barack Obama whose popularity amongst swinging voters swept him into the White House.[44] Satel and Lilienfeld caution against a narrow focus on the brain's physical processes that suggests our subjective experiences can be explained by biology alone and ignores or discounts psychology and human experience.

ARE PRAYERS REALLY ANSWERED?

I was once due to hear a case in which a church was being sued for negligent praying. A woman had been standing at the altar of a pentecostal church seeking prayer and, when the pastor prayed for her, she was, in the words of the Statement of Claim, "slain in the spirit." Unfortunately, this allegedly caused her to fall on top of another woman who had already fallen to the floor due to a similar phenomenon and she suffered quite significant injuries. The case raised some interesting legal questions. To my surprise, the insurance company that had taken over the defense of the claim did not deny liability on the ground that this was an "act of God." It did, however, suggest that the injured woman had been guilty of contributory negligence, presumably on the ground that she should have realized that churches are

---

42. Gajilan, "Are humans hard-wired for faith?"
43. Newberg, "Divining the brain." See also Newberg, "The neuroscientific study of spiritual practices."
44. Satel and Lilienfeld, *Brainwashed: The Seductive Appeal of Mindless Neuroscience,* at xii.

dangerous places and worn a crash helmet or at least a woman-proof vest. To my disappointment, the case was resolved by agreement, but I did spend some time musing about what evidence might have been available on the power of prayer.

Perhaps surprisingly, some people have philosophical or even religious objections to what is usually described as intercessory prayer. The philosopher, William Paley, thought that prayer for particular favors involved attempting to dictate to divine wisdom.[45] That rather overstates the ambition of most of us and I doubt that God feels threatened by pleas for the odd favor. Another philosopher has suggested that a belief that God answers prayers requires a conclusion that he is immoral.[46] The rationalization for this extraordinary proposition is ingenious, but I suspect that an omnipotent God might take the view that he is free to intervene in his creation whenever he chooses. And mortals facing serious problems such as financial crises, debilitating illness or fear of imminent death are unlikely to fear that God may feel maligned by our prayers; their dominant concern is whether he will answer them.

Countless people in different ages and different cultures have not only asserted that he does, but also claimed that their own prayers have been answered. Many have spoken of seemingly miraculous episodes of physical or emotional healing. Whilst prayer for healing is often associated with the Pentecostal and Charismatic movements, claims of this nature are not new. Both the Old and New Testaments are replete with accounts of divine healing and some, like the story of Lazarus being raised from the dead, have echoed down the ages and struck responsive chords in the hearts of countless sick and needy people. Many churches regularly pray for the sick and at the time of writing Amazon lists more than 7,000 books on the topics of prayer and healing.

Some studies have seemed to confirm that prayer for healing may have a significant effect. For example, a study conducted at Duke University involved 150 patients scheduled for invasive cardiac procedures, one group of whom had the benefit of "healing touch" or intercessory prayer. The prayers were conducted off-site without either the patient or the physician's knowledge in order to avoid any possibility of placebo effects. Patients who received some form of non-traditional therapy, including prayer, proved to have a 25 to 30% reduction in adverse outcomes

---

45. Paley and Valpy, *Paley's moral and political philosophy*, 157.
46. Veber, "Why Even a Believer Should Not Believe That God Answers Prayers."

compared to standard forms of treatment.[47] Other studies have also reported better outcomes after prayer.[48]

On the other hand, Richard Dawkins cites a study conducted at six US hospitals in which patients awaiting coronary artery bypass graft surgery were divided into two groups, with the experimental group being prayed for by members of three churches and those in the control group ostensibly receiving no prayer. The authors of the study concluded that intercessory prayer itself had no effect on complication-free recovery, but certainty of receiving intercessory prayer was associated with a higher incidence of complications.[49] Christopher Hitchens seemed to think this demonstrated that prayer was ineffective.[50] Various explanations were suggested for the disappointing nature of the results. Some of those asked to pray for the patients later complained about the scripted nature of the prayers they were required to use and the lack of information about the patient's age, gender or progress reports on their medical condition. Richard Swinburne also protested that God answers prayers only if offered "for good reasons."[51] Some Christians would regard such tests as futile since they believe prayer needs to be guided by the Holy Spirit,[52] and others might fear that studies of this kind breached the commandment: "You shall not put the Lord your God to the test."[53]

But there are other questions that can be raised about the reliability of studies of this nature. The most obvious, though it never seems to be discussed, is that the tests were dependent upon assumptions that whilst nominated people prayed for some patients, no one would pray for those in the control groups. Did the researchers really imagine that none of these seriously ill people would pray for their own healing? And that none would receive prayers from parents, partners, children, friends or even concerned strangers, like those who prayed for Hitchens when he was terminally ill? Did they think that the patients would all implore God to let them become

---

47. Krucoff, "Integrative noetic therapies as adjuncts to percutaneous intervention during unstable coronary syndromes."

48. Byrd, "Positive Effects of Intercessory Prayer in a Coronary Care Unit Population"; Harris et.al., "A Randomized, Controlled Trial of the Effects of Remote, Intercessory Prayer on Outcomes in Patients Admitted to the Coronary Care Unit,"; and Leibovici, "Effects of Remote, Retroactive Intercessory Prayer on Outcomes in Patients with Bloodstream Infection: Randomised Controlled Trial."

49. Benson et al, "Study of the therapeutic effect of intercessory prayer in cardiac bypass patients."

50. Hitchens, *Mortality*, 18.

51. Swinburne, "Response to a Statistical Study of the Effect of Petitionary Prayer".

52. Spear, *Talking to God: The theology of prayer*.

53. Deuteronomy 6:16.

martyrs in the cause of experimental objectivity should they happen to be in the wrong group? This problem necessarily undermines any conclusions that might otherwise be drawn from what are touted as double blind studies.

A meta analysis first published in 2000 nonetheless considered 23 studies, involving a total of 2774 patients. The analysis found that 13 of the studies had revealed statistically significant positive results, 9 had shown no effect from prayer, and one study had shown a negative result. The authors concluded that "a relationship between religion or spirituality and physical health does exist but that it may be more limited and more complex than has been suggested by others."[54] A subsequent review undertaken by David Hodge in 2007 noted that, of the 17 studies he regarded as acceptable, 7 had revealed that patients who had received intercessory prayer demonstrated significant improvement compared to those who received standard treatment. Similar results had not been revealed by the other studies, which had included some of the most methodologically rigorous, though in 5 of those 10 studies, "the trend favored the prayer group." Hodge also noted a suggestion that studies linking prayer with salutary outcomes might be more likely to be rejected during the peer-review process because of their controversial nature.[55] He described the results of his review as inconclusive and said that the only certain result was that the findings were "unlikely to satisfy either proponents or opponents of intercessory prayer."[56]

Few religious believers are unlikely to base their beliefs on studies of this kind, but many are influenced by their own experiences. Such people are not necessary naive. Some are hard-headed realists who have been surprised by what has occurred. Of course, many such experiences could be explained by natural events. Even when something quite extraordinary has happened, proof that it was a response to the prayer may be impossible. In a large population even highly improbable things may due to chance and people may sometimes experience psychological or even neurological reactions they do not understand. Yet many remain convinced of the reality of their spiritual experiences and make the valid point that the uniquely personal

---

54. Powell, Shahabi, and Thoresen, "Religion and spirituality. Linkages to physical health."

55. Hodge, "A Systematic Review of the Empirical Literature on Intercessory Prayer." See also Koenig, H.G., M.E. McCullough, and D.B. Larson, *Handbook of religion and health*, New York: Oxford University Press, 2001.

56. Hodge, "A Systematic Review of the Empirical Literature on Intercessory Prayer." See also Schlitz et al, "Distant Healing Of Surgical Wounds: An Exploratory Study"; and Radin, Schlitz, and Baur, "Distant Healing Intention Therapies: An Overview of the Scientific Evidence."

nature of some such experiences necessarily means that others have only limited bases upon which to make judgements about their validity.

Those who doubt the reality of such experiences sometimes suggest that, if there were a god who truly intervened in human affairs, he would overcome every problem we face and heal every illness. When the novelist, Anatole France was shown the many crutches left behind by those who had been healed at the Grotto of Lourdes, he is said to have asked, "What? No artificial limbs?" But few religious believers expect God to grant every request and the implicit suggestion that he could not intervene in some ways because he does not seem to intervene in others is far from compelling.

A PERSONAL PERSPECTIVE

Whilst I am rarely accused of being coy, I have found myself reluctant to mention my own spiritual experiences. In writing this book I have tried to assume a role akin to that of a judge intent upon remaining objective and pointing out the strengths and weaknesses in both cases. I cannot quite dispel the feeling that it is vaguely inappropriate to then put myself forward as a witness whose evidence might be weighed in the balance. I am also conscious of the fact that some of the experiences that have most influenced my own beliefs have involved other family members whose privacy should be respected. Hence, any picture that emerges from the brief account that follows will necessarily be incomplete. On the other hand, it would seem less than candid for me to fail to mention my own belief in God and to offer at least some explanation of the personal circumstances that have led to or strengthened that belief.

I grew up in the church. My father was the superintendent of the local Methodist Church and he and my mother were Christians in every sense; they had a strong faith in God, but saw the gospel as a call to love and serve others. My brother was already ten years old when I arrived as the fruit of an obvious, if forgivable, miscalculation, and I promptly shattered the remnants of my parents' equanimity. I developed eczema and asthma before my first birthday and the latter quickly became a serious problem. Asthma was a little understood illness in those days, there were no puffers or steroidal drugs and attacks were usually treated by injections of adrenalin to which I soon developed a tolerance. There were many rushed trips to hospital and many hours spent waiting as initial doses proved inadequate and successively higher ones gave rise to a need for me to be monitored. This often took most of the night and, after waiting with me for hours, my father sometimes had to take me home, change his clothes and go straight to work. At other times I was admitted for longer periods. I was not expected to survive childhood and when, despite this dismal prognosis, I wheezed into my mid teens, a thoracic physician urged me to accept a disability pension rather than try for employment he thought I would be unable to sustain.

Uncontrolled asthma attacks are frightening experiences and in the days before puffers they were terrifying. I was often very afraid and, even as a young child, frequently thought of death, not as something that befell old people, but as something that might happen in minutes if I could not drag more air into my lungs. So I suppose it was inevitable that I would be open to belief in God. The first overtly religious experience I can remember occurred when I was ten years old. I had been taken to an evangelistic meeting attended by several hundred people and, whilst I had already heard numerous sermons, I found the words of this speaker strangely moving. Of course decades have passed and I can no longer remember what the man said or recreate the feelings his words engendered, but when he invited people to come forward, I was the first to reach the foot of the podium. The faith I then embraced has been substantially sustained, though I had a brief flirtation with atheism in earlier years and, like many skeptics, I often find myself questioning my beliefs. There have also been times when they have seemed lost in a rising tide of anxiety and depression.

My health improved during my teenage years, but soon deteriorated again. By my mid 20s I was taking the maximum doses of cortisone based drugs that could be safely prescribed, supplementing them with other medication and constantly doubling the recommended maximum daily use of my 'puffer'. I had several spells in hospital, usually in coronary care wards, and I was repeatedly warned that my heart had been strained. The sudden illness and death of our first child, then 22 months old, had left my wife, Pam, and I emotionally shattered, but two things occurred when I was twenty-seven that changed my attitude to prayer and, perhaps paradoxically, brought renewed hope.

The first concerned another family member and I will omit some otherwise relevant information in order to avoid identifying her. She had been gravely ill and Pam and I lived with the constant fear that she would die. She had been in hospital several times, but there was no wholly effective treatment and we were advised to treat her constantly recurring fevers by putting water into her mouth with an eye dropper every 15 minutes. In the early hours of one morning I reached the point of despair. I looked up and tried to pray, but found myself saying that I did not know whether anyone was there or whether I was just talking to the paint on the ceiling. I said that I was very afraid and did not know how I would survive as an integrated person if she also died. The church in which I had been raised had stressed the need for faith and, in mounting distress, I realized that it was beyond me. I could only say, "If you want me to have faith, you'll have to give it to me, because I can't feel anything but despair." Then something amazing happened. I suddenly knew that, if I prayed for her, she would be healed. I had never experienced anything like this before. There was no gradual rekindling of optimism; it was an instantaneous and certain awareness, as if I had noticed something already present but previously overlooked. So I prayed a simple prayer, like "Lord, please heal her" and, as I watched, the flush faded from her face, she stopped twitching, sighed and then slept. She had no further symptoms and the illness never returned. Of course, I cannot prove that she would not have recovered in the ordinary course of events. Yet I have never been able to explain the certainty I suddenly felt, nor explain the observable changes in her condition that immediately followed.

Then, months later, I had an especially severe asthma attack due to smoke from a fireworks display. A hastily summoned GP came to my home, stayed with me for some time and gave me several injections. Their effect was short lived. Within an hour of his departure, he had been called again. He gave me further injections but eventually told Pam that I would have to go to hospital. He made the necessary arrangements and left. A neighbor, Colin, thought we might need some help and offered to drive us to the hospital, but he had just begun to reverse our car down the driveway when I stopped breathing altogether and slumped over. I was hastily dragged from the back seat onto the lawn and, as Pam began mouth to mouth resuscitation, the doctor returned. He thought he had left his prescription pad behind. He immediately began cardiac massage, but the minutes ticked by and I did not resume breathing. He eventually stopped, looked at Pam and said, "I'm sorry. It's no use, he is dead." My wife is a woman of many accomplishments, but she is not adept at taking "no" for an answer, and she met this statement with an implacable response: "I'm not having that! I'm praying for him. You keep working on him."

Of course, I was oblivious of this contretemps until the following day when I woke up in an intensive care ward with wires attached to my chest. A doctor duly assessed me and told me that I seemed to have recovered from the asthma attack and could be discharged. Then, some time, later he returned and, to my surprise, demanded to know why I had not told him about my cardiac arrest. He was visibly skeptical when I said that I had no idea what he was talking about. Later in the day the GP who had treated me at my home burst into the hospital room and announced, "You have no right to be here!" I was monetarily uncertain whether he meant that I was unjustly occupying a bed or whether he had made a moral judgment about the justification for my continued presence on earth. But he proceeded to to explain that since the resuscitation attempts had been unsuccessful for so long, he had thought there was no longer any reasonable prospect of revival. He added, with disarming candor, that he had resumed cardiac massage only to humor my wife and avoid any risk of criticism at an inquest into my death.

It is true, of course, that I could have just been very lucky. We now have a much better appreciation of the potential effectiveness of cardiac massage and, despite his conviction that further efforts were futile, our local GP may have given up hope too quickly. His belief that he had forgotten his prescription pad may have occurred by chance, his arrival just as I landed on the grass in need of resuscitation may have been a matter of coincidence, my wife's direction for him to keep working on me may have been merely fortuitous, and I may just have hit the jackpot when he proved sufficiently nervous about potential criticism to comply. But, to me, my survival seemed attributable to more than an improbable series of flukes.

My hopes that I may have been healed from the underlying asthmatic condition were soon dashed, but this experience encouraged me to ask others to pray for me when I had further attacks and the results were sometimes surprising. On one occasion I rang an Anglican priest in the middle of the night. I was suffering another severe asthma attack and about to head back to the hospital emergency department when my fear overcame my reticence about waking this poor man from a sound sleep. I could barely breathe, let alone talk, and it took some time for him to realize who I was. But he then prayed a simple one sentence prayer and it felt as though someone had reached out and cut the steel band constricting my chest. Within a minute or two I was breathing normally. Asthma attacks can be precipitated by emotional factors and it may be suggested that the prayer merely caused me to relax, but, despite the earlier experiences, I had actually remained very frightened.

Yet again my hopes of a complete cure were dashed. Subsequent attacks occurred and some of them were very severe. There were other occasions when I made an uncharacteristically fast recovery following prayer, but that did not always occur and another twenty years were to pass before the attacks finally ended. Throughout these years I found myself on a constant quest to understand how these things were possible and why they seemed to happen in response to some prayers but not others. Why was I not completely healed? Why did some people seem to make full recoveries? Why did even young people die? Some of the more fundamentalist preachers and writers suggested that God always wanted to heal people; if that did not occur, then there must be some explanation, such as lack of faith or some unconfessed sin. Most baulked at nakedly asserting that, if you remained sick, it must be your fault; but such claims often added burdens of guilt to shoulders that already had too much to carry. The theory was also sabotaged by numerous people of undoubted decency and compassion who had the temerity to die rather than recover. So what is the true explanation? I still do not know. For me, the holy grail of a coherent set of principles that would fully explain my experiences and those of other people I have known remains out of reach.

Some believe that prayer merely has a placebo effect, but that does not seem to be a wholly adequate explanation. There are too many times when something extraordinary seems to occur. It is true that some people see miracles in things readily explicable by chance and that even 'long shots' are bound to occur from time to time, but chance is a less plausible explanation when a series of long shots occur within a single life rather than across a broad population. My own perception is that there are answers to prayer, but that they are not always predictable and they are rarely, if ever, scientifically verifiable.

This also seems to be true of other spiritual experiences. Neither visions of God nor talking fireballs have ever blown me off my feet, but there have been times when I have been conscious of a sense of a spiritual reality. Some time ago I wandered around the famous cathedral at Chartres, looking at the magnificent stained glass windows and taking the odd photograph. I was not feeling guilty about anything and, as a lawyer of many years standing, I had long assumed that I had successfully anesthetized my conscience. But amidst the splendor of centuries-old artwork was a relatively small cardboard poster with a picture and the words, "Neither do I condemn you. Go." I had been familiar with these words for decades, but for reasons I cannot understand let alone explain, I had a sudden and almost overwhelming feeling of forgiveness and acceptance. The feeling remains with me still. Was this a spiritual experience? Some skeptics could reasonably protest that this may have been nothing more than an emotional reaction triggered by the poster. That is possible. I can only say that it was very real to me.

William James proclaimed that "God is real since he produces real effects."[57] For many, spiritual experiences have led them to believe in God or confirmed their existing faith. Reports of such experiences should not be immune from skeptical scrutiny. The possibility of fabrication, exaggeration or psychological manifestations of various kinds should obviously be considered and in many cases they may seem obvious explanations. But the evidence does not really support the view that all such experiences are attributable to mental or physical disorders or neurological activity. The truth,

---

57. William, *The Varieties of Religious Experience*, Lecture XX Conclusions.

unpalatable as it may be to religious fundamentalists and atheists alike, is that we live with mysteries we cannot wholly fathom.

8

Does The Fat Lady Sing at Funerals?

The Venerable Bede once told a now famous story of the counsellor who, when asked to advise King Edwin (586 – 632 or 633 AD) whether he should accept Christianity, spoke of a sparrow:

> *The present life of man, O king, seems to me, in comparison of that time which is unknown to us, like to the swift flight of a sparrow through the room wherein you sit at supper in winter, with your commanders and ministers, and a good fire in the midst, whilst the storms of rain and snow prevail abroad; the sparrow, I say, flying in at one door, and immediately out at another, whilst he is within, is safe from the wintry storm; but after a short space of fair weather, he immediately vanishes out of your sight, into the dark winter from which he had emerged. So this life of man appears for a short space, but of what went before, or what is to follow, we are utterly ignorant. If, therefore, this new doctrine contains something more certain, it seems justly to deserve to be followed.*[1]

There is much to be said for the wisdom of this unknown counsellor. Despite the enormous scientific advances made in the succeeding centuries and the apparent assurance of fundamentalists and atheists alike, we still lack the means to ascertain what may have come before and what is to follow our brief lives. The crucial question is, of course, whether we cease to exist as soon as we fly out the other door. The prospect of life after death has enchanted humanity for millennia. The theologies of most religions include conceptions of some form of afterlife. Judaism, Christianity and Islam all maintain belief in the resurrection of the dead, whilst beliefs in

---

1. Bede, *The Ecclesiastical History of the English People*, book II, chapter 13.

reincarnation or rebirth are held by Hindus, Buddhists and devotees of other ancient and modern religions. But are any of these beliefs sustainable? Was Plato right to insist that the soul is immortal?

Plato supported his view by four arguments. First, since the living are generated from the dead and the dead from the living, the souls of the dead must exist somewhere. Second, since we possess some non-empirical knowledge at birth, the soul must have had a prior existence. Third, some things are invisible, immortal, and incorporeal, whilst are others visible, mortal, and corporeal and, since our souls are amongst the former, they will live on. Fourth, as beautiful things participate in the Form of beauty, so we are infused with the Form of soul. The soul is that which renders the body living, and "the soul will never admit the opposite of what she always brings."[2]

Aquinas argued that human souls are incorruptible whereas the souls of other animals are not and that Christ's resurrection affirms that we will be saved by our bodies rising from the dead.[3] Kant invoked reason, arguing that, since morality requires the highest good and such holiness is not achieved in this life, the soul must live on to achieve and enjoy this in an afterlife. Hence, immortality is 'a postulate of pure practical reason.'[4] Other philosophers have argued that the soul is simple and hence must be immortal.[5]

Of course, I have adverted to these arguments only in very broad terms and a grumpy Plato, Aquinas or Kant might even now be glowering down at me in justified pique. However, I suspect that few people come to believe in life after death by reading such philosophical arguments and this is not the place for a discussion of their merits.

On the other hand, atheists insist that such feelings are the product of religious indoctrination, wishful thinking and perhaps a simple lack of imagination. How does one form a mental image of perpetual oblivion? They maintain that life and consciousness are merely manifestations of our physical being and that both are extinguished upon death. Sean Carroll complains that. "Among advocates for life after death, nobody even tries to sit down and do the hard work of explaining how the basic physics of atoms and electrons would have to be altered in order for this to be true."[6] This

---

2. Plato, *Plato: Phaedro*, edited by R Hackforth, Cambridge, Cambridge University Press, 1972, 100c–104c.

3. McInerny, "Saint Thomas Aquinas," 9.

4. Kant, *Critique of Practical Reason*, book 2, 1–2 para 35.

5 Sassen, Brigitte (2008). "Kant and Mendelssohn on the Implications of the 'I Think,'" 215–233.

6. Carroll, Sean, "Physics and the Immortality of the Soul," *Discover*, May 23

seems to reflect an assumption that life after death could only be achieved by physical resurrection and that anyone who believes that this occurs should be able to explain the precise physical mechanisms by which it is achieved.

The beliefs of some people are influenced by their experiences or perceptions. A survey in 2009 revealed that 29% of Americans claimed to have been in touch with the dead and 18% claimed to have seen a ghost.[7] Such perceptions are sometimes caused by the misinterpretation of phenomena for which there are purely physical explanations, though in other contexts one might hesitate to dismiss such an enormous body of eye-witness evidence on the assumption that all must be mistaken.

Many years ago Pam and I occupied a run down, inner city terrace house that had reputedly been occupied by people involved in occult practices. One moonless night I thought I sensed a presence of some kind in the pitch black interior of a small open shed in the rear yard. The house was in an area with a high crime rate and there was more to worry about than the risk of disembodied intruders. I did not know what to expect but, summoning my courage, I stood at the doorway and commanded whoever or whatever was in there to come out. An unseen thing immediately hurtled towards me and crashed into my legs, nearly knocking me over backwards. The fight response instinctively kicked in but, before I could even regain my balance, let alone offer any resistance, I realized that my assailant was neither human nor ghost, but a startled black Labrador, almost invisible in the dark, who proved anxious to make amends by licking my hand.

Whatever the causes, there can be no doubt that belief in some kind of afterlife is widespread. The *Cognition, Religion and Theology Project*, a three year international study completed in 2011, found that people from many different cultures instinctively believe that some part of their mind, soul or spirit lives on after death. A co-director, Roger Trigg, explained that "attempts to suppress religion are likely to be short-lived as human thought seems to be rooted to religious concepts, such as the existence of supernatural agents or gods, and the possibility of an afterlife or prelife."[8] One could almost hear the grinding of atheistic teeth.

Of course, the possibility that death may not be the end of our conscious existence but a doorway to another form of life inevitably raises further questions. What would such a life be like? Would we have resurrected or new bodies? Would we live on as purely spiritual beings? Would we face a divine judgment that would determine our eternal destiny? Would we

---

2011.

7. Lipka, "18% of Americans say they've seen a ghost."
8. University of Oxford, "Humans 'predisposed' to believe in gods and the afterlife."

be welcomed home like the prodigal son returning to his father? Would the unrepentant face unimaginable punishment? Such questions are profoundly important, but I am concerned in this chapter with only one: is death the end?

There may be numerous theological answers to that question but, for present purposes, I am more interested in any available evidence. Tales of people consulting the dead have been recorded throughout history, with one of the most famous accounts involving King Saul calling up the ghost of the prophet, Samuel.[9] But few lawyers have reported successfully cross-examining ghosts and forensic science laboratories have not taken up the challenge to establish approved protocols for seances. Hence, it seems, one is substantially reliant upon near death experiences for evidentiary support.

THE PHENOMENON OF NEAR DEATH EXPERIENCES

These tantalizing phenomena became the subject of public awareness largely due to Raymond Moody's books *Life after Life* first published in 1975[10] and *The Light Beyond* published in 1988.[11] Suggestions that they might actually provide evidence of life after death were initially derided by many as the product of naivety or religious opportunism, but as further cases were reported it became increasingly difficult to dismiss them on those bases and even some medical specialists began to suspect that they were not attributable to either physiology or psychology alone. More reports occurred as people became emboldened by the prospect of being taken seriously, and in many cases medical or hospital notes were still available to reveal patients' conditions at the relevant times. As a consequence, there has been a flood of recent books on the topic.[12] There are still some grounds for skepticism. The experiences are subjective and, perhaps with rare exceptions, unverifiable, they fly in the face of the purely physicalist paradigm that many scientists

---

9. 1 Samuel 28.
10. Moody, *Life after Life*.
11. Moody, *The Light Beyond*.

12. See, for example, van Lommel, *Consciousness Beyond Life: The Science of the Near-Death Experiences*; Long, Jeffrey, *Evidence of the Afterlife*; Miller J Steve, *Near-Death Experiences as Evidence for the Existence of God and Heaven: A Brief Introduction in Plain Language*; Neal, Mary C., *To Heaven and Back*; Anderson, Reggie, *Appointments with Heaven*; Sartori, Penny, *Wisdom of Near Death Experiences*; McVea, Crystal *Waking Up in Heaven: A True Story of Brokenness, Heaven, and Life Again*, Brentwood, Howard Books, 2013; Piper, Don, *90 Minutes in Heaven: A True Story of Death and Life*; and Burke, John, *Imagine heaven*.

seem to accept as a bedrock of faith, and the stories recounted often seem like the stuff of dreams. Yet there is a mounting body of evidence and attempts to explain them in purely medical terms have not been as compelling as the more emphatic declamations might suggest.

Whilst such experiences were once thought to be rare, they have been reported more frequently since the advent of modern resuscitation techniques. Surveys have generally revealed that they now occur in 10% to 20% of cases in which people survive cardiac arrest.[13] Pin van Lommel, a cardiologist, whose own surveys found that 18% of patients surviving cardiac arrest reported such experiences, could find no evidence that their frequency was influenced by the duration of cardiac arrest, the duration of unconsciousness, the need for intubation in complicated CPR, induced cardiac arrest, drugs, fear of death before the arrest, foreknowledge of near death experiences, religion or education.[14]

These and other studies have revealed that such experiences are characterized by a number of common elements, though not all are present in every case:

- intense emotions, usually of peace and love, but occasionally of fear, horror or loss;
- the perception of looking down on one's own body, sometimes observing resuscitation attempts or even moving into other rooms or areas;
- moving through darkness, often toward an indescribably bright light, often perceived as a being of light;
- a sense of being in a spiritual realm;
- clear thinking and vivid observations;
- meeting loved ones who have previously died and sometimes other people;
- images of one's past life and the impact certain actions may have had on others;
- sometimes receiving knowledge about life and the universe; and
- a reluctance to return to the body and sometimes a conscious decision to do so.[15]

13. Greyson, "Near-Death Experiences."
14. van Lommel, "Pathophysiological Aspects of Near-Death Experiences."
15. International Association for Near Death Studies Inc, *Characteristics of Near Death Experience*. See also Williams, *Common Elements are Found in Near-Death Experiences*; Woodruff, Sherwood, and Johnson, "Ask the Experts: What Is a Near-Death Experience?"; Bethune, *Why so many people–including scientists–suddenly believe in an*

Whilst such experiences are described by people of varying religious and cultural backgrounds, enculturation may influence their interpretation of them. For example, whilst Christians might see the being of light as Jesus, non-Christians might associate the figure with other religious identities or none at all. But those who have such experiences invariably see them as foretastes of an afterlife and, for many, they are life changing. In some cases those who report meeting children or other family members who have died find emotional healing in an assurance that they bear no blame and will not be exposed to judgment. And those who choose to return, however reluctantly, do so with a sense of purpose and sometimes even a specific agenda of tasks or responsibilities.[16]

Whilst individual anecdotes may not provide adequate support for general conclusions, they may sometimes create a more vivid picture than that which can be painted by bare descriptions of common features and statistical analyses. For the sake of brevity, I will mention just a few.

THE MAN WHO LOST HIS TEETH

Van Lommel mentions the case of a comatose patient who was treated by a nurse during the pilot phase of his studies. The nurse reported that the 44 year old man was brought to the coronary care unit by ambulance. He was found to be cyanotic and comatose. Artificial respiration with heart massage and defibrillation was administered, but when intubation was attempted he was found to have upper dentures. The nurse removed them and put them onto the 'crash cart'. The patient was still comatose and receiving artificial respiration when transferred to the intensive care unit about an hour and a half later. When he saw the nurse again more than a week later, he immediately said "Oh, that nurse knows where my dentures are." The nurse was surprised by this statement, but the patient continued, "Yes, you were there when I was brought into hospital and you took my dentures out of my mouth and put them onto that cart, it had all these bottles on it and there was this sliding drawer underneath and there you put my teeth." The nurse remembered this happening while the patient had been in deep coma. The patient proceeded to explain that he had seen his prone body from above and observed the nurses and doctors busy with CPR. He was able to describe correctly and in detail the small room in which he had been resuscitated as well as the appearance of those present. He said that he had

---

afterlife.

16. Bethune, *Why so many people–including scientists–suddenly believe in an afterlife.*

been very much afraid that they would stop CPR and that he would die. He had tried unsuccessfully to let them know that he was still alive and that they should continue. The experience made a deep impression on him and he said that he was no longer afraid of death.[17]

This account has been questioned, with C. C. French querying whether any attempt was made to corroborate details with the patient,[18] and G. M. Woerlee suggesting that the patient would have regained consciousness as a result of cardiac resuscitation.[19] However, the nurse confirmed that the patient had been clinically dead: no heartbeat, no breathing, no blood pressure, and "cold as ice." The dentures had been removed from his mouth immediately after he entered the hospital and it was "simply unthinkable" that he could have made any "normal" observation of this occurring. He had never been in that hospital before, let alone in the resuscitation room, and the crash cart he had accurately described had been a unique hand-made product of ramshackle quality, stationed only in that room.[20]

Woerlee responded by conceding the accuracy of the nurse's observations, but suggesting that he may have failed to recognize that people suffering from hypothermia may retain consciousness with little if any blood flow. He insisted that the patient would have been conscious as a result of cardiac massage from a machine called the "thumper," but paralyzed due to oxygen starvation and hypothermia. Hence he could have felt his dentures being removed, heard them placed on a tray and made visual observations when his eyes were opened to check his reflexes.[21] In fact, the nurse subsequently confirmed that the thumper had been turned on only after the dentures had been removed. He added that the patient had had no blood circulation and that his pupils had remained unresponsive even when a bright light had been shone into them. He also said that details the patient described could not have been seen from his bed, but only from a different perspective.[22]

---

17. van Lommel et al. "Near-death experiences in survivors of cardiac arrest: A prospective study in the Netherlands."

18. French, "Dying to know the truth: Visions of a dying brain, or false memories?"

19. Woerlee, "Cardiac arrest and near-death experiences."

20. Smit, "Corroboration of the Dentures Anecdote Involving Veridical Perception in a Near-Death Experience."

21. Woerlee, "Response to "Corroboration of the Dentures Anecdote Involving Veridical Perception in a Near-Death Experience."

22. Smit, and Rivas, "Rejoinder to "Response to 'Corroboration of the Dentures Anecdote Involving Veridical Perception in a Near-Death Experience.'"

THE WOMAN WHO SAW A SHOE

An earlier case involved a patient named Mary who had a cardiac arrest whilst being treated in the Harborview Medical Center in Seattle following a heart attack three days earlier. She said she had looked down at the attempts to resuscitate her and noted printouts coming from the machines monitoring her vital signs. She had been distracted by something over the area surrounding the emergency room entrance and, "willing herself" outside of the hospital," went to have a look. She accurately described the area surrounding the emergency room entrance, despite the fact that a canopy would have obscured the view from her hospital room window. She then noticed something on a third-floor window ledge on the far side of the hospital and, 'willing herself' to this location, found a man's left-foot tennis shoe on a third-floor window ledge. She described the shoe as dark blue with a worn-out patch over the little toe and a single shoelace tucked under its heel. When she regained consciousness, she asked her critical care social worker, Kimberly Clark, to look for the shoe. Clark was initially skeptical but agreed to conduct a search. She first went outside and, when unable to see it, went from room to room on the floor above Maria's room, pressing her face against the glass so she could see the window ledges. She eventually found the shoe, but later explained that she had been unable to see the worn out toe that had been facing outwards or the tucked in lace until she had removed the shoe from the ledge.

In an article written in 2012, Loren Lemos suggested that this story had been "totally demolished." Hospital reports for Maria could not be found and "little details are all inflated; for instance the claim that details of a shoe on a ledge could not possibly be discerned has been tested on that hospital building, and it turns out that a shoe on the ledge actually is really easy to see and jumps out to the eye of people passing beneath."[23] In making these dismissive statements, Lemos was apparently relying upon an investigation by Hayden Ebbern and Sean Mulligan in 1994, some 17 years after the incident.[24] They were unable to locate Maria, who had been a migrant worker visiting from interstate, but interviewed Clark and formed various hypotheses. They thought Maria "could have been" familiar with hospital equipment and procedures, so assumed it was "quite possible" that her observation of the monitoring machine streaming out chart paper could have been a visual memory incorporated into an hallucination. She may have deduced the appearance of the driveway and entrance to the

23. Lemos, Loren *The NDE delusion*.
24. Ebbern, Hayden, Sean Mulligan, and Barry L Beyerstein, "Maria's Near-Death Experience: Waiting for the Other Shoe to Drop."

emergency room from observations made when she was brought in to the hospital at night three days earlier, if then conscious, and from sounds she subsequently heard. They placed a running shoe of their own in the area Clark had described, but found that it was easily visible both from ground level and from inside the adjacent room. Maria had not been on the ground outside the hospital or in that room, but in a room below that level and the shoe would have been on the ledge above her. Nonetheless, they concluded that it was "not far fetched to assume" that she "could have" overheard others discussing it and "could have" unintentionally filled in details to flesh out the story, such as the state of the shoe. They also suggested that Clark may have come to honestly misremember how closely the facts matched Maria's account. None of this was particularly compelling.

    A number of questions might be asked. Did they find the right room? Had it been changed? The original hospital was opened in 1931, a time not renowned for floor to ceiling windows, and it has had "numerous, difficult to chronicle additions and alterations" since its opening.[25] A shoe on a ledge outside a room with the smaller windows may not have been visible unless an occupant pressed her face against the glass as Clark described.

    Ebbern and Mulligan actually saw some construction work being undertaken whilst they were present in 1994. Were other changes made during the 17 years that had elapsed prior to their inspection? The work being done in 1994 meant that they had to view the shoe they had placed on the ledge from some distance away. They assumed that it would have been more clearly visible to a closer observer, but is that a valid assumption? Or could it have been visible only from an oblique angle but obscured by the ledge itself when someone looked up from below? Was it placed in the same position on the same ledge? The report published two years after their inspection, does not suggest that these questions were considered or that Clark was ever asked to explain any apparent inconsistencies.

    Ebbern and Mulligan did not suggest that either she or Maria had fabricated the incident. Nor did they suggest that her account of what occurred had been demolished. On the contrary, whilst they thought the case was far from unassailable, they fairly conceded that their investigation did not prove that Maria had not had an out of body experience or that Clark's recollections and interpretations had been wrong. Of course, none of this proves that her observations were accurate, but is also worth remembering that Clark was not the patient; she was a critical care social worker who was initially skeptical of the claim and became involved only when she agreed

---

25. Mitchelson, Alan, "Harborview Medical Center, Campus, First Hill, Seattle, WA" *PCAD* http://pcad.lib.washington.edu/building/3642/.

to see if the shoe had been in the position Maria had described. There is no reason to imagine that she was delusional or prone to flights of fancy.

THE MUSICIAN WHO HEARD A PERFECT 'D'

In 1991 Pam Reynolds had an extraordinary operation to remove a giant basilar artery aneurysm in her brain. As Michael Sabom explains,[26] the procedure involved lowering her body temperature to 60 degrees Fahrenheit, stopping her heart, ensuring there was no detectable brain activity and draining the blood from her head. She was placed under general anesthesia, electroencephalogram electrodes were attached to monitor her brain activity, her eyes were taped shut and moulded earplugs were inserted into both ears, with speakers administering clicking sounds so that her brain response to these sounds could be measured. Her head was shaved and clamped to the operating table. The operation itself involved the use of a pneumatic bone saw to create a hole in her skull and give the surgeon, Dr Spetzler, access to the brain.

During the course of the operation she heard a sound. She was a musician and to her it seemed to be a natural D. She felt it was pulling her out of the top of her head. The further she got out of her body, the clearer the tone became. She found herself looking down into the operating theatre and felt more aware than she had ever been in her entire life. She was "metaphorically sitting on Dr Spetzler's shoulder." Her vision was brighter, more focused and clearer than normal vision. There was much in the operating theatre she did not recognize and many people. She was surprised by the manner in which her head had been shaved as she had expected them to remove all of the hair. She saw a "saw thing" that looked like an electric toothbrush. It had a dent, "a groove at the top where the saw appeared to go into the handle, but it didn't." It also had interchangeable blades that were in a case. She heard the saw "crank up." She didn't see them use it on her head, but heard it humming at a relatively high pitch and then it suddenly "went Brrrrrrrr!"

Whilst Spetzler was opening her head to reveal the brain, a female cardiac surgeon located the femoral artery and vein in Reynold's right groin, but found them too small to cope with the flow of blood needed for the cardiopulmonary bypass machine. Pam later recalled that someone had said something about her veins and arteries being very small. She believed it was a female voice and that it was the cardiologist. She also recalled seeing the

---

26. Sabom, *Light and Death*. In his preface Sabom notes that Dr Robert Spetzler assisted him by ensuring that his reconstruction of the surgical procedure on Pam Reynolds was accurate.

heart-lung machine, the respirator and a lot of tools and instruments that she did not recognize.

Sabom, who is also a cardiologist, explains that the aneurysm proved to be as large as had been feared and hypothermic cardiac arrest was required. Blood was pumped from her body, chilled and returned to facilitate cooling. Cardiac arrest occurred and her brain waves flattened into "complete electrocerebral silence" before the blood was drained from her body "like oil from a car." Sabom records that "sometime during this period" Reynold's near death experience progressed.

There was a sensation of being pulled. It was not a physical sensation but she felt like she was entering something that was like a tunnel. She became aware of her grandmother calling her and continued down this dark shaft towards a pinpoint of light that became larger and larger. The light became incredibly bright but she could discern figures of light that began to form shapes she could recognize. One of them was her grandmother. She also recognized other relatives and noted that their appearances fitted perfectly into her understanding of what each person had looked like when at their best during their lives. They were looking after her, but would not permit her to go further into the light and she understood that, if she did, they would be unable to reconnect her to her body. She wanted to go on into the light, but she also wanted to go back because she had children to raise. Her relatives were nourishing her with something that was not a physical thing but gave her a sensation of being fed and made strong. Her uncle subsequently took her back through the tunnel. Everything was fine until she saw her body, which looked dead. She was afraid and, when she re-entered it, "it was like diving into a pool of ice water . . . It hurt!" She then heard the medical staff playing the song, "Hotel California." She later remembered the line "You can check out anytime you like, but you can never leave," which she said, with some amusement, had seemed incredibly insensitive.

Alas, none of her dead relatives volunteered to be interviewed, but the doctors confirmed the accuracy of her observations about the operation. She had initially thought her experiences might have been hallucinations; it was actually the doctors who told her they had been real. The sound which, to Reynolds, was a natural D, had apparently been the sound of the surgical drill being used to make the initial hole into her skull. The instrument she saw in Dr Spetzler's hand had apparently been a Midas Rex craniotomy saw. The conversation about the size of her arteries had occurred as she remembered it and she had correctly recalled the choice of music. Yet, Dr Spetzler later said that these observations "were just not available to her." The instruments like the drill were kept inside their packages and not opened until the patient was unconscious. He also explained that at that stage in the operation, patients cannot make observations or hear things and added, "I don't have an explanation for it. I don't know how it's possible for it to happen, considering the physiological state she was in."[27]

Woerlee has mounted an extensive argument in support of his contention that Reynolds merely had "a typical period of conscious awareness under general anesthesia." He maintains that she was awakened by the vibration and sound of the drill, but felt no pain because of the high doses of the drugs and heard the sounds clearly because they were transmitted through the bones of her skull. The drugs also caused her to be calm and indifferent and, he suggests, caused her to have an out-of-body experience by altering her mental function.[28] There are several problems with this argument. Perhaps most obviously, it assumes that Reynolds recovered consciousness; not merely some vestige of consciousness in which things were dimly perceived through a drug induced haze, but a consciousness that was abnormally clear and vivid. Given the depth of her anesthesia and the extremity of her physical condition, that seems highly unlikely.

Woerlee remains undeterred by this, insisting that, "both the awareness and the out of body experience are conscious experiences, and can only occur in a conscious brain." Since he agrees that consciousness is impossible when the electroencephalogram is flat, this view would also require an assumption that her experiences occurred whilst she was under anesthesia, but not during her period of hypothermic cardiac arrest. Yet she described a continuous experience. Her observations of the drill and the saw could only have occurred during the early part of the operation and the music she heard was played near the end. Hence, even if otherwise credible, Woerlee's suggested explanation would require there to have been at least two separate episodes of consciousness, with the narrative she was experiencing being picked up seamlessly on the second occasion. Awareness during anesthesia is said to occur in 1 or 2 cases per 1,000 patients[29] and two episodes in the course of a single operation would seem to strain the laws of probability unless, perhaps, she had been only lightly anesthetized which, given the nature of the operation, seems highly improbable. Furthermore, the EEG failed to detect any indication of awareness, a fact Woerlee can explain only by suggesting that such monitoring is not 100% reliable. This adds a further long shot to the mix.

27. Mango, Barbara, *Cardiac Arrest and the Near Death*.

28. Woerlee, G.M., "Pam Reynolds Near Death Experience," *Near Death Experiences. Is there a life after death?* (2008 updated 2014) http://neardth.com/pam-reynolds-near-death-experience.php.

29. Sandhu K.and H.H. Dash, "Awareness During Anaesthesia," *Indian Journal of Anaesthesia*. (April 2009) 53(2): 148–157.

One must also ask how she could have heard what was said? She was not only under anesthesia but, her ears were blocked and subjected to auditory clicking sounds. One ear was subjected to 'white noise' at 40 decibels and the other to 100 microsecond square-wave pulses, at a frequency of 11.3 Hz, and an intensity of 95 decibels. Moulded earplugs were used and her ears were covered with tape and cotton gauze. Yet she heard the drill, the surgical saw, the conversation about the size of her veins and later the music. Woerlee nonetheless insists that she could hear external sounds by air and bone conduction. In support of this contention, he proposed a test using a computer program called "Test Tone Generator" which permitted a user to produce similar levels of sound in headphones. Rudolf Smit, who was unimpressed by Woerlee's theory, tried it out and later reported that the clicking sounds were very irritating and impossible to filter out and ignore. Despite his resolution to stick with the test for at least a few minutes, he found it virtually impossible to persist for more than a few seconds. Woerlee actually cites this response as a success. He notes that Smit found the experience unpleasant, but claims that "his letter did reveal the main point of the test—she could hear."[30]

Of course, this is simply wrong; the test only revealed that Smit could hear. The earphones he used were not the same as the combination of speakers, moulded earplugs, tape and gauze used on Reynolds and Smit had not arranged for someone to anesthetize him and cut his head open. Furthermore, even if one were to cross the fingers of both hands and assume for the sake of argument that this was a fair comparison, one would still be left with the fact that the sounds Reynolds reported were quite different from the intolerable cacophony of noise reported by Smit. She made no mention of any clicking sounds. Woerlee is undaunted by this, suggesting that musicians, like Reynolds, are better at extracting meaningful signals from a noisy background and she might have simply filtered out the clicking sounds. This again strains credulity. Smit found that clicking so loud that it actually hurt his ears. It is difficult to believe that a musician, sensitive to sound, would not even have noticed it.

So what did the senior surgeon, who had actually performed the operation, think? In an interview which forms part of a videotaped presentation published in 2010, Dr Spetzler referred to the conversation that Reynolds overheard about her artery and veins and then said:

> At that stage in the operation nobody can observe, (or) hear in that state and I find it inconceivable that her normal senses such

30. G M Woerlee, "Test of the Possibility that Pam Reynolds Heard Normally During Her NDE."

> as hearing, let alone the fact that she had clicking modules in each ear, that there was any way for her to hear those through normal auditory pathways.[31]

Then there is the problem of her visual observations. This was a woman with no medical training whose eyes were taped shut and yet was apparently able to look down on the operation and describe various things in detail, including the appearance of an instrument unknown even to Sabom, a medical specialist. How can that be explained? Again Woerlee is undaunted. Reynolds subsequently discussed her experiences with medical staff and Woerlee speculates that they might have shown her photographs of their instruments, or even the instruments themselves, to make it clear what she had heard. Then "she remembered all these things, and combined them into a story she reported to Michael Sabom during 1994." There is no evidence to support this speculation and Dr Spetzler has never suggested that she made any changes to her description of the instrument and other things since she first explained her experiences to him after the operation.

THE NEUROSURGEON WHOSE OWN BRAIN SHUT DOWN

In 2008 Dr Eben Alexander developed severe bacterial meningitis. E. coli bacteria had penetrated his cerebrospinal fluid and attacked his brain. He went into a deep coma and was not expected to live. Yet, whilst in this state he had vivid conscious experiences. This should not have been possible as his cortex had been shut down and brain was essentially inactive. His subsequent book, *Proof of Heaven*, provoked considerable controversy because he reported finding himself in the "invisible, spiritual side of existence" which proved to be a place of unconditional love. He moved around in this realm, often guided by a beautiful girl riding a giant butterfly, and encountered God. He understood that love was the only thing that truly matters and received a reassuring message: "You are loved and cherished. You have nothing to fear. There is nothing you can do wrong."

It might be easy to dismiss his experiences as fantasy, though I do nurture some hope that heaven will be well stocked with beautiful girls riding butterflies. One may, perhaps, speculate that if there is life after physical death it takes a different form and people who have previously died may be recognized only by images that will be significant to those still attached to a physical body. Of course, it might also be suggested that this had been a

---

31. Video, *The Near Death Experience of Pam Reynolds*.

simple case of hallucination. But there was an intriguing postscript to the story. Alexander was an adopted child whose natural parents had later married and had other children. One daughter had subsequently died. Some time after his experience he received a photograph of her and he recognized her; she was the girl on the butterfly. This could perhaps be explained as an emotional reaction that had led him to subconsciously graft the face of his sister onto memories of hallucinations.

But even hallucinations should not have been possible if consciousness is wholly attributable to brain activity and his brain was effectively shut down. So how could any awareness have been possible? He later said that his recovery had been a miracle in itself, but it was his experiences whilst still in the coma that he found life changing. In his early life he had adhered to the Christian beliefs of his childhood, but he had later become an agnostic and, like many neuroscientists, had accepted that the brain generated consciousness. What happened to him destroyed that belief.

The philosopher, Victor Stengar, responded to Alexander's account of his experiences with the line, "Hell, he's a surgeon, not a neuroscientist. Why should he know?"[32] In fact, Alexander had been a neurosurgeon for more than 25 years and had both taught and researched neurosurgery at Harvard Medical School. Sam Harris insisted that Alexander could not reasonably claim that the relevant parts of his brain had been completely shut down and added that "it's just not a factual statement."[33] Harris has a PhD in neuroscience, but that was still quite a diagnosis for someone who is not a medical practitioner, had apparently not consulted the treating specialists and had not seen the hospital records. Alexander insists that it was also quite wrong; isolated preservation of cortical regions could not have explained "the overall odyssey of rich experiential tapestry."

Van Lommel has also rejected suggestions that near death experiences may be explained in this manner, noting that the relevant issue is not whether there could have been any residual brain activity at all, but whether there could have been the kind of activity that can permit conscious experience "with visible and measurable simultaneous activities in many neural centers." He says that it has been proven that such activity does not occur during cardiac arrest.[34] It does seem unlikely that clear and vivid observations could be explained by brain activity too faint to cause even a flicker on EEG monitors. If anything, there would be a form of consciousness that was

32. Tsakiris, "Sam Harris and Steve Novella offer half-witted attack of Eben Alexander's Near-Death Experience."

33. Tsakiris, "Sam Harris and Steve Novella offer half-witted attack of Eben Alexander's Near-Death Experience."

34. Pin van Lommel, "Pathophysiological Aspects of Near-Death Experiences," 92.

much more vague, confused and dim.[35] Van Lommel also points out that a flat-line EEG is one of the major bases for a diagnosis of brain death and he makes that point that, when that is the issue, quibbles about the need to exclude any brain activity whatever are never mentioned.[36]

Harris also suggests that Alexander's experience may have occurred as his brain was coming back "on line," a suggestion echoed by a psychologist, Steven Novella. The suggestion has been flatly rejected by Alexander who maintains that he knows his experiences happened within the coma because of certain anchors to "earth time" in his memory. Novella even pontificated that Alexander had failed to be true to his calling as a scientist because "he did not step back from his powerful experience and ask dispassionate questions."[37] In fact, Alexander apparently spent months attempting to find a physical explanation for what occurred, read widely, consulted other neurologists and ultimately included in his book an appendix of nine hypotheses derived from conversations with colleagues, though he found none of them capable of explaining the nature of his experiences in any "brain-based" manner.

Alexander complains that few of his critics read his book or consulted him and suggests that anyone convinced that his experiences can be explained as brain-based would need to address the broad clinical experience in transpersonal psychology and "the overwhelming tsunami of evidence of the phenomena of non-local consciousness" cited in the books, *Irreducible Mind*[38] and *Consciousness Beyond Life*.[39] One may doubt some of his perceptions, but his plea for people to consider the evidence rather than simply dismiss any facts that challenge any entrenched opinions should be received sympathetically by any skeptic.

HOW CAN THIS BE?

The most recent champion of the proposition that near death experiences are foretastes of an afterlife is Dr Jeffrey Long, a radiation oncologist and author of the book, *Evidence of the Afterlife*.[40] When interviewed in 2010, he

---

35. Taylor, Steve, "The Puzzle of Near-Death Experiences."

36. van Lommel, "Pathophysiological Aspects of Near-Death Experiences," 92.

37. Tsakiris, "Sam Harris and Steve Novella offer half-witted attack of Eben Alexander's Near-Death Experience."

38. Kelly et al, *Irreducible Mind: Toward a Psychology for the 21st Century*.

39. van Lommel, *Consciousness Beyond Life. The Science of the Near-Death Experience*.

40. Long, Jeffrey, *Evidence of the Afterlife*.

revealed that he had, even then, studied more than 280 cases of near-death experiences involving out-of-body observations. In his book he explores what he describes as nine lines of evidence. He claims that his own research and all prior scholarly research in relation to each of these lines provide "proof of the reality of near-death experiences."[41] The nine lines of evidence Long claims can be drawn from his extensive studies can be briefly summarized:

1. People have clear and lucid experiences whilst clinically dead. This is medically inexplicable.

2. Many report having been in an out-of-body state in which they could move about and make observations. They are able to provide clear descriptions of the things they saw and heard and, in more than sixty of the cases studied, they were later able to verify that their observations had been correct in every detail.

3. People see things during out-of-body experiences when such observations should not be possible. Even blind people may perceive clear visual images.

4. Near death experiences occur during anesthesia when consciousness should not be possible.

5. Life reviews that sometimes occur during these experiences accurately reflect real events and this points to a reality beyond what we know from our present existence.

6. Many report meeting with family members or friends who had previously died and, in some cases, whose existence was previously unknown.

7. Near death experiences reported by children are consistent with those of adults and apparently unrelated to socio-cultural influences.

8. Reports of such experiences in different countries are similar and this suggests that they are not merely products of religious or cultural beliefs or prior life experiences.

9. They have long term effects, with those who survive them typically becoming more social and empathic, and many losing their fear of death because of what they perceive to have been a foretaste of another life to come.

---

41. Tsakiris, *Dr. Jeffrey Long's Near-Death Experience Research a "Game Changer" for Science*.

Long insists that he has considered every skeptical argument he could find, but has no doubt that such experiences provide "a profound and reassuring message that we all have an afterlife." Woelee emphatically rejects this proposition. He warns that Long's book may "hurl uncritical readers back into a new dark age of superstition" concerning these experiences, and dismisses it as "an outstandingly good example of bad science"[42] Other medical scientists have joined the fray on both sides. The issues raised by Long have been seriously debated and it may be worth considering at least the main competing arguments.

Long's first point, that there is no reasonable medical explanation for people to have lucid experiences whilst clinically dead, might seem to be a self evident proposition, but there have been a number of attempts to explain such experiences as neurological or psychological reactions to physical changes.[43] Woerlee insists that, whilst they may have seemed to be unconscious, all of the patients were actually awake. He argues that cardiac massage restores blood flow and, in some cases, perhaps even the electrical activity of the brain, though the latter proposition is supported only by the citation of a single case reported in 1961. Whilst initially suggesting that all those who survived cardiac arrest would have received cardiac massage, he now concedes that other means of CPR are usually used when someone has a cardiac arrest in a hospital and that cardiac massage is often the last resort.[44] Nonetheless, he maintains that one may "predict" that 15–20% of cardiac arrest survivors will report being fully or partially conscious during resuscitation. He also points out that hypoxia may cause paralysis and that immobility does not prove someone is unconscious. In his view, the very fact that people report observing verifiable things during out-of-body experiences, demonstrates that they can see with physical light waves and hear with physical sound waves. Hence, they are not unconscious. "After all," he adds reassuringly, "an unconscious person has no experiences."[45]

Long agrees, that according to conventional medical theory, it should not be possible for unconscious people to have such experiences. Yet he maintains that the evidence is clear; some are seeing things when unconscious and, in some cases, when their eyes are taped shut. One may question the truth of the evidence or try to explain it in some way, but the mere insistence that they must be conscious and able to see physically does not

42. Woerlee, G.M., *Review of "Evidence of the Afterlife."*

43. See, for example, Augustine, Keith "Hallucinatory Near-Death Experiences."

44. Tsakiris,, *Near-Death Experience Skeptic, Dr. G.M. Woerlee Alex Tsakiris , Takes Aim at Dr. Jeffrey Long's, Evidence of the Afterlife*; Tsakiris, *Near-Death Experience Skeptics Running Out of Excuses.*

45. Woerlee, G.M., *Review of "Evidence of the Afterlife."*

substantially advance the debate. Theories must give way to evidence, not vice versa. Woerlee's explanation would require more than an assumption that the medical specialists treating them were unable to tell the difference between conscious and unconscious patients. It would also require an assumption that those undergoing emergency resuscitation whilst conscious, but paralyzed and unable to breathe, were somehow able to remain free from shock, fear and pain and able to have vivid experiences characterized by love and peace.

In a book published in 1993, Susan Blackmore suggested that a lack of oxygen during the dying process might affect the part of the brain that controls vision and hence cause the visual illusion of a bright light at the end of a dark tunnel.[46] This explanation has been embraced by other psychologists and neurologists and it is true that a lack of oxygen to brain tissue may cause "cortical disinhibition" that could affect the visual cortex and perhaps explain visions of tunnels and lights. A sense of well-being could perhaps be caused by the release of endorphins from a dying brain. But such conditions should produce uncontrolled brain activity resulting in a chaotic jumble of experiences and perceptions, not the usually serene, well ordered and integrated experiences reported. It is also difficult to imagine how thousands of disinhibited brains could produce such relative uniformity of experiences.[47] Less traumatic brain states do not produce such conformity. We do not all have similar dreams and those who use hallucinogenic drugs do not all have similar 'trips'.

Van Lommel has suggested that, if a lack of oxygen were the real explanation, then all of his comatose patients should have had near death experiences because they had all been unconscious due to lack of oxygen in the brain. He is understandably skeptical of any theory that such exceptionally intense and vivid experiences can be explained by brains starved of oxygen.[48] Sam Parnia also points out that some patients who have had near death experiences would have had normal oxygen levels and adds that, in any event, low oxygen levels are associated with acute confusional states, not the lucid states of consciousness typically reported.[49]

More recently, there have been attempts to attribute perceptions of a tunnel of light to excessive carbon dioxide in the blood or even to a sleep disorder in which rapid eye movements are said to cause hallucinations

46. Blackmore, Susan *Dying to Live*, New York: Prometheus, 1993.
47. Taylor, "The Puzzle of Near-Death Experiences."
48. van Lommel, "Pathophysiological Aspects of Near-Death Experiences."
49. Parnia, Sam, *What Happens When We Die? A Groundbreaking Study into the Nature of Life and Death*; Parnia, Sam, and Josh Young, *Erasing Death: The Science That Is Rewriting the Boundaries Between Life and Death*.

and a feeling of being detached from the body.[50] The idea that near death experiences are merely hallucinations is not new,[51] and these new theories of causation do not really add much to the debate. There may well be delusional aspects to some near death experiences; it would be remarkable if a cocktail of fear, strong drugs, cardiac arrest and/or surgery did not produce some disordered thoughts. However, the reality of some observations by comatose patients have been confirmed by medical staff.

It may also be significant that people report observations, perceptions and insights they do not normally have during their conscious lives. Conventional theory does not explain how the suppression of almost all brain activity could lead to heightened awareness and intellectual ability, but perhaps we should all ask our friendly local neurologist to book us in for induced comas now and again, just in case the theory proves to be correct. Hypotheses about hypnosis or some similar phenomenon are also untenable. Hypnosis is not the product of a substantially disabled brain. It works by modulating activity in regions of the brain associated with focussed attention and may not work in those with little functional connectivity between two crucial parts.[52] The alternative explanation suggested by Harris and others, that such experiences may occur as the patients' brains are coming back "on line," is also unsatisfactory. It ignores the reports of observations made when there is no sign of such a recovery.

Long's second point, that people perceive they are moving about and are able to make clear observations, is also supported by van Lommel, who insists that none of these explanations could account for the whole spectrum of experiences, involving verifiable perceptions, a panoramic life review, an encounter with deceased persons and a conscious return to the body.[53] Some who reject the Long's conclusions seem oblivious of the need to address this whole spectrum, rather than merely picking out particular aspects that may be compatible with their theories. Others take the view that, even if the current 'scientific' hypotheses are inadequate, some physiological explanation will eventually be found. That is still possible, but even scientists may need to remind themselves of the difference between expectations arising from a fair and dispassionate analysis of the evidence and those arising from articles of faith or a reluctance to leave the safe shore of conventional theory.

50. Bethune, *Why so many people–including scientists–suddenly believe in an afterlife.*
51. Augustine, "Hallucinatory Near-Death Experiences."
52. Brandt, Michelle, *Not getting sleepy? Research explains why hypnosis doesn't work for all.*
53. van Lommel, "Pathophysiological Aspects of Near-Death Experiences," 90.

Long's third point, that even blind people may perceive visual images during near-death experiences, is confirmed by numerous cases.[54] Lukas Konopka argues that this provides further support for the conclusion that people may have visual perception without "physiological substrate,"[55] though the same point could be made about comatose patients under anesthesia with their eyes taped shut. At face value, this evidence would appear to refute any theory that all of the observations made during near death experiences are seen with physical light waves by conscious people.

Woerlee responds that the 'visual' perceptions of some of the people mentioned in *Mindsight* are understandable because were partially sighted or became blind later in life. Hence, they would have known what color was, had the experience of sight and the relevant parts of their brains would have developed. He acknowledges that the book mentions visual experiences by some people who were born blind, but questions whether they were really born wholly blind and maintains that mental images based upon information derived from their other senses could explain their perceptions of sight. He dismisses a case in which a blind person was able to describe the color and texture of a new tie on the grounds that his account of the incident was not corroborated and he may have been told about the tie. Whilst these speculations may seem to involve clutching at straws, Worlee cites Susan Blackmore's opinion that such observations can be explained by prior knowledge, fantasy, lucky guesses, the remaining operating senses of hearing and touch and by the way memory works.[56] He then makes the startling statement: "As yet, no-one has managed to provide evidence to the contrary. So the third line of evidence postulated by Jeffrey Long is clearly no evidence at all."

This is a strikingly illogical statement. When witnesses describe what they saw, that is evidence. It does does not cease to be evidence merely because someone tries to explain it away by speculation that it may be attributable to factors such as fantasy or lucky guesses or because no has proved that such speculation is false. Can you really imagine a lawyer arguing that there was no evidence against his or her client because there was no proof that all of the eyewitnesses had not been fantasizing or guessing? In reality, of course, it is Woerlee's response that offers no evidence at all; merely broadbrush speculation.

---

54. See, for example, Ring and Cooper, *Mindsight: near-death and out-of-body experiences in the blind.*

55. Konopka, "Near death experience: neuroscience perspective."

56. Blackmore, *Dying to Live. Near-Death Experiences*, 115.

Long's fourth point, that near death experiences occur during anesthesia when consciousness should not be possible, again seems compelling, but Woerlee insists that even those patients are really awake. Anesthesiologists nearly always begin by injecting morphine-like painkilling drugs and those who use heroin, which is a similar drug, experience euphoria. He suggests that this explains why "some people who are aware during general anesthesia feel euphoric, feel wonderful, feel that their consciousness is clearer than normal, feel unconcerned, and feel no pain." He announces that "clear and transcendent" consciousness under general anesthesia is possible and recycles the claim that this is "clearly no evidence at all."

This statement is again misconceived. Intravenous injections of heroin, which is converted to morphine upon entering the body, do produce a "rush" of euphoria,[57] but this is usually short lived and accompanied by clouded mental functioning.[58] Heroin trips may produce all manner of perceptions but they are not characterized by the common cluster of phenomena, such as life reviews and meetings with dead relatives, that characterize near death experiences. Furthermore, studies of patients who have found themselves conscious during surgery suggest less rosy experiences. Pain is the most distressing feature reported, but other complaints include anxiety, feelings of helplessness, panic attacks and fear of impending death. In some cases there are psychological consequences including anxiety, flashbacks, and post traumatic stress disorders.[59] It is true that not all who wake during surgery experience pain, but there are few, if any, who report euphoria, let alone transcendence. Perhaps there is the odd patient who finds transcendence in having his or her body cut open whilst awake to enjoy it, but I suspect they are a rather small group.

At face value, Long's fifth point, that life reviews during some near death experiences point to a reality beyond our earthly existence, seems reasonable. Woerlee suggests that panoramic reviews of earlier events may help people understand their lives better and evaluate them, "acting as a sort of psychotherapy." The events initiating life reviews are diverse and there is currently no adequate medical explanation for them, but he makes the

---

57. Halbsguth et al, "Oral diacetylmorphine (heroin) yields greater morphine bioavailability than oral morphine: Bioavailability related to dosage and prior opioid exposure."

58. See for example, National Institute on Drug Abuse, "What are the immediate (short-term) effects of heroin use?"; Castle Craig Hospital, *Heroin*.

59. Ghoneim, M.M.,"Awareness during Anesthesia"; Sandhu and Dash, "Awareness During Anaesthesia; Bruchas R.R. et al, "Anesthesia awareness: narrative review of psychological sequelae, treatment, and incidence."

reasonable point that this does not mean there is no medical explanation; merely that it is not known at this time.

Woerlee responds to Long's sixth point, that people report meeting with others who have previously died, by suggesting that these experiences are either memories or hallucinations. Of course, this would not explain those cases in which people report meeting long dead siblings or other family members they never knew existed. It is sometimes suggested that they must have subconsciously picked up clues during the course of their lives and then, whilst comatose, assimilated the clues, realized the truth and created an hallucination of a meeting with an adult version of an unknown person who may have died in infancy. The obvious difficulty with any such hypothesis is that the necessary insights and creative imagination must have occurred only when the patients had little, if any residual brain activity and not during all of the years in which they had perfectly functional brains. Whilst a study has revealed that the brain can continue to process some tasks after a person has fallen asleep,[60] I have been unable to find any study suggesting that comas bring insights denied to the conscious.

In response to Long's seventh point, about the near death experiences reported by children, Woerlee points out that the bodies of children are similar to those of adults and that they respond to diseases and drugs in a similar manner. That is largely true, but it misses Long's relatively modest point. The dreams and fantasies of children are generally different from those of adults. There have been no monsters under my bed since I was a small boy. Children may be more impressionable than adults, but they inhabit more limited social and intellectual worlds. Even in western societies, few hear bedtime stories involving out-of-body experiences or turn off the cartoons on television to read books by people like Long or Woerlee. Most probably have religious beliefs of some kind, but they are unlikely to explain why children of different faiths and cultures have similar types of experiences or why those experiences are similar to those reported by adults. This suggests that enculturation is not an adequate explanation.

Long's eight point makes a somewhat similar point about the commonality of near death experiences in different countries. Woerlee responds by arguing that the commonality of the experiences merely reflects the commonality of human body structure and function and he suggests that they are caused by oxygen starvation or the affects of drugs, poisons or disorders. The viability of such explanations has already been discussed. Long's essential point, that the commonality of experiences cannot be explained by

---

60. Kouider et al., "Inducing Task-Relevant Responses to Speech in the Sleeping Brain."

religious or cultural beliefs or by life experiences, seems to have remained substantially unchallenged.

Long's ninth and final point is that near death experiences have long term effects, with those reporting them becoming more social and empathic and losing their fear of death. Woerlee predictably remains unimpressed. He argues that oxygen starvation can generate near death experiences and cause long-lasting changes in mental function. Life reviews and life-threatening experiences may also cause a person to re-evaluate their life and change. Whilst anything may be possible, the impression that one has died, stepped into an afterlife and yet been able to return does seem likely to have a special impact. The positive impact on character was highlighted by the wife of the former atheist, A J Ayer, who held out hope for other troubled wives by mentioning that "Freddie has been so much nicer since he died."[61]

So, what inferences can be drawn from all this?

OTHER POSSIBILITIES

Lukas Konopka acknowledges that it is scientifically challenging to ask whether near death experiences are perceptions of what lies beyond our normal sensorium and understanding of consciousness, but suggests that we may need to step out of our currently accepted physiological paradigms to embrace other explanations. He speculates that these experiences may open a window to the concept of a universal consciousness that is free of time and space.[62] That is an evocative concept and one that may find some resonance with those who believe in an omnipresent and omniscient god, but it is essentially speculative. More than one writer has suggested that the stances taken by scientists on this issue have little to do with clinical findings and almost wholly reflect their personal beliefs. That should not be surprising. As mentioned earlier, scientists are not immune from the influence of presuppositions and they may have a powerful effect when entrenched by professional paradigms. But what inferences would you draw? Are these experiences really glimpses of another life after physical death?

It would be nice to be certain of the existence of an afterlife but, unfortunately, complete verification is impossible without undertaking the ultimate experiment. My own cardiac arrest was many years ago. Sadly, I saw no tunnel of light and was left to wonder whether I had offended my

---

61. Williams, Kevin, *An Analysis of the Near-Death Experiences of Atheists* (2014) http://www.near-death.com/religion/atheism/an-analysis-of-the-ndes-of-atheists.html.

62. Konopka, "Near death experience: neuroscience perspective."

deceased family members, none of whom showed up to meet me. I would love to obtain a guest pass that would enable me to accompany some of Long's patients to the pearly gates, shake hands with St Peter and return to write an endorsement for Long's next book. But, at least in this life, we can only do the best we can with the available evidence and that consists largely of the reports of those who have near death experiences. The overwhelming majority of those who have actually had such experiences find explanations, such as those suggested by Woerlee, wholly inadequate. For them, the experiences were real and the implications are clear.

So perhaps it is not surprising that some scientists are now questioning their earlier commitment to a purely material world, with consciousness attributed solely to the physical brain. The intriguing phenomenon of near death experiences suggests the existence of a separate mind, perhaps even a soul capable of living on after the body dies. Of course, the tantalizing prospect of life after death remains unproven, but despite simplistic suggestions that science has revealed this as mere superstition, the grounds for such a belief are now stronger than they have ever been.

So will the fat lady sing at your funeral? And, if she does, will you be able to hear the song?

9

A Way Forward?

There has long been some debate about Albert Einstein's views on religion, with both theists and atheists seeking to posthumously recruit him to their camp. The former may have been encouraged by his statement that "If I were not a Jew I would be a Quaker"[1] The latter may have been equally heartened by his statement: "I cannot accept any concept of God based on the fear of life or the fear of death or blind faith. I cannot prove to you that there is no personal God, but if I were to speak of him I would be a liar."[2] The apparent incongruity may reflect Einstein's admiration for the Quaker insistence that their faith be expressed in their lives, a commitment that led them to shelter numerous Jews sought by the Nazis and openly oppose Hitler despite the sometimes brutal consequences. It does not appear that he shared their religious beliefs. He famously declared that believed in "Spinoza's God who reveals Himself in the orderly harmony of what exists, not in a God who concerns himself with the fates and actions of human beings."[3]

Spinoza said that he understood God to be "a being absolutely infinite, i.e., a substance consisting of an infinity of attributes, of which each one expresses an eternal and infinite essence." He rejected any anthropomorphic conception of God, "like man, consisting of a body and a mind, and subject to passions."[4] It was understandable that Einstein, who died when computer science was still in relative infancy, might have struggled to accept the idea

---

1. Schlipp, *Albert Einstein: Philosopher-Scientist*, 659 – 660 (originally reported in the *New York Times* on 25 April 1929.
2. Schlipp, *Albert Einstein: Philosopher-Scientist*, 659–660.
3. Schlipp, *Albert Einstein: Philosopher-Scientist*, 659–660.
4. Spinoza, "The Ethics," Part 1, proposition 15.

of a god able to be concerned with the affairs of billions of people and to respond to individual prayers, but life and technology have moved on. We are now on the cusp of an age in which even computers endowed with artificial intelligence may be capable of communicating with billions of people simultaneously and the idea that the God who maintains the orderly harmony of existence might also be capable of concern for our individual lives no longer seems implausible. Even claims that he may hear silent prayer no longer seem untenable in light of emerging technology enabling us to communicate unspoken questions or commands to computers by brain signals.[5]

Einstein went on to make an interesting and often overlooked statement:

> . . . if you ask me to prove what I believe, I can't. You know them to be true but you could spend a whole lifetime without being able to prove them. The mind can proceed only so far upon what it knows and can prove. There comes a point where the mind takes a higher plane of knowledge, but can never prove how it got there. All great discoveries have involved such a leap.[6]

When the trail of evidence has been duly followed and the competing arguments duly explored, one must still confront the great questions of life knowing that absolute proof is impossible. Science has permitted us to gain insights into reality that would have been unimaginable for earlier generations, but there is still fundamental uncertainty about the extent to which physical sciences can be expected to probe the existence and nature of non-physical realities. One may try to test claims about physical effects attributed to non-physical realities, such as answers to prayers for healing, but, as mentioned earlier, no one has invented a god-detection machine. Does that mean that we have come to the end of the road and can proceed no further? Or was Einstein right? Does there come a point where the mind takes a higher plane of knowledge, though unable to prove how it got there?

It would be nice to imagine that all we know as reality could be assessed by linear streams of logic, but reality is not always so accommodating. Our opinions are often dependent upon subconscious reflection that may defy analysis but nonetheless coalesce to create an impression of the truth. Of course, such impressions can be wrong. One melancholy truism about which theists and atheists should agree is that none of us are infallible (sorry about that, Your Holiness). But the possibility of error does not prevent us from forming views about whether friends are trustworthy, colleagues are competent and numerous other things that may be incapable of

---

5. White, Chelsea, "Google with your mind."
6. Clark, *Einstein: The Life and Times*, 659–660.

proof. The cumulative effect of numerous minor events, many perhaps no longer consciously remembered, may be compelling.

And what of the claims of those who insist that there are spiritual realities? Might they also reflect this process? Are religious believers right to insist that God may bring conviction as to the truth?[7] Many will protest that this is an invitation to step out on thin ice, but sometimes there is little choice. One may share Einstein's caution about beliefs based upon nothing more substantial than fear of life or death or of blind faith, but even the most wary wayfarers may be unable to ascertain whether ice will support their weight until they have stepped out onto it and tested it. And, of course, this is what many people claim to be doing when they attempt to live their lives in accordance with their religious beliefs. Those left standing on the bank may also feel that it would be nice to have their doubts dispelled by a voice from Heaven, but when the skies offer nothing but the odd rumble of thunder one may have to seek answers by other means. It is often wise to begin with what seems reasonably clear. So what can be included in that category?

First, the existence of God has neither been proven nor disproven by science. Nor is it likely to be. Science has already revealed aspects of reality that earlier generations could not have imagined and the curtains will no doubt be drawn back from many more windows, but there are some challenges that may continue to defy the most brilliant boffins. We may forever be unable to verify the existence of other universes, let alone cross the barriers of space and interrogate their inhabitants about whether we are avatars in their computer games. We may discover more about the cosmos and perhaps gain new insights into issues such as the nature of consciousness and the neurological changes accompanying spiritual experiences. But, whilst the tools of our natural sciences might enable us to further explore relevant physical phenomena, they are unlikely to ever provide any adequate means of probing the supernatural.

Second, if any religion is to be taken seriously by skeptical people, it must embrace the reality of the cosmos. There have always been religious believers who have responded to science with enthusiasm, seeing it as the study of God's creation. They see no reason to be afraid of what it might reveal. For them, the pursuit of truth can only lead to a better understanding of God and his creation. If God is real, he must be a being of unimaginable power, complexity and creativity; a creator concerned with the vast sweep of galaxies and the smallest detail of sub-atomic particles. This may trouble those who see God as a grandfather figure with magical powers, like a heavenly version of Tolkien's character, Gandalf, but it should not trouble

---

7. John 16:13.

conservative theologians who have long taught that God is an omnipresent spirit who pervades the universe.[8]

Third, whilst there are numerous arguments for and against the existences of such a God, there are two obvious sources of evidence; the objective reality of the cosmos and the subjective reality of our human experience.

We now know much more about the cosmos than earlier generations, but there are still mysteries to unravel. To take a few examples, we still do not understand the nature of dark energy and dark matter and we do not know why the the universe was apparently so well ordered at its beginning or why there is more matter than antimatter. Even the concept of the initial singularity that is said to have fueled the Big Bang is a hypothesis dependent upon mathematical extrapolations and there are alternative theories. But if one accepts the standard conception of Big Bang theory, one could formulate a contemporary version of the creation story that could be acceptable even in an atheists' bible[9]:

> *In the beginning there was a singularity. The singularity consisted of all the matter in the universe piled on top of itself in an infinite density unconstrained by the laws of physics.*[10] *Then, some 13.8 billion years ago, an unknown something somehow caused this infinitely small and infinitely dense spot of matter to explode. It was not an explosion of any kind with which we might be familiar, but a cataclysmic event that somehow created both space and time.*[11] *Space expanded, causing objects to move apart faster than the speed of light.*[12] *Particles of matter coalesced, forming galaxies, planets and other physical objects. Life somehow popped into existence and an almost unimaginable diversity of plant and animal life evolved. More complex forms somehow acquired consciousness and humanity developed reasoning, and imagination.*

---

8. The proposition is vividly expressed in Psalm 139: 7–12: "Where can I go from your Spirit? Where can I flee from your presence? If I go up to the heavens, you are there; if I make my bed in the depths, you are there. If I rise on the wings of the dawn, if I settle on the far side of the sea, even there your hand will guide me, your right hand will hold me fast. If I say, 'Surely the darkness will hide me and the light become night around me,' even the darkness will not be dark to you; the night will shine like the day, for darkness is as light to you."

9. There are, in fact, several books called "The Atheist's Bible," but my suggested opening does not appear in any of them.

10. Hawking, *The Beginning of Time.*

11. Davies, Paul, "What came before the big bang," boingboing.net, May 20 2014 http://boingboing.net/2014/05/20/what-came-before-the-big-bang.html.

12. Aaronson, Scott, *Quantum Computing since Democritus,* Cambridge, Cambridge University Press, 2013, 329 et seq.

> *People began to form religious beliefs and music, art, science and philosophy flourished.*

These statements should not trouble anyone committed to following the path of truth. They reflect the current scientific understanding of the way in which this astonishing creative process has actually unfolded. The crucial question is, why? The odds of the universe emerging in a manner that would permit planets and galaxies to form, let alone prove hospitable to life, were astronomically small. Chance alone can be confidently excluded unless one assumes the existence of an infinite number of unknown universes all created randomly and with an infinite variety of physical laws and properties, and even then the likelihood of a sentient designer would not be excluded.

There are many things for which religious believers have no adequate explanation. Why would an intelligent creator cause a universe to develop over billions of years rather than instantly pop into existence? Why go through the slow process of evolution from creature to creature when, as a literal interpretation of the Adam and Eve story suggest, we could have been introduced as a fully formed species? Why do we have to face deterioration and death? Why is the world afflicted by pain and suffering? I do not have adequate answers to these questions and, if you meet fervent souls who claim to be able to explain it all, I can only suggest you try to remain patient and change the subject; they may be able to say something useful about basket weaving or petunias.

Nonetheless, religious believers do have a strong case. Even when one makes due allowance for the possibility of multiverses, the passage of time and the processes of natural selection, it still strains credulity to imagine that a purely spontaneous event created space and time and formed the stars, planets and galaxies of our universe. There are so many fundamental questions to be addressed. What was the first cause? Why was there something rather than nothing? Why was there a Big Bang? How could it have produced the apparently finely tuned laws and conditions necessary for the universe and the life we know? Was it all a matter of chance, aided perhaps by infinite throws of the dice? Or was the process initiated, planned or directed in some way? And why do our brains seem to be structured in a way that makes it easy for us to have spiritual experiences? Of course, there may be explanations of which we are unaware, but the single proposition that God created the universe and all it contains does provide plausible answers to all these questions. God was the first cause. There is something rather than nothing because he created it. The Big Bang occurred as the start of a creative process he initiated. The universe looks like it was designed because it was designed. It is hospitable to life because it was intended to accommodate living beings. Life, consciousness and the capacity for free will were all created by God. The brain is structured in a manner that facilitates spiritual experiences because we are meant to have them. It is true that none of this actually proves the existence of God, but the case for theism has been strengthened rather than diminished by modern cosmology.

We also know more about neurology and psychology than earlier generations and, in western countries at least, this had led to understandable caution, if not overt cynicism, about spiritual experiences. We now understand that some experiences may be caused by delusional disorders. We also know that embracing a positive attitude may improve a person's health and that some apparent answers to prayer could be due to a placebo effect or explained by statistical probability. But recognition of the need for caution does not justify a wholesale rejection of the reality of spiritual experiences. Literally millions of people remain convinced that God has touched them in a way they may be unable to define or adequately describe but which has nonetheless affected them deeply. Perhaps ironically, this point has been made with admirable clarity by an atheist, Clive Davies-Frayne, who concedes that he knows people who sense the presence of God in their lives and recognizes that this "gives meaning to their personal journey and their struggle to understand themselves and life." He accepts that such personal experiences are real and acknowledges that those who have them find the non-existence of God inconceivable because they have "the anecdotal and experiential proof in their daily lives."[13]

The apparent incongruity between these acknowledgements and his commitment to atheism seems to be explained by his view that the objective existence of God is an untestable hypothesis and hence has to be given a null or zero rating. This is logically misconceived. Neither the existence of God nor the non-existence of God may be testable in the sense used by Davies-Frayne, but if you do not know whether something is true or false, you cannot simply pick one alternative, assign a zero probability to it and act on the assumption that the other is true. You have to do the best you can to grapple with whatever evidence is available and try to make a rational assessment of the relative probabilities.

The realm of science now embraces many theories that are not presently testable. Perhaps the most interesting are those involving the possibility of other universes and other dimensions of space and time. Whilst some scientists still seem anxious to keep a divine foot from the door, belief that there may be other realities, even other planes of existence, can no longer be dismissed as mere superstition.

13. Davies-Frayne, "What is the best positive case for atheism?"

Skeptics may follow the path of reason as far as it may lead and try to make sense of whatever they encounter, but even the most rational inevitably reach chasms impassable by logic alone. And some must be crossed; we all experience tragedy and we all eventually die. Grief, fear and guilt are all sadly impervious to logic. Those who face them may review the available evidence about the existence of God and weigh the competing arguments with all the objectivity they can muster but, ultimately, they have few options; they may simply hope for the best, succumb to despair, or they may pray and trust that God will somehow sustain them through it all. Many draw faith from those occasions when they chose the third of these option and found consolation and strength and, in some cases, even an indefinable awareness of the presence of a God of compassion.

Are these beliefs mere phantasms? The products of disordered minds? Imaginings woven into explanations for neurological aberrations? Or is there a spiritual reality? And, if there is, might our lives continue beyond the death of our bodies? Might we move on to another life, like a butterfly emerging from a chrysalis, a life perhaps glimpsed in near death experiences? If you are truly a skeptic, you will not walk away from these questions, but wrestle with them, consider your experiences, make your own judgments and, above all, resolve to pursue the truth, no matter what the implications. Do not be afraid to pray. It is not irrational to call for help when you are lost in a forest, even if unsure whether anyone is present to hear you. And, you never know, there may be a response of some kind.

Bibliography

Aaronson, Scott, *Quantum Computing since Democritus,* Cambridge, Cambridge University Press, 2013.

Ackrill, J. L., *Aristotle the Philosopher*. Oxford, Oxford University Press, 1981.

Adams, Robert, "Flavors, Colors and God" in *Contemporary Perspectives on Religious Epistemology, Oxford: Oxford University Press,* 1992.

Adams, Robert, "Moral Arguments for Theism," in *The Virtue of Faith and Other Essays in Philosophical Theology*, New York: Oxford University Press, 1987, 144–163.

Adler, Mortimer J, *Aristotle for Everybody,* New York, Macmillan,1978.

Aaen-Stockdale, Craig, "Neuroscience for the Soul," *The Psychologist* 25 (7) (2012) 520–523.

Ali, Ahmed Farag and Saurya Das. "Cosmology from quantum potential," *Physics. Lettters B,* 741 (2015) 276–279.

Albert, David, *Quantum Mechanics and Experience,* Harvard University Press, 1994.

Albert, David, "Sunday Book Review: On the Origin of Everything, 'A Universe From Nothing,' by Lawrence M. Krauss," *The New York Times*, March 23, 2012.

Alighier, Dante, *Dante's Inferno (The Divine Comedy): Volume I, Hell,* Digireads, 2016.

Andersen, Ross, "Has Physics Made Philosophy and Religion Obsolete?" *The Atlantic*, April 23 2012.

Anderson, Reggie, *Appointments with Heaven,* Chicago: Tyndale House, 2013.

Anselm, Saint, "Proslogion." *St. Anselm: Basic Writings*. trans. by Sidney D. Deane. Chicago: Open Court, 1962.

Appleyard, Bryan, "The God Wars," *New Statesman*, 28 February 2012.

Aquinas, St Thomas *Summa Theologica*, Thomas More Publishing; New edition, 1981.

Armstrong, Karen, *Fields of Blood: Religion and the History of Violence,* New York: Alfred A Knopf, 2014.

Shields, Christopher, "Aristotle," *Stanford Encyclopedia of Philosophy*, revised July 29, 2015.

Aristotle *Physics,* Translated by R. P. Hardie and R. K. Gaye, Lincoln, University of Nebraska, 1961.

Aristotle, *The Works of Aristotle*, edited by W. D. Ross, Oxford, Clarendon Press, 1912.

Aronson, Elliott, *The Social Animal*, 8th edition, Duffield: Worth Publishers, 1999.

Augustine, Keith "Hallucinatory Near-Death Experiences" (2003, updated 2008), *The Secular Web,* http://infidels.org/library/modern/keith_augustine/HNDEs.html (accessed January 2, 2019).

Augustine, Keith, "Religious Experience," *The Secular Web*, http://infidels.org/library/modern/theism/experience.html (accessed 1 January, 2019).

Augustine, Saint, "The beauty of the unchangeable creator is to be inferred from the beauty of the changeable creation," *Sermons of St. Augustine*, 241, Easter: c.411 AD, The Vatican, http://www.vatican.va/spirit/documents/spirit_20000721_agostino_en.html.

Augustine, Saint, *De Genesi Contra Manichaeos*, I: 5: 9. 'Two Books On Genesis Against the Manichees' in *The Fathers of the Church: A New Translation*, Vol. 84.

Augustine, Saint "Excursus on Time," *The Confessions*. Translated by Henry Chadwick, Oxford, Oxford University Press, 2009.

Augustine, Saint 'On Genesis: A refutation of the Manichees.' in *On Genesis*, edited by. J. E. Rotelle, Hyde Park, New York: New City Press, 2002.

Baddely, Alan, Michael Eysenck, and Michael Anderson, *Memory*, New York: Psychology Press, 2009.

Bagchi, Arjun, Rudranil Basu, Daniel Grumiller, Max Riegler. Entanglement Entropy in Galilean Conformal Field Theories and Flat Holography. *Physical Review Letters*, (2015) 114 (11) DOI: 10.1103/PhysRevLett.114.111602.

Baggott, Jim, *Farewell to Reality*, London, Constable and Robinson, 2013).

Balko, Radley, "Eyewitness Testimony on Trial," *reason.com*, April 8, 2009, http://reason.com/archives/2009/04/08/eyewitness-testimony-on-trial.

Ball, Philip,"We might live in a computer program, but it may not matter," *Earth*, BBC, 5 September 2016.

Barker, J A, *Paradigms* (1992) Melbourne: The Business Library.

Barnes, Luke, 'A universe from nothing? Putting the Krauss-Craig debate into perspective', *ABC Religion and Ethics*, 13 Aug 2013, https://www.abc.net.au/religion/a-universe-from-nothing-putting-the-krauss-craig-debate-into-per/10099686.

Barrow, John D. and Frank J. Tipler, *The Anthropic Cosmological Principle*, New York: Oxford University Press, 1986.

Basil, Robert *Not Necessarily the New Age*, New York, Prometheus, 1988.

Basil, Saint, *Hexaemeron*. Translated by B.l. Jackson, St Basil the Great Resources, Elpenor, https://www.elpenor.org/basil/hexaemeron.asp.

Bastardi, A., et,"Wishful Thinking: Belief, Desire, and the Motivated Evaluation of Scientific Evidence." *Psychological Science* 22 (6) (April 22 2011) 731–732.

Beall, Abigail, "Theory claims to offer the first 'evidence' our Universe is a hologram," Wired, 31 January 2017, https://www.wired.co.uk/article/our-universe-is-a-hologram

Beane, Silas R., Zohreh Davoudi and Martin J. Savage, *Constraints on the Universe as a Numerical Simulation*, NT@UW-12-14 INT-PUB-12-046, November 12, 2012, http://arxiv.org/pdf/1210.1847v2.pdf.

Bear, Adam and Paul Bloom, "A Simple Task Uncovers a Postdictive Illusion of Choice," *Psychological Science*, Volume: 27 issue: 6 (April 28, 2016) 914–922.

Bechara A, H Damasio, and A.R. Damasio, "Emotion, decision making and the orbitofrontal cortex," *Cereb Cortex* 10(3) (March 2000) 295–307.

Bechara, A., "The role of emotion in decision-making: evidence from neurological patients with orbitofrontal damage," *Brain Cogn*. 55(1) (June 2004) 30–40.

Bede, *The Ecclesiastical History of the English People*, translated by Bertram Colgrave, Translated by Bertram Colgrave, Oxford, Oxford University Press, 1999.

Behe, Michael, *Darwin's Black Box*, New York: Free Press, 1996
Bennett, Dennis J., *Nine o'Clock in the Morning*, Los Angeles: Bridge, 1994.
Benson, H., et al, "Study of the therapeutic effect of intercessory prayer in cardiac bypass patients," *American Heart Journal* 151: 4 (2006) at 934–942.
Berkson, Joseph et al, "The Error of Estimates of the Blood Cell Count as made with the Hemocytometer," *American Journal of Physiology*, Vol 128, issue 2 (December 1939) 309–322.
Bethune, Brian, *Why so many people–including scientists–suddenly believe in an afterlife*, May 7, 2013 http://www.macleans.ca/society/life/the-heaven-boom/.
Bett, Richard, "Pyrrho," *The Stanford Encyclopedia of Philosophy*, first Mon Aug 5, 2002; substantive revision Tue Oct 23, 2018, https://plato.stanford.edu/entries/pyrrho/.
Blackmore, Susan *Dying to Live*, New York: Prometheus, 1993.
Bogen, James, "Theory and Observation in Science" (2009 revised 2013), in *Stanford Encyclopedia of Philosophy*, https://plato.stanford.edu/entries/science-theory-observation/.
Boring, Edwin G, *A History of Experimental Psychology*, New York: D Appleton-Century Co, 1929.
Boring, Edwin G, "Newton and the Spectral Lines," *Science*, Volume 136, Issue 3515, (1962) 600–601.
Boyle, Robert, *The Sceptical Chymist: Chymico-Physical: Doubts & Paradoxes (Alchemy and Alchemists)*, London: J Crooke, 1661.
Bostrom, Nick, 'Are you living in a computer simulation?' *Philosophical Quarterly* Vol. 53, No. 211 (2003) 243–255.
Boyer, R.W., "Did the Universe Emerge from Nothing? Reductive vs. Holistic Cosmology," *NeuroQuantology*, Volume 12, Issue 4, (December 2014) 424–454.
Brandt, Michelle, *Not getting sleepy? Research explains why hypnosis doesn't work for all*, Stanford Medicine News Centre, http://med.stanford.edu/news/all-news/2012/10/not-getting-sleepy-research-explains-why-hypnosis-doesnt-work-for-all.html (accessed January 2, 2019).
Brewster, Sir David, *Memoirs of the Life, Writings, and Discoveries of Sir Isaac Newton*, Edinburgh, Edmondston & Douglas, 1855. Volume II.
Bridgham, J.T., S.M. Carroll & J.W. Thornton,. "Evolution of hormone-receptor complexity by molecular exploitation," *Science* 312 (5770) (April 2006) 97–101.
Brodsky, Stanley L. Et al, "Credibility in the courtroom: how likable should an expert witness be?" *J Am Acad Psychiatry Law*, 37(4) (2009) 525–32.
Brooks, Michael, "What we'll never know," *Mind expanding Ideas, New Scientist, The Collection*, (2016) Volume 3, Issue 5.
Brorson, J.R., and K. Brewer, "Matters arising: St Paul and temporal lobe epilepsy," *Journal of Neurology, Neurosurgery, and Psychiatry* (1988) 51; 886–87.
Bruchas R.R. et al, "Anesthesia awareness: narrative review of psychological sequelae, treatment, and incidence," *Journal of Clinical Psychology in Medical Settings* (September 2011) Volume 18, Issue 3, 257–267.
Brunetti, M, et al, "Framing deductive reasoning with emotional content: An fMRI study," *Brain and Cognition* 87 (2014) 153–160.
Bryant, David, "God is unknowable—stop looking for him and you will find faith," *The Guardian*, 8 January, 2013.
Burke, John, *Imagine heaven* (2015) Ada: Baker Books.

Byrd, Randolph C., "Positive Effects of Intercessory Prayer in a Coronary Care Unit Population," *Southern Medical Journal* 81 (1988), 826-82
Caius Julius Caesar, *"De Bello Gallico and other commentaries"* Project Gutenberg ebook loc 1201 (Jan 9 2004) ebook #10657.
Campbell, Andy, "Elon Musk Thinks That Our Existence Is Someone Else's Video Game," *The Huffington Post Australia*, June 3, 2016.
Campbell, Richard, *From Belief to Understanding*, Canberra, Australian National University, 2016.
Campbell, Richard, *The Metaphysics of Emergence* London: Palgrave Macmillan, 2015.
Campbell, Richard and Mark Bickhard, "Physicalism. Emergence and Downward Causation' in *Axiomathes*, Volume 21, Issue1 (March 2011) 33-56.
Campbell, Richard, *Rethinking Anselm's Arguments: A Vindication of his Proof of the Existence of God*, Leiden: Brill, 2018.
Campbell, Richard, *That Anselm's God Exists but Gaunilo's Island is Lost Forever*, paper presented at Lehigh University, 24 April 2018.
Carey, Benedict, "A Neuroscientific Look at Speaking in Tongues," *New York Times* 7 November, 2006.
Carroll, Lewis , *Through the Looking Glass*, London: Macmillan, 1872.
Cambridge Dictionary of Philosophy, 2nd edition, edited by Robert Audi. Cambridge University Press,1999.
Carroll, Sean, "Falsifiability" in *This Idea Must Die*, edited by John Brockman, New York: Harper Perennial, 2015.
Carroll, Sean, "Physics and the Immortality of the Soul," *Discover*, May 23 2011.
Carruthers, Peter , *Human Knowledge and Human Nature: A New Introduction to an Ancient Debate*, Oxford: Oxford University Press, 1992.
Carruthers, Peter, Stephen Laurence, ,and Stephen P. Stich. *The Innate Mind: Structure and Contents*, New York: Oxford University Press, 2005.
Caruso, Eugene M. and Francesca Gino "Blind ethics: Closing one's eyes polarizes moral judgments and discourages dishonest behavior," *Cognition* 118 (2011) 280-285.
Caruso, Eugene M. et al,, "Political partisanship influences perception of biracial candidates' skin tone." *Proceedings of the National Academy of Sciences*, 106, (2009) 20168-20173.
Castle Craig Hospital, *Heroin* http://www.castlecraig.co.uk/resources/drugs/types-drugs/heroin (accessed January 2, 2019).
Chalmers, David J., *The Conscious Mind in Search of a Fundamental Theory*, Oxford: Oxford University Press, 1996.
Chalmers, David J., "Facing up to the Problem of Consciousness." In *Journal of Consciousness Studies* (1995) 2: 200-219.
Chalmers, David, "How Can We Construct a Science of Consciousness?," *The Cognitive Neurosciences III*, edited by Michael Gazzaniga, Cambridge Mass.: MIT, 2004.
Cho Adrian, "Higgs Boson Makes Its Debut After Decades-Long Search." *Science* 337 (6091), 141–143, 13 July 2012.
Chomsky, Noam, *Aspects of the Theory of Syntax*, Cambridge Mass.: MIT, 1965.
Clarke, Arthur C. *Profiles of the Future*, London, Indigo, 2000.
Clark, Ronald W., *Einstein: The Life and Times* (World Pub. Co. , New York, 1971.
Cleland, Carol E. and Christopher F. Chyba, "Defining 'Life,'" *Origins of Life and Evolution of the Biosphere* Vol 32, Issue 4 *(2002)* 387–393.

Clement, Saint of Alexandria, *Stromata or Miscellanies,* Savage, Minnesota: Lighthouse, 2018.
Cloninger, C. Robert *Feeling Good: The Science of Well-Being,* Oxford: Oxford University Press, 2004.
Collins, Francis, "Dr Francis S. Collins and Barbara Bradley Hagerty at the May 2009 Faith Angle Forum," *EPPC*, https://eppc.org/publications/francis-s-collins-and-barbara-bradley-hagerty-at-the-may-2009-faith-angle-forum/.
Collins, Francis, *The Language of God,* New York, Simon and Schuster, 2007.
Collins, Tim, "Could an ancient virus be responsible for human consciousness? Scientists claim our ability to have thoughts may have evolved from alien genetic code over the past half billion years." Daily Mail Australia, 7 February, 2018.
Committee on Identifying the Needs of the Forensic Sciences Community, National Research Council, *Strengthening Forensic Science in the United States: A Path Forward,* Washington, National Academies, 2009 at 161.
Conifer, Steven J.,"The Argument from Consciousness Refuted" (2001) *TheSecularWeb*, http://infidels.org/library/modern/steven_conifer/ac.html.
Costello, Tim, *Faith,* Hardie Grant, 2006.
Coughlan, Sean "What does post-truth mean for a philosopher?" *BBC News*, 12 January 2017
Cox, Brian, and Andrew Cohen, *The Human Universe* London: William Collins, 2014
Cox, Brian, Interview: "Parallel universes are real, say physicists," *The Day*, 1 October, 2014. http://theday.co.uk/chosen-by-you/parallel-universes-are-real-say-physicists
Coyne, Jerry, "David Albert pans Lawrence Krauss's new book," *Why Evolution is true,* https://whyevolutionistrue.wordpress.com/2012/04/02/david-albert-pans-lawrence-krausss-new-book/.
Coyne, Jerry A., "You Don't Have Free Will," *The Chronicle of Higher Education* March 18, 2012.
Craig, William Lane, *The Cosmological Argument from Plato to Leibniz* London: Macmillan, 1980.
Craig, William Lane, 'Barrow and Tipler on the Anthropic Principle vs. Divine Design'. *British Journal for the Philosophy of Science* 38 (1988): 389–395.
Craig, William Lane, "The Problem of Evil," *Reasonable Faith,* https://www.reasonablefaith.org/writings/popular-writings/existence-nature-of-god/the-problem-of-evil/.
Cramer, R.J. et al, "Expert witness confidence and juror personality: their impact on credibility and persuasion in the courtroom," *J Am Acad Psychiatry Law,* 37(1) (2009) 63–74.
Crane, Tim, and Craig French, "The Problem of Perception," *Stanford Encyclopedia of Philosophy,* (revised Dec 31, 2015).
Crispin, Ken, *The Quest for Justice,* Melbourne: Scribe, 2010.
Cyprian, Saint, *Treatises,* New Advent, Translated by Robert Ernest Wallis. From Ante-Nicene Fathers, Vol. 5. Edited by Alexander Roberts, James Donaldson, and A. Cleveland Coxe. Buffalo, NY: Christian Literature Publishing Co., 1886.
Darling, David, "On creating something out of nothing," *New Scientist*, Vol 151, No. 2047, 14 September 1996, 49.
Darwin, Charles, "Letter 12041 Darwin C. R. To Fordyce, John 7 May 1879," *Darwin Correspondence Project,* https://www.darwinproject.ac.uk/letter/DCP-LETT-12041.xml.

Darwin, Charles, Letter to Joseph Hooker, 1 February, 1871, *Darwin Correspondence Project*, https://www.darwinproject.ac.uk/letter/DCP-LETT-7471.xml.

Davies, Brian, "Anselm and the ontological argument," *The Cambridge Companion to Anselm*, Cambridge: Cambridge University Press.

Davies, Lizzy, "Descartes was 'poisoned by Catholic priest'", *The Guardian*, 15 February, 2010.

Davies, Paul, *The Goldilocks Enigma*, London: Allen Lane, 2006.

Davies, Paul, "Particles do not Exist" in *Quantum Theory of Gravity* Bristol: Adam Hilger, 1984 66-77.

Davies, Paul, "What came before the big bang," *boingboing.net*, May 20 2014 http://boingboing.net/2014/05/20/what-came-before-the-big-bang.html.

Davies-Frayne, Clive, "What is the best positive case for atheism?" *Quora* (updated Jan 24, 2011) https://www.quora.com/What-is-the-best-positive-case-for-atheism.

Davis, Phillip J. and Reuben Hirsh, *Descartes' Dream*, Boston: Houghton Mifflin.

Dawkins, Richard, *The Blind Watchmaker*, London: Penguin, 2006.

Dawkins, Richard, *The God Delusion*, London: Black Swan, 2006.

Dawkins, Richard, *Harris and Free Will*, Richard Dawkins Foundation, Sep 4 2013, https://richarddawkins.net/2013/09/harris-and-free-will/.

Dawkins Richard, *Militant Atheism*—ted.com. February, 2002, https://www.ted.com/talks/richard_dawkins_on_militant_atheism.

Dawkins, Richard, "'Never be afraid of stridency': Richard Dawkins' interview with Christopher Hitchens." *New Statesman* 2 September 2015.

Deecke, L., "The Bereitschaftspotential as an electrophysiological tool for studying the cortical organization of human voluntary action," chap 27, *Supplements to Clinical Neurophysiology*, vol 53 (2000) at 199-206.

Delfgaauw, Bernard, *Evolution: The Theory of Teilhard de Chardin* London: Fontana, 1969.

Dembski, William A, *No Free Lunch: Why Specified Complexity Cannot Be Purchased without Intelligence*, New York: Rowman & Littlefield, 2001

Dennett, Daniel C., *Darwin's Dangerous Idea: Evolution and the Meaning of Life*, New York: Touchstone, 1996.

Descartes, Rene, *Meditations on First Philosophy*, translated by John Cottingham, Cambridge: Cambridge University Press, 1986.

Desnues, Christelle, Mickael Boyer, and Didier Raoult, "Sputnik, a Virophage Infecting the Viral Domain of Life," *Advances in Virus Research*, Volume 82 (2012) 63-89.

Devinsky, Julie and Steven Schachter, "Norman Geschwind's contribution to the understanding of behavioral changes in temporal lobe epilepsy: The February 1974 lecture," *Epilepsy & Behavior* (2009) 15 (4): 417-24.

Dittrich, Walter and Holger Gies, *Probing the quantum vacuum: perturbative effective action approach*. Berlin: Springer, 2000

Doctrinal Commission of International Catholic Charismatic Renewal Services, *Baptism in the Holy Spirit, Catholic Charismatic Renewal, Holy Spirit, Theology* (2012) National Service Committee of the Catholic Charismatic Renewal in the U.S.

Dodson, Brian, "Einstein's biggest blunder beats dark energy in explaining expansion of the universe," *Gizmag*, January 16, 2013, http://www.gizmag.com/einstein-cosmological-constant-dark-energy/25809/.

Dougherty, Elizabeth, *What are thoughts made of?* MIT School of Engineering, http://engineering.mit.edu/ask/what-are-thoughts-made.

Doyle, Bob, *Free Will: The Scandal in Philosophy,* Tulsa: IPhI, 2011.Drange, Theodore M., "Nonbelief vs. Lack of Evidence: Two Atheological Arguments," *The Secular Web,* (1998) https://infidels.org/library/modern/theodore_drange/anbvslea.html.

Dunning, Brian, "What is Skepticism?," *Skeptoid,* http://skeptoid.com/skeptic.php.

Dubrow, Aaron, "Testing Technicolor Physics," *Live Science,* April 29, 2011 http://www.livescience.com/13954-higgs-lhc-technicolor-physics-bts.html.

Dyson, Freeman, 'Disturbing the Universe', 250—in Barrow & Tipler, *The Anthropic Cosmological Principle* Oxford: Clarendon, 1988.

Ebbern, Hayden, Sean Mulligan, and Barry L Beyerstein, "Maria's Near-Death Experience: Waiting for the Other Shoe to Drop," *The Skeptical Inquirer,* Vol 20, No 4, (July/August 1996).

Egner, Robert E. and Lester E. Denonn, *The Basic Writings of Bertrand Russell* 1903–1959 New York: Touchstone, 1961

Ehrenfreund, Max, "Obama's skin looks a little different in these GOP campaign ads," *The Washington Post,* December 29, 2015.

Elders, Leo, *The Philosophical Theology of St. Thomas Aquinas,* Leiden, Brill, 1990.

Ellis, George, "83 years of general relativity and cosmology: Progress and problems," *Classical and Quantum Gravity,* Vol 16, number 12A (1999).

Ellis, George, "Scientific American, Does the Multiverse Really Exist?," *Scientific American* 305 (August 2011) 38–43.

Ellis, George, & Joe Silk, 'Scientific method: Defend the integrity of physics' *Nature,* vol 516, issue 7531, 16 December 2014.

Emonds, G. et al, "Comparing the neural basis of decision making in social dilemmas of people with different social value orientations, a fMRI study." *Journal of Neuroscience, Psychology, and Economics,* 4 (2011) 11–24.

Evans, C. Stephen "Moral Arguments for the Existence of God" (Jun 12, 2014) *Stanford Encyclopedia of Philosophy*

Fabry, Alexander , "Welcome to the Multiverse!," *The Daily Beast,* 2.11.11. http://www.thedailybeast.com/articles/2011/02/11/brian-greenes-the-hidden-reality-review.html.

Farrell, John, "A Physicist Talks God And The Quantum," *Forbes,* Jan 29, 2017.

Fatoohi, Louay, "One Night in a Cave that Changed History Forever," *Qur'anic Studies* (2007) http://www.quranicstudies.com/quran/one-night-in-a-cave-that-changed-history-forever/.

Ferreira, Pedro J., *The Perfect Theory* London: Little, Brown, 2014.

Feser, Edward, *Aquinas : a beginner's guide,* Oxford: Oneworld, 2009. at 99–109.

Filoramo, Giovanni, *A History of Gnosticism,* Oxford: Basil Blackwell, 1990.

Fisher, Roger, "He who pays the piper," *Harvard Business Review,* 63 (1985) 150.

FitzPatrick, William, "Morality and Evolutionary Biology" (revised July 23, 2014) *Stanford Encyclopedia of Philosophy.*

Flew, Antony, *The Presumption of Atheism and Other Philosophical Essays on God, Freedom, and Immortality,* New York: Barnes and Noble, 1976.

Follmann, Hartmut and Carol Brownson, "Darwin's warm little pond revisited: from molecules to the origin of life," *Naturwissenschaften,* Volume 96, Issue11 (November 2009) 1265–1292.

Fowler, William A., "William A. Fowler—Autobiography," *Nobelprize.or*g. 1983.

Frampton, Paul H, *Did Time Begin? Will Time End?*, Singapore: World Scientific, 2010.
Frankel, Marvin, *Partisan Justice*, New York, Hill & Wang, 1978.
Frankel, Victor E., *Man's Search for Meaning*, Boston: Beacon, 2006.
French, Christopher C., "Dying to know the truth: Visions of a dying brain, or false memories?" *Lancet* (2001) 358, 2010–2011.
French, C. C. et al, „The 'Haunt' project: An attempt to build a 'haunted' room by manipulating complex electromagnetic fields and infrasound". *Cortex* (2009) 45 (5): 619–629.
Fried, Itzhak, Roy Mukamel, and Gabriel Kreiman, "Internally generated preactivation of single neurons in human medial frontal cortex predicts volition," *Neuron* 69(3) (10 Feb 2011) 548–562.
Fretheim, Terence, *The New Interpreter's Bible*, volume 1, Nashville, Abingdon, 326
Frye, Roland Mushat (ed), *Is God a Creationist? The Religious Case Against Creation-Science*, New York: Charles Scribner's Sons, 1983.
Fromm, Eric, *The Fear of Freedom* (1960) London: Routledge & Kegan Paul, 1960.
Fury, J.B., *History of Freedom of Thought*. London: Williams & Norgate, 1914.
Gajilan, A. Chris, "Are humans hard-wired for faith?" *CNN* April 5, 2007, http://edition.cnn.com/2007/HEALTH/04/04/neurotheology/.
Gallagher, Jonathan, *Biblical Prophets, Modern Critics*, 2003, http://www.pineknoll.org/references/2003/q4/jonah01-05.pdf.
Gamov, George, *My World Line*, New York, Viking Press, 1970.
Garrett, Brian, 'On Behalf of Gaunilo', *Analysis*, 73(3) (2013) 481–82.
Garvey, Brian, "Absence of Evidence, Evidence of Absence, and the Atheist's Teapot," *Ars Disputandi*, Volume 10 (2010) 9—22.
Gatti, Hilary (2002). *Giordano Bruno and Renaissance Science: Broken Lives and Organizational Power*. New York: Cornell University Press, 2002.
Gaunilo. "Reply on Behalf of the Fool." In *Proslogion, with the Replies of Gaunilo and Anselm*. Translated by Thomas Williams, 27–33. Indianapolis: Hackett, 2001.
Gendle, M. H., and M. G. McGrath, "Can the 8-coil shakti alter subjective emotional experience? A randomized, placebo-controlled study." *Perceptual and Motor Skills* (2012) 114 (1): 217–235.
Gflhus, Ingvild Stolid, "The Gnostic Demiurge—An Agnostic Trickster," *Religion* 14 (1984) 301–311
Ghoneim, M.M.,"Awareness during Anesthesia," *Anesthesiology*, February 2000, Vol.92, 597.
Gifford, E. H., translator, Eusebius, *Praeparatio evangelica*, http://www.tertullian.org/fathers/eusebius_pe_14_book14.htm.
Gish, Duane, *Creation Scientists Answer Their Critics* (1993) Dallas: Institute for Creation Research, 1993.
Glick, Thomas F, *The Comparative Reception of Darwinism* Chicago: University of Chicago Press, 1988.
Goldsmith, Donald, *Einstein's Greatest Blunder? The Cosmological Constant and Other Fudge Factors in the Physics of the Universe*, Cambridge, Mass: Harvard University Press, 1997.
Gould, Stephen Jay. *Rocks of Ages: Science and Religion in the Fullness of Life*, New York: Ballantine Books,1999.
Gould, Stephen Jay, "Nonoverlapping Magisteria," *Natural History*, 106 (March 1997): 16–22 and 60–62.

Gräslund, Bo, "Prehistoric Soul Beliefs in Northern Europe," *Proceedings of the Prehistoric Society*, Volume 60 (1994) 15–26.
Green, Peter, *Alexander of Macedon 356–323 B.C*, University of California Press, 1991.
Greene, Brian, *The Elegant Universe,* London: Random House, 2000.
Greene, Brian *The Fabric of the Cosmos: Space, Time, and the Texture of Reality,* New York: Knopf, 2004.
Greene, Brian, *The Hidden Reality*, New York: Vintage, 2011.
Gregory, Jane, *Fred Hoyle's Universe*. Oxford, Oxford University Press, 2005.
Greyson, Bruce, "Near-Death Experiences," in Corsini *Encyclopedia of Psychology*, New York: Wiley and sons, 2010.
Guth, Alan H., "Eternal inflation and its implications." *Journal of Physics* A40:6811–6826,2007, arXiv.hep- th/0702178, 2007.
Guth, Alan H. *The Inflationary Universe: The Quest for a New Theory of Cosmic Origins*, New York: Basic, 1997.
Haldane, J.B.S.,*What Is Life?* New York: Boni and Gaer 1947.
Halford, Joseph Taylor and Scott H. C. Hsu, *Beauty is Wealth: CEO Appearance and Shareholder Value,* December 19, 2014, https://ssrn.com/abstract=2357756.
Hall-Flavin, Daniel K.,"Is there a link between pain and depression? Can depression cause physical pain?" *Diseases and Conditions,* Mayo Clinic. http://www.mayoclinic.org/diseases-conditions/depression/expert-answers/pain-and-depression/faq-20057823 (accessed 31 December, 2018).
Halbsguth U, et al, "Oral diacetylmorphine (heroin) yields greater morphine bioavailability than oral morphine: Bioavailability related to dosage and prior opioid exposure." *British Journal of Clinical Pharmacology* (2008) 66 (6): 781–791.
Hansen, Katgherine et al, "People Claim Objectivity After Knowingly Using Biased Strategies," *Personality and Social Psychology Bulletin*, 40 (March 2014) 691–699.
Harrell, Eben, "Collider Triggers End-of-World Fears," *Time*, Sept 4 2008.
Harris, Sam, *Free Will,* New York: Free, 2012.
Harris, William S., et.al., "A Randomized, Controlled Trial of the Effects of Remote, Intercessory Prayer on Outcomes in Patients Admitted to the Coronary Care Unit," *Archives of Internal Medicine* 159 (1999), 2273–2278.
Hart, William et al, "Feeling Validated Versus Being Correct: A Meta-Analysis of Selective Exposure to Information," (2009) *Psychological Bulletin*, Vol. 135, No. 4, 555–588.
Hartmann, William K., "Chelyabinsk, Zond IV, and a possible first-century fireball of historical importance." *Meteoritics & Planetary Science* (2015) 50, 368.
Hathaway, Bill, "You may have already decided to read this article," *Yale News*, May 2 2016.
Hawking, Stephen, *A Brief History of Time*, London, Bantam Books, 1988.
Hawking, Stephen, *"The Beginning of Time, http://www.hawking.org.uk/the-beginning-of-time.html.*
Hawking Stephen, *The Universe in a Nutshell,* New York: Bantam Books, 2001.
Head, Tom, *Conversations with Carl Sagan* Jackson: University of Mississippi, 2006.
Heckert, Paul, *Was the Big Bang an Explosion?* https://suite.io/paul-a-heckert/67e2dj.
Heimlich, Russell, "Mystical Experiences," *Factank*, Pew Research Centre, December 29, 2009.
Henderson, Barney, "On in four Americans 'do not know the earth circles the sun'" *The Telegraph* (UK) 25 February, 2014.

Henry, Richard Conn, "2008: A New Introductory Essay," in Sir Arthur Stanley Eddington, *The Nature of the Physical World*, Electronic Edition, 2007 November, vi.

Hespos, Susan J. and Kristy van Marle, "Physics for infants: characterizing the origins of knowledge about objects, substances, and number," *Wiley Interdisciplinary Reviews: Cognitive Science*, Volume 3, Issue 1, (January/February 2012) 19–27.

Hicks, John W, *Microscopy of Hair. A practical Guide and Manual*, FBI, January 1977.

Highfield, Roger, "Parallel universe proof boosts time travel hopes." *The Telegraph*, 21 September 2007.

Hilberry, Sir Malcolm, *Duty and Art in Advocacy*, London: Sweet & Maxwell, 1959.

Himma, Kenneth Einar, "Anselm: Ontological Argument for God's Existence," *Internet Encyclopaedia of Philosophy*, http://www.iep.utm.edu/ont-arg/#SH2b.

Hitchens, Christopher, *God is not Great*, New York: Twelve, 2007.

Hitchens, Christopher, *Mortality*, Sydney: Allen & Unwin, 2013.

Internet Encyclopedia of Philosophy, http://www.iep.utm.edu/skepanci/.

Hobson, J. Allan, "Neuroscience and the Soul:The Dualism of John Carew Eccles," *Cerebrum*, The DANA Foundation, Thursday, April 1, 2004.

Hodge, David, "A Systematic Review of the Empirical Literature on Intecessory Prayer" Research on Social Work Practice" (March 2007) 17(2):174–187.

Hoffmann, R Joseph, "Five Good Things about Atheism," *The New Oxonian*, September 28, 2010, https://rjosephhoffmann.wordpress.com/2010/09/28/five-good-things-about-atheism/.

House of Lords in *Royal Bank of Scotland v Etridge* [2001] UKHL 44.

Hoyle, Fred, "The Big Bang in Astronomy," *New Scientist*, Vol. 92, No. 1280 (November 19, 1981) 521–527.

Hoyle, Fred, *Evolution from Space*, Omni Lecture, Royal Institution, London, 12 January 1982. Hoyle, Fred, *Evolution from Space*, New York: Simon and Schuster, 1981.

Hoyle, Fred, *The Intelligent Universe*, Austin: Holt, Rinehart and Winston, 1988

Hoyle, Fred, "A New Model for the Expanding Universe," Monthly Notices of the Royal Astronomical Society, 108 (1948) 372.

Hoyle, Fred, "The Universe: Past and Present Reflections." *Engineering and Science*, (November, 1981) 8–12.

Human Benchmark, "Reaction Time Statistics," 2018, http://www.humanbenchmark.com/tests/reactiontime/statistics.

Hume, David, *Dialogues Concerning Natural Religion*, 1779. Second edition, edited by Richard H. Popkin, Indianapolis, Hackett, 1998.

Hume, David, *Enquiry Concerning Human Understanding*, edited by L. A. Selby Bigge, Oxford: Oxford University Press.

Hume, David, *A Treatise of Human Nature: Being an Attempt to Introduce the Experimental Method of Reasoning into Moral Subjects*, London: Penguin, 1985.

Hunt, Matthew R. and Franco A. Carnevale. "Moral Experience: A framework for Bioethics Research" *Journal of Medical Ethics* (November 2011) Volume 37, issue 11.

Huxley, Leonard, *Life and Letters of Thomas Henry Huxley*, Vol 2, London: Macmillan, 1900.

Huxley, T. H., *Lessons in Elementary Physiology*, London: Macmillan, 1986.

International Association for Near Death Studies Inc, *Characteristics of Near Death Experience*, Wednesday, 08 July 2015, http://iands.org/ndes/about-ndes/characteristics.html.

International Council of Science, Advisory Note *"Bias in science publishing"* (Sep 2011) http://www.icsu.org/publications/cfrs-statements/bias-in-science-publishing.

Jambaqué, Isabelle, Maryse Lassonde, and Olivier Dulac, *Neuropsychology of Childhood Epilepsy,* Dordrecht: Klewer Academic Publishing, 2001.

James, William, *The Varieties of Religious Experience,* New York: Dover 2018.

Janis, Irving, "Groupthink," *Psychology Today* 5 (November 1971) 43–46, 74–76.

Janko, Richard, 'Socrates the Freethinker', in *A Companion to Socrates,* edited by Sara Ahbel-Rappe and Rachana Kamtekar, New York: John Wiley, 2009, 48–62.

Jefferson T. et al, "Effects of editorial peer review: a systematic review," *JAMA* (June 5, 2002) 2784–2876, https://jamanetwork.com/journals/jama/fullarticle/194989.

Johnson, M.L., "Seeing's Believing," 15 *New Biology* (1953) 60–79.

Johnson, Phillip, *Darwin on Trial,* Washington: Regnery Publishing, 2015.

Jonas, Hans, *The Gnostic Religion: The Message of the Alien God,* Boston: Beacon, 1963.

Jones, Owen D., "The End of (Discussing) Free Will," *The Chronicle of Higher Education,* March 18, 2012.

Kahneman, "Daniel, Bias, Blindness and How We Truly Think" (Part 2), *Brophy.net* (October 25, 2011) http://www.brophy.net/PivotX/?e=325&w=pattys-recipes.

Kahneman, Daniel *Thinking Fast and Slow* New York: Farrar, Straus and Giroux, 2011.

Kaminer, Ariel, "Where Theory and Research Meet to Jam About the Mind," *New York Times*. Dec 9, 2012.

Kant Immanuel, *Critique of Pure Reason*, translated by Werner Pluhar, Indianapolis: Hackett Publishing, 1996.

Kaptchuk, T J., "The double-blind, randomized, placebo-controlled trial: gold standard or golden calf?" *Journal of Clinical Epidemiology*, volume 54, issue 6, (June 2001) 541–9.

Kelly, Edward F., *Beyond Physicalism: Toward Reconciliation of Science and Spirituality,* Lanham: Rowman & Littlefield, 2015.

Kelly, Edward F., et al, *Irreducible Mind: Toward a Psychology for the 21st Century,* Lanham: : Rowman & Littlefield, 2007.

Kelly, Kyle, "Is the Weak Anthropic Principle Compatible With Divine Design?," *The Secular Web*, (1997) https://infidels.org/library/modern/kyle_kelly/wap.html.

Kierkegaard, Soren, *Works of Love,* (1847) Translated by Howard & Edna Hong, New York: HarperPerennial, 2009.

Klemm, W. R, "Free will debates: Simple experiments are not so simple," *Advances in Cognitive Psychology*, Vol. 6 (August 30, 2010) 47–65.

Klyce, Brig, 'What is life?,' *Cosmic Ancestry,* http://www.panspermia.org/whatis2.htm#%2010ref.

Koenig, H.G., M.E. McCullough, & D.B. Larson, *Handbook of religion and health,* New York: Oxford University Press, 2001.

Koenig, H.G., M.E. McCullough, and D.B. Larson, *Handbook of religion and health,* New York: Oxford University Press, 2001.

Kohn, Alexander, *False Prophets,* Oxford: Basil Blackwell, revised edition 1989.

Konopka, Lucas M., "Near death experience: neuroscience perspective," *Croatian Medical Journal,* (2015 Aug) 56(4): 392–393.

Kouider et al., "Inducing Task-Relevant Responses to Speech in the Sleeping Brain," *Current Biology* (2014), http://dx.doi.org/10.1016/j.cub.2014.08.016.

Kragh, Helge. *Cosmology and Controversy: The Historical Development of Two Theories of the Universe*, Princeton, Princeton University Press, 1999.

Kramer, Miriam, "Our Universe may Exist in a Multiverse, Cosmic Inflation Discovery Suggests," *space.com*, March 18, 2014. https://www.space.com/25100-multiverse-cosmic-inflation-gravitational-waves.html.

Krane, D. et al, "Sequential unmasking: A means of minimizing observer effects in forensic DNA interpretation," *Journal of Forensic Sciences* 53 (4) (2008) 1006–1007.

Krauss, Lawrence M., *A Universe from Nothing*, New York, Free Press, 2012.

Kreeft, Peter, *Twenty Arguments For God's Existence*, Peter kreeft.com. (accessed December 31, 2018).

Krucoff, Mitchell W., et al, "Integrative noetic therapies as adjuncts to percutaneous intervention during unstable coronary syndromes," *American Heart Journal* 142 (2001), 760–769.

Ku, John Baptist, "Interpreting Genesis 1 with the Fathers of the Church," *Thomist Evolution: A Catholic Approach to Understanding Evolution in the Light of Faith*, http://www.thomisticevolution.org/disputed-questions/interpreting-genesis-1-with-the-fathers-of-the-church/.

Kuhn, Robert Lawrence, "Physicist Paul Davies' Killer Argument Against The Multiverse," *Uncommon Descent*, August 14, 2015. http://www.uncommondescent.com/intelligent-design/physicist-paul-davies-killer-argument-against-the-multiverse/.

Kuhn, Thomas S, *The Structure of Scientific Revolutions*, 2nd edition, Chicago, University of Chicago Press, 1970.

Kurzweil Digest, May 4, 2016, http://www.kurzweilai.net/more-evidence-that-youre-a-mindless-robot-with-no-free-will.

Kushner, Harold, *When Bad Things Happen to Good People*, New York: Shocken Books, 1981.

Lagemann, R.T.. "New light on old rays: N rays." *American Journal of Physics* 45 (3) (1977) 281–284.

Lambrecht, Astrid, "Observing mechanical dissipation in the quantum vacuum; an experimental challenge" in Laser physics at the limits edited by Hartmut Figger, Dieter Meschede, Claus Zimmermann, Berlin/New York: Springer, 2002.

Landsborough, D., "St. Paul and Temporal Lobe Epilepsy," *Journal of Neurology, Neurosurgery, and Psychiatry* (1987) 50; 659–64.

Larson, M.S.,*The Rise of Professionalism: a Sociological Analysis*, Berkeley: University of California Press, 1977.

Lerner, Jonah, "The Mysterious Decline Effect," *Wired Science Blog*s, (9 December 2010)bFrontal Cortex 12. 09.10 http://www.wired.com/wiredscience/2010/12/the-mysterious-decline-effect/.

Leibniz, Gottfried W., "Monadology," in *G. W. Leibniz: Philosophical Essays*, Translated by R. Ariew and D. Garber, Indianapolis: Hackett, 1989.

Leibniz, Gottfried W., *New Essays on Human Understanding*, Translated by Peter Remnant and Jonathan Bennett, Cambridge, Cambridge University Press, 1996.

Leibovici, Leonard, "Effects of Remote, Retroactive Intercessory Prayer on Outcomes in Patients with Bloodstream Infection: Randomised Controlled Trial," *British Medical Journal* 323 (2001), 1450–1451.

Lemonick, Michael D. "New model of the cosmos: a Universe that begins again," *Cosmos*, 14 September 2015.
Lemos, Loren *The NDE delusion*, http://freethoughtblogs.com/pharyngula/2012/04/24/the-nde-delusion/.
Lennox, James G, *Aristotle's Philosophy of Biology: Studies in the Origins of Life Science*. Cambridge: Cambridge University Press, 2001.
Levine, Joseph, "Materialism and Qualia: The Explanatory Gap," *Pacific Philosophical Quarterly*, 64 (1983) 354–361.
Levine, Joseph, *Purple Haze: The Puzzle of Conscious Experience*, Cambridge Mass:MIT, 2001.
Lewis, C.S., *The Abolition of Man*, London: Fontana, 1947.
Lewis, C.S., *Mere Christianity*, London: Fontana, 1952.
Lewis, C.S., *The Problem of Pain*, New York: MacMillan, 1944.
Lewontin, Richard, "Review of 'Carl Sagan's The Demon-Haunted World: Science as a Candle in the Dark,'" *New York Review of Books*, January 9, 1997.
Libet, Benjamin, "Do We Have Free Will?" in *Oxford Handbook on Free Will*. New York: Oxford: Oxford University Press, 2002, 551–564.
Libet, Benjamin, "Theory and evidence relating cerebral processes to conscious will," *Behavioural and Brain Sciences* (1985) Volume 8, Issue 4
Linde, Andre and Vitaly Vanchurin, "How many universes are in the multiverse?" *High Energy Physics—Theory*, (2010) Cornell University, https://arxiv.org/abs/0910.1589v3
Linde, Andrei, *Inflationary Cosmology after Planck 2013*, arXiv:1402.0526 [hep-th].
Lipka, Michael, "18% of Americans say they've seen a ghost," *Factank*, Pew research Centre, October 30, 2015, http://www.pewresearch.org/fact-tank/2015/10/30/18-of-americans-say-theyve-seen-a-ghost/.
Locke, John, *An Essay Concerning Human Understanding*, edited by Kenneth P. Winkler, Indianapolis: Hackett, 1998.
Logan, Ian, *Reading Anselm's Proslogion*, London: Routledge, 2016.
Long, A. A., and D. N. Sedley, *The Hellenistic Philosophers*. vol. 1, Cambridge: Cambridge University Press, 1987.
Long, Jeffrey, *Evidence of the Afterlife*, HarperOne, 2010.
Loria, Kevin, "Scientists discovered an absurdly easy way to seem convincing," *Business Insider*, December 26 2016, https://www.businessinsider.com.au/how-to-convince-people-of-something-2016-12.
Lowder, Jeffery Jay, "Is a Sound Argument for the Nonexistence of a God Even Possible?" *The Secular Web* (1998) http://infidels.org/library/modern/jeff_lowder/ipnegep.html.
Lowe, E. J., 'The ontological argument', in *The Routledge Companion to Philosophy of Religion*, London: Routledge (2007) 331–340.
Macchia, Frank D., *Baptized in the Spirit: A Global Pentecostal Theology*, Grand Rapids: Zondervan, 2006.
Mango, Barbara, *Cardiac Arrest and the Near Death Experience*, https://www.nderf.org/NDERF/Articles/barbara_cardiac.htm (accessed 1 January, 2019).
Margulis, Lynn, *Symbiotic Planet: A New Look at Evolution*, New York: Basic, 1998 at 69.
Markie, Peter, "Rationalism vs. Empiricism," in *The Stanford Encyclopedia of Philosophy*, edited by Edward N. Zalta, Summer 2013

Marshall, Barry J., "Barry J Marshall—Biographical," *Nobelprize.org*, http://www.nobelprize.org/nobel_prizes/medicine/laureates/2005/marshall-bio.html.
Marsden, George M., *Fundamentalism and American Culture*, Oxford, Oxford University Press, 2006.
Matthews, Gareth, "The ontological argument," in *Blackwell Guide to Philosophy of Religion*, edited by William E Mann, Blackwell, 2004
Marx, Karl, *Introduction to A Contribution to the Critique of Hegel's Philosophy of Right*. Translated by Annette Jolin and Joseph O'Malley, Cambridge: Cambridge University Press, 1970 (firs pub 1843).
Maydole, Robert E., *The Blackwell Companion to Natural Theology*, New York: John Wiley, 2011.
McEvilley, Thomas, The Shape of Ancient Thought: Comparative Studies in Greek and Indian Philosophers, New York: Allworth Press, 2002.
McFadden, Johnjoe, "It seems llfe really does have a vital spark: quantum mechanics," *The Drum*. Mon 8, February 2016, ABC News, https://www.abc.net.au/news/2016-02-08/mcfadden-it-seems-life-really-does-have-a-vital-spark/7148448 (accessed 31 December 2018).
McGauran, Natalie et al, "Reporting bias in medical research—a narrative review," *Trials* 11: 37 (April 13 2010) https://trialsjournal.biomedcentral.com/articles/10.1186/1745-6215-11-37.
McGinn, Colin "Can we solve the Mind-Body Problem?" *Mind* 98 (1989) 349–66.
McGrath, A. E., *Darwinism and the Divine: Evolutionary Thought and Natural Theology*, New York: John Wiley, 2011.
McInerny, Ralph and John O'Callaghan, "Saint Thomas Aquinas" (revised May 23, 2014) *Stanford Encyclopedia of Philosophy*.
McKie, Robin, "Fred Hoyle: the scientist whose rudeness cost him a Nobel prize," *The Guardian*, 3 October 2010.
McLain Sylvia, "Not breaking news: many scientific studies are ultimately proved wrong!," *The Guardian*, 17 September 2013, http://www.theguardian.com/science/occams-corner/2013/sep/17/scientific-studies-wrong.
McVea, Crystal, *Waking Up in Heaven: A True Story of Brokenness, Heaven, and Life Again*, Brentwood, Howard Books, 2013.
MDU, "Bias in medico-legal decisions," *MDU Journal*, November 2012.
Mele, Alfred R., *Effective Intentions: The Power of Conscious Will* Oxford: Oxford University Press, 2009.
Merrett, Rebecca, "Self-programming machines next phase of computer science: Wozniak," *CIO*, 29 May 2015, http://www.cio.com.au/article/576144/ai-machines-self-programming-next-phase-computer-science/.
Merriam-Webster, "Materialism," https://www.merriam-webster.com/dictionary/materialism.
Merriam Webster Dictionary, "anthropic principle," https://www.merriam-webster.com/dictionary/anthropic%20principle.
Mexted, Kathy, "The music of recovery," *Slow Living Magazine* (Autumn 2016) 38–39.
Meyer, Marvin, (ed), *The Gnostic Gospels*, London:The Folio Society, 2007.
Mill, J. S. *Nature, The Utility of Religion, and Theism*, London: Longmans, 1874.
Millican, Peter, "The one fatal flaw in Anselm's argument," *Mind*, 113 (2004) 437–476.
Miller, Kenneth R, *Finding Darwin's God*, New York, Harper Collins, 2000.

Miller, Kenneth R, *Only a Theory: Evolution and the Battle for America's Soul*, New York: Viking, 2008.

Miller J Steve, *Near-Death Experiences as Evidence for the Existence of God and Heaven: A Brief Introduction in Plain Language*, Acworth, Wisdom Creek Press, 2012

Miller, Stanley L., "A Production of Amino Acids Under Possible Primitive Earth Conditions." *Science* Volume 117, Issue 3046 (15 May 1953) 528–529.

MIT (writer not identified) "Astronomers Find First Evidence of Other Universes" *MIT Technology Review* December 13 2010.

Mitchelson, Alan, "Harborview Medical Center, Campus, First Hill, Seattle, WA" *PCAD* http://pcad.lib.washington.edu/building/3642/.

Mitton, Simon, *Fred Hoyle a life in science*," Cambridge: Cambridge University Press, 2011.

Mizrachi, N., "Epistemology and legitimacy in the production of anorexia nervosa in the journal Psychosomatic Medicine 1939–1979." *Sociology of Health & Illness*, 24 (2002) 462–490.

Monroe, M. H., "Stromatolites, Australia: The Land Where Time Began," 24 March 2003, https://austhrutime.com/stromatolites.htm.

Montaigne, Michel de, *Essays of Montaigne*, translated by Charles Cotton. Adelaide, The University of Adelaide, updated Tuesday, January 27, 2015, https://ebooks.adelaide.edu.au/m/montaigne/michel/essays/index.html.

Moody, Raymond, *Life after Life*, New York: Bantam, 1976.

Moody, Raymond, *The Light Beyond*, New York: Bantam, 1988.

Morgan, David L, 'We came from your Future' in *Planet of the Apes and Philosophy*, edited by J Huss, Chicago: Open Court, 2013.

Morin CM et al, "How 'blind' are double blind placebo-controlled trials of benzodiazepine hypnotics?" *Sleep* 18(4) (May 1995) 240–245

Moreland, J.P., *Consciousness and the Existence of God: A Theistic Argument*, New York, Rutledge, 2008.

Moser, Scott, "Confirmation Bias: The Pitfall of Forensic Science," (2013) *Themis: Research Journal of Justice Studies and Forensic Science*: Vol. 1: Issue. 1, Article 7.

Moskowitz, Clara , "Right Again Einstein! New Study Supports 'Cosmological Constant'," *SPACE.COM*, Jan 16 2013 http://www.space.com/19282-einstein-cosmological-constant-dark-energy.html.

Mounce, Howard, *The Two Pragmatisms: From Peirce to Rorty*, London: Routledge, 1997.

Moyal, Ann, *Platypus: The Extraordinary Story of How a Curious Creature Baffled the World*, Sydney: Allen & Unwin, 2002.

Murphy, Todd and Michael A. Persinger, *Debate concerning the God Helmet, Behavioral Neuroscience Program*, Laurentian University, Sudbury, Ontario, Canada, 2011, http://www.innerworlds.50megs.com/The_God_Helmet_Debate.htm (accessed 1 January, 2019).

Murray, E. D., M. G. Cunningham and B. H. Price, "The role of psychotic disorders in religious history considered," *Journal of Neuropsychiatry and Clinical Neurosciences* (2012) 24 (4) 410–426.

Musgrave, Ian, "Lies, Damned Lies, Statistics, and Probability of Abiogenesis Calculations," *TalkOrigins Archive*, http://www.talkorigins.org/faqs/abioprob/abioprob.html.

Nagel, Thomas, *The Last Word*, Oxford: Oxford University Press, 1997.

National Aeronautic and Space Administration, "What is a Cosmological Constant?," *Universe 101*, http://map.gsfc.nasa.gov/universe/uni_accel.html (accessed 31 December 2018).

Nagel, Thomas, *The View from Nowhere*, *Oxford:* Oxford University Press, 1986.

Nagel, Thomas, "What is it like to be a Bat?" In *Philosophical Review* (1974) 83: 435–456.

National Institute of Neurological Disorders and Stroke (writer/s not identified), *Brain Basics: Understanding Sleep*, http://www.ninds.nih.gov/disorders/brain_basics/understanding_sleep.htm.

National Institute on Drug Abuse, "What are the immediate (short-term) effects of heroin use?," *Heroin* https://www.drugabuse.gov/publications/research-reports/heroin/what-are-immediate-short-term-effects-heroin-use (accessed January 2, 2019).

Neal, Mary C., *To Heaven and Back* Waterbrook, 2012.

Neff, Bryan D & Julian D Olden, "Is Peer Review a Game of Chance?" *Bioscience*, Vol 56 Issue 4 at 333–340.

Nelson, R.J., "Libet's dualism," *Behavioral and Brain Sciences*, Vol 8, Issue 4 (December 1985) 550- 550.

Newberg, Andrew B., "Divining the brain," *Salon*, 20 Sep 2006, interview. http://www.salon.com/2006/09/20/newberg/.

Newberg, Andrew B., Interview by Neal Conan, "Neurotheology: This Is Your Brain On Religion," December 15, 2010, Author interviews, NPR Books, December 15, 2010, http://www.npr.org/2010/12/15/132078267/neurotheology-where-religion-and-science-collide.

Newberg, Andrew B., "The neuroscientific study of spiritual practices" *Frontiers in Psychology* (2014) 5: 215.

Newberg, Andrew B., *Principles of Neurotheology*, Farnham: Ashgate, 2010.

Newberg, Andrew B., "Religion, Evolution and the Brain: What Caused What?," *Religion and the Brain: A Debate* (December 01, 2009) The Dana Foundation, http://www.dana.org/Cerebrum/Default.aspx?id=39426.

Newman, John. Henry., *An Essay in Aid of a Grammar of Assent*, London: Burns, Oates, and Co. 1870.

Noble, John, Wilford, "Novel Theory Challenges The Big Bang," *New York Times*, February 28, 1989.

Nolan, Lawrence, "Descartes' Ontological Argument," *The Stanford Encyclopedia of Philosophy*, edited by Edward N. Zalta, Summer 2011.

Nordquist, Richard, "The Value of Analogies in Writing and Speech" (August 14, 2017) *ThoughtCo*, https://www.thoughtco.com/what-is-an-analogy-1691878.

Norman, Abby, "Scientists Have an Experiment to See If the Human Mind Is Bound to the Physical World," *Futurism*, May 23, 2017

O'Connor, Timothy, "Degrees of Freedom," *Philosophical Explorations* (2009) 12 (2), 119–125.

Oppy, Graham, "Ontological Arguments." (revised 15 July 2011) *Stanford Encyclopedia of Philosophy*.

Origen, Saint, *De Principiis*, Translated by Frederick Crombie. From Ante-Nicene Fathers, Vol. 4. Edited by Alexander Roberts, James Donaldson, and A. Cleveland Coxe, Buffalo, NY: Christian Literature Publishing Co., 1885. (Book IV), paragraph 16.

Ostrowick, John M., "The Timing Experiments of Libet and Grey Walter," *South African Journal of Philosophy* 26(3) (2007) 9–26.

Overbye, Dennis, "The Collider, the Particle and a Theory About Fate," *The New York Times,* October 12, 2009.

Overbye, Dennis, "Detection of Waves in Space Buttresses Landmark Theory of Big Bang," *The New York Times,* 17 March 2014.

Oxford English Reference Dictionary, 2nd edition, 1996.

Padmanaghan, T., "Dawn of Science: 14 The Galilean World," *Resonance,* Volume 16, Issue 7 (July 2011) 663–669.

Paley, William. *Natural Theology: or, Evidences of the Existence and Attributes of the Deity,* Suzeteo, 2012.

Paley, William, and Abraham John Valpy, *Paley's moral and political philosophy,* Philadelphia: Uriah Hunt, 1835.

Palmer, B. J. (editor) "Julius Caesar," *The Oxford Library of Words and Phrases,* 2nd edition, London, *BCA*, 1990.

Parkinson, G. H. R., *An Encyclopedia of Philosophy.* Taylor & Francis, 1988.

Parnia, Sam, *What Happens When We Die?: A Groundbreaking Study into the Nature of Life and Death,* Hay House, 2007.

Parnia, Sam, and Josh Young, *Erasing Death: The Science That Is Rewriting the Boundaries Between Life and Death,* HarperCollins, 2014.

Pascal, Blaise, *Thoughts,* The Harvard Classics, Vol 48, New York: Collier, 1909.

Peebles, P. J. E., *Principles of Physical Cosmology.* Princeton: Princeton University Press, 1993.

Penrose, Roger, *Cycles of Time: An Extraordinary New View of the Universe* New York: Vintage, 2012.

Penrose, Roger. *The Road to Reality: A Complete Guide to the Laws of the Universe,* New York: Knopf, 2004.

Penzias, A.A. and R. W. Wilson, "A Measurement of Excess Antenna Temperature at 4080 Mc/s." *The Astrophysical Journal,* 142 (1) (1965) 419–421.

Persinger, M. A., and S. A. Koren, "A response to Granqvist et al. 'Sensed presence and mystical experiences are predicted by suggestibility, not by the application of transcranial weak magnetic fields,'" *Neuroscience Letters,* 2005 Jun 3;380(3)

Persinger, M. A., "The Sensed Presence Within Experimental Settings: Implications for the Male and Female Concept of Self." *The Journal of Psychology: Interdisciplinary and Applied* (2003) 137 (1): 5–16.

Peters, Ted and Martinez Hewlett, *Evolution from Creation to New Creation: Conflict, Conversation, and Convergence,* Nashville, Abingdon, 2003.

Petrement, Simone, *A Separate God: The Christian Origins of Gnosticism,* San Francisco, Harper, 1990.

Pew Research Center, *Public's Views on Human Evolution,* December 30, 2013, http://www.pewforum.org/2013/12/30/publics-views-on-human-evolution/.

Pham, Michel Tuan, "Emotion and Rationality: A Critical Review and Interpretation of Empirical Evidence" *Review of General Psychology,* Vol. 11, No. 2 (2007) 155–178.

Phillips, Ron, *An Essential Guide to Baptism in the Holy Spirit,* Lake Mary: Charisma House, 2011.

Pilkington, Ed, 'The man who was jailed for 22 years—on the fantasy evidence of a single hair', *The Guardian,* 23 June 2015

Piper, Don, *90 Minutes in Heaven: A True Story of Death and Life,* Ada: Revell, 2015.

Plantinga, Alvin, "Kant's objection to the ontological argument," *The Journal of Philosophy*, 63 (1996) 537–546.
Plantinga, Alvin, *Warranted Christian Belief*, Oxford: Oxford University Press, 2000.
Plato, *The Dialogues of Plato*. Translated by B. Jowett, Oxford: Oxford University Press, 1892.
Plato, *The Laws of Plato*, Translated by Thomas L. Pangle, New York: Basic, 1980
Plato, *The Republic*. edited by R.E. Allen, New Haven: Yale University Press, 2006.
Polanyi, Michael, "Scientific Outlook: Its sickness and cure", *Science*, vol 125 issue 3246 (March 15 1957) 480–484.
Polis, Dennis F., *God, Science and Mind*, lulu.com, 2012.
Pope Pius XII, *Humani Generis,* Vatican City, Vatican,1950.
Powell, L.H., L. Shahabi and C.E. Thoresen, "Religion and spirituality. Linkages to physical health." *The American Psychologist* (January 2003) 58 (1) 36–52.
Priscu, John C., *Origin and Evolution of Life on a Frozen Earth*, National Science Foundation (undated) https://www.nsf.gov/news/special_reports/darwin/textonly/polar_essay1.jsp.
Quach, James Q., et al "Domain structures in quantum graphity," *Physical Review* D, 86, 044001, 2012.
Radin, D., M. Schlitz and C, Baur, "Distant Healing Intention Therapies: An Overview of the Scientific Evidence," *Global Advances in Health and Medicine*. (November 2015) 4 (Suppl) 67–71.
Ramachandran, V., and S. Blakeslee, *Phantoms in the Brain*, New York: William Morrow, 1998.
Rand, Ayn, *For the New Intellectual*, Toronto, University of Toronto Press, 1967.
Ray, Christopher, *Time, space and philosophy*, London/New York: Routledge, 1991.
Rees, Martin, *Just Six Numbers*, New York: Basic, 2001, 176.
Regosin, Richard L., "Montaigne and His Readers,"*A New History of French Literature*, edited by Denis Hollier, 248–252, Cambridge, Massachusetts: Harvard University Press, 1995.
Rescher, Nicholas *Epistemology*, Albany: State University of New York, 2003.
Rey, Georges, "A Reason for Doubting the Existence of Consciousness," i *Consciousness and Self-Regulation Vol 3.*, New York: Springer, 1983, 1–39.
Reynolds, R.G., "The Principles of Advocacy" in *Selected Papers on Advocacy and the Presentation of Evidence* Canberra: Australian National University, 1980.
Ricker, Jeffry, *Psy 101—Introduction to Psychology*, Section 5-5: Encoding, Storing, & Retrieving Memories, (undated) https://sccpsy101.com/home/chapter-5/section-5/.
Ring, Kenneth and Sharon Cooper, *Mindsight: near-death and out-of-body experiences in the blind*, Bloomington: iUniverse, 2008.
Ritchie, Angus *From Morality to Metaphysics: The Theistic Implications of our Ethical Commitments*, Oxford: Oxford University Press, 2012.
Risinger, D Michael et al, "The Daubert/Kumho Implications of Observer Effects in Forensic Science: Hidden Problems of Expectation and Suggestion," *California Law Review*, Volume 90, no 1. (2002) 1–41.
Ritvo, Harriet, *The Platypus and the Mermaid: and Other Figments of the Classifying Imagination*, London: Harvard University Press, 1997.
Rizvi, Sajjad H. "Avicenna (Ibn Sina) (c. 980—1037)" in *Internet Encyclopaedia of Philosophy*, http://www.iep.utm.edu/avicenna/#H5.

Rizvi, Sajjad, "Mulla Sadra" (9 June 2009) *Stanford Encyclopedia of Philosophy.*
Rizzieri, A., *Pragmatic Encroachment, Religious Belief and Practice,* Kindle edition, Palgrave Macmillan, 2013.
Rorty, Richard, "In Defence of Eliminative Materialism" in *The Review of Metaphysics XXIV,* Philosophy Education Society, 1971.
Rosemond, Marleen, *Descartes's Dualism*, Cambridge, Massachusetts: Harvard University Press, 1998.
Rosen, Jill, "Hopkins neuroscientists pinpoint part of brain that taps into our memory banks," *Hub,* August 20, 2015, http://hub.jhu.edu/2015/08/19/brain-science-memory-hippocampus.
Rosenthal, R., *Experimenter Effects in Behavioral Research,* New York: Appleton-Century-Crofts, 1966.
Ross, Hugh, *The Creator and the Cosmos,* Colorado Springs: NavPress, 2001.
Ross, William David, *Plato's Theory of Ideas,* Oxford: Clarendon Press, 1951.
Rusbridger, "Interview with Rowan Williams," *The Guardian,* 21 March 2006.
Russell, Bertrand, *The Analysis of Matter,* London: Kegan Paul, 1927
Russell, Bertrand,"Is There a God?" In Slater, John G. *The Collected Papers of Bertrand Russell, Vol. 11: Last Philosophical Testament, 1943-68.* London: Routledge, 1997, 542–548
Russell, Bertrand, "What Is an Agnostic?" In *The Basic Writings of Bertrand Russell,* London, George Allen & Unwin, 1961.
Russell, Bertrand, *An Outline of Philosophy,* London: George Allen & Unwin, London, 1927.
Russell, Bertrand, *History of Western Philosophy* New York: Simon & Schuster, 1945.
Russell, Paul, and Anders Kraal, "Hume on Religion" (revised Mar 27, 2017) *Stanford Encyclopedia of Philosophy.*
Russell, Michael, *Origins, Abiogenesis and the Search for Life,* Cambridge, Mass.: Cosmology Science, 2011.
Sabom, Michael, *Light and Death,* Grand Rapids: Zondervan, 1998.
Sackett, D. L., "Bias in analytic research," *Journal of Chronic Diseases* 32 (1979) 51- 63.
Sagan, Carl, *Contact,* New York: Simon and Schuster, 1985.
Sagan, Carl, "God and Carl Sagan: Is the Cosmos Big Enough for Both of Them? Edward Wakin interviews Carl Sagan," *U.S. Catholic,* No. 5 (May 1981), 19–24.
Sagan, Carl, *Pale Blue Dot: A Vision of the Human Future in Space*, New York: Ballantine Books, 1994.
Saks, M. J., W.C. Thompson and R. Rosenthal, "The Daubert/Kumho Implications of Observer Effects in Forensic Science: Hidden Problems of Expectation and Suggestion," *California Law Review,* 90 (1) (2002) 1–56.
Sample, Ian, et al, "Gravitational waves discovery: 'We have a first tantalising glimpse of the cosmic birth pangs," *The Guardian,* 23 March, 2014.
Sample, Ian, "Nobel winner declares boycott of top science journals" *The Guardian,* 10 December 2013.
Sandhu' K. and H.H. Dash, "Awareness During Anaesthesia," *Indian Journal of Anaesthesia.* (April 2009) 53(2): 148–157.
Sarfati, Jonathan, *Refuting Evolution* (5th ed) Powder Springs: Creation Book Publishers, 2012.
Sarkar, Husain, *Descates' Cogito Saved from the Great Shipwreck* (2003) Cambridge : Cambridge University Press.

Sartori, Penny, *Wisdom of Near Death Experiences*, London: Watkins, 2014.
Sassen, Brigitte (2008). "Kant and Mendelssohn on the Implications of the 'I Think," in Lennon T.M., Stainton R.J. (eds) *The Achilles of Rationalist Psychology.(Studies in the History of Philosophy of Mind)* vol 7. Dordrecht: Springer, 2008.
Satel, Sally and Scott O. Lilienfeld, *Brainwashed: The Seductive Appeal of Mindless Neuroscience*, New York: Basic, 2013.
Schacter, Daniel, *Searching for memory: The brain, the mind, and the past*. New York: Basic, 1996.
Schlipp, Paul Arthur, *Albert Einstein: Philosopher-Scientist*, 3rd edition, Chicago: Open Court, 1970.
Schlitz, Marilyn, et al, "Distant Healing Of Surgical Wounds: An Exploratory Study," *Explore* (July 2012) 8(4): 223–230.
Schrödinger, Erwin, *What is Life?* Cambridge: Cambridge University Press, 2012.
Seeskin, Kenneth, *Maimonides*, Stanford Encyclopedia of Philosophy (first pub2006; substantive 2013) https://plato.stanford.edu/entries/maimonides/.
Sewell, Marilyn, "Was Christopher Hitchens Religious?," *Huffington Post*, February 21, 2015.
Shanks, Niall, and Karl H. Joplin, "Redundant Complexity: A Critical Analysis of Intelligent Design in Biochemistry," *Philosophy of Science*, 66, no. 2 (Jun., 1999): 268-282.
Shapiro, Robert, *Origins: A Skeptic's Guide to the Creation of Life on Earth* Toronto: New York, 1987 at 110.
Sheldrake, Rupert, *The Sense of Being Stared at and other aspects of the Extended Mind*, London: Hutchinson, 2003.
Shikhovtsev, Eugene, *Biographical Sketch of Hugh Everett, III* (2003) https://space.mit.edu/home/tegmark/everett/everett.html.
Shimojo, Shinsuke, "Postdiction: its implications on visual awareness, hindsight, and sense of agency," *Frontiers in Psychology*, March 31 2014.
Silk, Joseph,*The Big Bang*, New York: Freeman/Owl, 2001.
Silk, Joseph, *Horizons of Cosmology*, Templeton, 2009.
Singer, Peter, "Afterword," in *A Companion to Ethics*, edited by Peter Singer, Oxford: Basil Balckwell, 1991.
Singh, Simon, *Big Bang: The Origin of the Universe*, Harper Perennial, 2005.
Skeptics Dictionary, edited by Robert T Carroll, http://skepdic.com/skepticism.html
Skrbina, David, *Panpsychism in the West*, Cambridge Mass.: MIT, 2007.
Smit, Rudolf H., "Corroboration of the Dentures Anecdote Involving Veridical Perception in a Near-Death Experience," *Journal of Near-Death Studies*, 27(1) (Fall 2008).
Smit, Rudolf H. and Titus Rivas, "Rejoinder to 'Response to 'Corroboration of the Dentures Anecdote Involving Veridical Perception in a Near-Death Experience'," *Journal of Near-Death Studies*, 28, January (2010).
Smith, C.L., "The large hadron collider: The edge of physics," *Scientific American*, (May, 2003) Special Edition.
Smith, Kerri, "Neuroscience vs philosophy: Taking aim at free will," *Nature* 477 (31 August 2011) 23–25.
Smith, John Maynard, *The Problems of Biology*, Oxford, Oxford University Press, 1986, 49.

Smith, Richard, "Peer review: a flawed process at the heart of science and journals," *Journal of the Royal Society of Medicine* 99(4) (April 2006) 178–182.
Smolin, Lee, *The Trouble with Physics: The Rise of String Theory, The Fall of a Science, and What Comes Next*, Boston: Houghton Mifflin, 2006.
Solomon, Robert, *A Passion for Justice* (1990) Reading Mass: Addison-Wesley, 1990.
Solovyova, Julia, *"Mustering Most Memorable Quips,"* The Moscow Times, 28 October 1997.
Soon, Chun Siong, et al, "Unconscious determinants of free decisions in the human brain," *Nature Neuroscience*, Vol 11, No 5 (May 2008) 543–5.
Spear, Wayne R., *Talking to God: The theology of prayer*, Pittsburgh: Crown & Covenant, 2002.
Spinoza, Benedict, *Ethics*, Translated by E. Curley, New York: Penguin, 2005.
Stanciu, Marius M., "The Explanatory Gap: 30 Years after," Procedia—Social and Behavioral Sciences, Volume 127 (22 April 2014) 292–296.
Stanford Encyclopedia of Philosophy, "Atheism and Agnosticism," 2004
Stanger, Melissa, "Attractive People Are Simply More Successful," *Business Insider*, October 10, 2012, https://www.businessinsider.com.au/attractive-people-are-more-successful-2012-9?r=US&IR=T.
Statt, Nick, "Scientists create 'alien' life form with artificial genetic code," *C/net*, 8 May 2014, http://www.cnet.com/au/news/scientists-create-alien-life-form-with-artificial-genetic-code/.
Steinhardt, Paul, "Big Bang blunder bursts the multiverse bubble," *Nature*, vol 510, issue 7503, 5 June 2014.
Steinhardt, Paul J. and Neil Turok, *Endless Universe: Beyond the Big Bang*, New York: Doubleday, 2007.
Steinhardt, Paul J., "Inflation Debate: Is the theory at the heart of modern cosmology deeply flawed?" *Scientific American*. 304 (4) (April 2011) 36–43.
Stoeger, W.R., G. F. R. Ellis & U. Kirchner (2006) "Multiverses and Cosmology: Philosophical Issues" *CiteSeer*, (2006) http://citeseerx.ist.psu.edu/viewdoc/summary?doi=10.1.1.255.2258.
Stoljar, Daniel, "Physicalism and phenomenal concepts." *Mind and Language* (2005) 20, 5, 469–494.
Stone, Jon R. *The Routledge Dictionary of Latin Quotations*, New York, Routledge, 2005.
Stone, Maddie, "There Is Growing Evidence that Our Universe Is a Giant Hologram," *Motherboard*, May 5 2015, https://motherboard.vice.com/en_us/article/jp59b8/there-is-growing-evidence-that-our-universe-is-a-giant-hologram.
Strassler, Matt, "Big Bang: Expansion, Not Explosion," *Of Particular Significance*, http://profmattstrassler.com/articles-and-posts/relativity-space-astronomy-and-cosmology/history-of-the-universe/big-bang-expansion-not-explosion/.
Strassler, Matt, "Which Parts of the Big Bang Theory are Reliable, and Why?," *Of Particular Significance*, March 26, 2014, http://profmattstrassler.com/2014/03/26/which-parts-of-the-big-bang-theory-are-reliable/.
Strawson, P. F., *Individuals: An Essay in Descriptive Metaphysics*, London: Methuen, 1959.
Strawson, Galen, *Real Materialism and Other Essays* Oxford: Oxford University Press, 2008.
Stroglatz, Steven V., *Sync: How Order Emerges from Chaos in the Universe* New York: THEIA, 2003.

Stubenberg, Leopold, Review of *Consciousness and Its Place in Nature: Does Physicalism Entail Panpsychism?* by Galen Strawson, Notre Dame Philosophical Reviews, May 4, 2007, https://ndpr.nd.edu/news/consciousness-and-its-place-in-nature-does-physicalism-entail-panpsychism/.

Suzuki, Fumitaka , "The Cogito Proposition of Descartes and Characteristics of His Ego Theory," in *Bulletin of Aichi University of Education*, 61(Humanities and Social Sciences) 73—80, March, 2012.

Swinburne, Richard., *The Existence of God,* 2nd edition, Oxford: Oxford University Press 2004.

Swinburne, Richard, *Faith and Reason*, 2nd edition, Oxford: Oxford University Press, 2005.

Swinburne, Richard, *Is there a God?* Oxford: Oxford University Press, 1996.

Swinburne, Richard, "Response to a Statistical Study of the Effect of Petitionary Prayer," *Science and Theology News* (2006).

Tait, David, "Juries can be influenced by where defendants sit in a courtroom, Australian study finds" ABC News 7 November 2014.

Tait, David, "Deliberating about terrorism: Prejudice and jury verdicts in a modern terrorist trial," *ANZ Journal of Criminology*, December 2011, Vol 44, No 3, 387–403.

Taylor, John, *Super Minds*, London: Picador, 1976.

Taylor, Rosie, 'Is our universe merely one of billions? Evidence for the existence of 'multiverse' revealed for the first time by cosmic map, *Daily Mail*, 19 May 2013.

Taylor, Steve, "The Puzzle of Near-Death Experiences" (October 15, 2014) *Psychology Today*, October 15, 2014.

Tegmark, Max, "Critique," *The Universes of Max Tegmark*: http://space.mit.edu/home/tegmark/mathematical.html (accessed 5 January, 2019).

Tegmark, Max, *Our Mathematical Universe: My Quest for the Ultimate Nature of Reality*, New York: Knopf, 2014.

Tegmark, Max, *The Mathematical Universe*, 2007, http://arxiv.org/pdf/0704.0646.pdf.

Tegmark, Max, "Parallel Universes," *Scientific American*, May 2003, 41–51.

Tegmark, Max, "The Universes of Max Tegmark," *space.mit.edu*, https://space.mit.edu/home/tegmark/crazy.html (accessed December 29, 2018).

Teilhard de Chardin, *The Phenomenon of Man*, London, Collins, 1940.

Tenney E.R. et al, "Calibration trumps confidence as a basis for witness credibility," *Psycholical Science*.18(1):46–50, February 2007.

Than, Ker, "Why Great Minds Can't Grasp Consciousness," *Live Science*, August 08, 2005, http://www.livescience.com/366-great-minds-grasp-consciousness.html?li_source=LI&li_medium=most-popular.

Thompson, S.P., *Life of William Thomson: Baron Kelvin of Largs*. London: Macmillan. vol 2, 1910.

Tooby, John, Leda Cosmides and H. Clark Barrett, "Resolving the Debate on Innate Ideas" in Peter Carruthers, Stephen Laurence & Stephen Stich, *The Innate Mind: Structure and Contents*. New York: Oxford University Press, (2005) 305-337.

Tiggs, Thomas J. and Walter G. Harris, *Reaction time of drivers to road stimuli*, Monash University, June 1982.

Tsakiris, Alex, *Dr. Jeffrey Long's Near-Death Experience Research a "Game Changer" for Science* (Feb 3 2010) http://www.skeptiko.com/94-jeffrey-long-near-death-experience-research/.

Tsakiris, Alex, *Near-Death Experience Skeptic, Dr. G.M. Woerlee Alex Tsakiris , Takes Aim at Dr. Jeffrey Long's, Evidence of the Afterlife*, http://www.skeptiko.com/near-death-experience-skeptic-gm-woerlee/ (accessed January2, 2019).

Tsakiris, Alex, *Near-Death Experience Skeptics Running Out of Excuses*, April 16, 2010, http://www.skeptiko.com/near-death-experience-skeptics-running-out-of-excuses/.

Tsakiris, Alex, "Sam Harris and Steve Novella offer half-witted attack of Eben Alexander's Near-Death Experience," *Skeptiko* (October 16, 2012) http://www.skeptiko.com/sam-harris-wont-debate-eben-alexander-on-near-death-experience-science/.

United States District Court for the Middle District of Pennsylvania, *Kitzmiller,, et al. v. Dover Area School District, et al.* (2005) 400 F. Supp. 2d 707, Docket No. 4cv2688.

University of Oxford (writer not identified) "Humans 'predisposed' to believe in gods and the afterlife." *ScienceDaily. ScienceDaily*, 14 July 2011. <www.sciencedaily.com/releases/2011/07/110714103828.htm>.

Ussher, J., *The Annals of the World*, Green Forest, Master Books, 2007 (originally published 1658), 17.

Vaidman, Lev, "Many-Worlds Interpretation of Quantum Mechanics," *Stanford Encyclopedia of Philosophy*, revised Jan 17, 2014.

van Lommel, Pim, *Consciousness Beyond Life: The Science of the Near-Death Experiences*, HarperOne, 2010.

van Lommel, Pim et al. "Near-death experiences in survivors of cardiac arrest: A prospective study in the Netherlands," *Lancet*, 358 (2001) 2039–2045.

van Lommel, Pim, "Pathophysiological Aspects of Near-Death Experiences," in *Making Sense of Near Death Experiences*, ed by M. Perere, K. Jagadheesan and A. Peake, Philadelphia: Jessica Kingsley Publishers, 2011, chapter 6.

Veber, M., "Why Even a Believer Should Not Believe That God Answers Prayers," *Sophia* (2007) 46: 177.

Victorinus, Saint, *On the Creation of the World*, Translated by Robert Ernest Wallis, Ante-Nicene Fathers, Vol. 7. Edited by Alexander Roberts, James Donaldson, and A. Cleveland Coxe., Buffalo, NY: Christian Literature Publishing Co., 1886.

Video, *The Near Death Experience of Pam Reynolds*, 31 Jan 2010, http://www.metacafe.com/watch/4045560/the_near_death_experience_of_pam_reynolds_video/ (accessed 2 January 2019).

Vilenkin, Alexander & Max Tegmark. 'The Case for Parallel Universes. Why the multiverse, crazy as it sounds, is a solid scientific idea," *Scientific American*, July 19 2011.

Villata, Massimo, "The matter-antimatter interpretation of Kerr spacetime," *Physick*, Vol 527, Issue 7–8 (August 2015) 507–512

Vorster, James M., "Perspectives on the Core Characteristics of Religious Fundamentalism Today," *Journal for the Study of Religions and Ideologies*, Vol 7 No 21 (2008) 44–65.

Wall, Robert, *New Interpreter's Bible* Vol. X, London: Abingdon Press 2002.

Ward, Keith, *The Evidence for God*, London: Darton, Longer and Todd, 2014.

Ward, Keith, *God, Chance and Necessity* Oxford: Oxford University Press, 1996.

Waters, Larry J (ed.) *When Suffering Is Redemptive: Stories of How Anguish and Pain Accomplish God's Mission*, Weaver, 2016.

Waugh, Evelyn, *Brideshead Revisited*, London: Penguin, 2011 (first pub 1945).

Webb, Mark, "Religious Experience," *The Stanford Encyclopedia of Philosophy* (revised Dec 13, 2017).

Webb, R.K., "The emergence of Rational Dissent" in *Enlightenment and Religion: Rational Dissent in eighteenth-century Britain* (1996) edited by Knud Haakonssen. Cambridge, Cambridge University Press, 1996.

Webster's Comprehension Dictionary, encyclopedic edition, 1986.

Wegner, Daniel, *The Illusion of Conscious Will*, Cambridge, Mass.: MIT, 2002.

Weinberg, Steven, "The Search for Unity—Notes for a History of Quantum Field Theory," Daedalus, Vol. 106, No. 4, Discoveries and Interpretations: Studies in Contemporary Scholarship, Volume II (Fall, 1977) 17–35.

Weinberg, Steven,*The Quantum Theory of Fields, Vol. I, Foundations* Cambridge: Cambridge University Press, 1995

Weinberg, Steven, *The Quantum Theory of Fields, Vol. 2, Modern Applications*, (1996) Cambridge: Cambridge University Press, 1996.

Weintraub, Pamela, "The Dr. Who Drank Infectious Broth, Gave Himself an Ulcer, and Solved a Medical Mystery," *Discover Magazine*, March 2010, http://discovermagazine.com/2010/mar/07-dr-drank-broth-gave-ulcer-solved-medical-mystery#.UyOv9ygoboc.

Weisberg, Josh, "The Hard Problem of Consciousness," *Internet Encyclopedia of Philosophy*, http://www.iep.utm.edu/hard-con/.

Wertheim, Margaret, "Physics Pangolin," aeon.co, http://aeon.co/magazine/science/margaret-wertheim-the-limits-of-physics/.

Wesley, Charles, *And can it be that I should gain?*, 1738, https://www.hymnal.net/en/hymn/h/296.

Westminster Abbey (writer/s not identified), "Charles Darwin," *Westminster Abbey website.* http://www.westminster-abbey.org/our-history/people/charles-darwin.

White, Chelsea, "Google with your mind," *New Scientist*, 7 April 2018 at 6–7.

Whyte, G., "Groupthink Reconsidered," *The Academy of Management Review*, 14 (1) (1989) 40–56.

Williams, Kevin, *An Analysis of the Near-Death Experiences of Atheists* (2014) http://www.near-death.com/religion/atheism/an-analysis-of-the-ndes-of-atheists.html.

Williams, Kevin, *Common Elements are Found in Near-Death Experiences*, http://www.near-death.com/science/evidence/common-elements-are-found-in-ndes.html.

Wiseman, Richard, "The Haunted Brain," *Skeptical Inquirer*, Volume 35.5, (September/October, 2011).

Withnall, Adam, "North Korean defector says she believed Kim Jong-il was a god who could read her mind," *Independent* 11 April, 2014.

Woerlee, G.M., "Cardiac arrest and near-death experiences" *Journal of Near Death Studies*, 22, (2004) 235–249.

Woerlee, G.M., "Pam Reynolds Near Death Experience," *Near Death Experiences. Is there a life after death?* (2008 updated 2014) http://neardth.com/pam-reynolds-near-death-experience.php.

Woerlee, G.M., "Response to "Corroboration of the Dentures Anecdote Involving Veridical Perception in a Near-Death Experience" (Summer 2010) *UNT Digital Library*, http://digital.library.unt.edu/ark:/67531/metadc461689/ (accessed January 1, 2019).

Woerlee, G.M., *Review of "Evidence of the Afterlife,"* http://neardth.com/evidence-of-the-afterlife.php (accessed January 2, 2019).

Woerlee, G.M., "Test of the Possibility that Pam Reynolds Heard Normally During Her NDE," *Near Death Experiences. Is there a life after death?* http://neardth.com/failed-hearing-test.php.

Woit, Peter, *Not Even Wrong: The Failure of String Theory and the Search for Unity in Physical Law,* New York: Basic, 2006.

Wolchover, Natalie, "Experiment Reaffirms Quantum Weirdness," *Quanta Magazine*, February 7, 2017.

Wolchover Natalie and Peter Byrne, "In a Multiverse, What Are the Odds?," *Quanta Magazine*, November 3, 2014.

Wolf, David, "World Thinkers 2013," *Prospect*, April 24, 2013.

Wolf, Gary, in "The Church of the Non-believers, *WIRED*, Issue 14.11, November 2006.

Wolterstorff, Nicholas, "In Defense of Gaunilo's Defense of the Fool," in C. Stephen Evans and Merold Westphal (eds.), *Christian Perspectives on Religious Knowledge,* Grand Rapids: Eerdmans, 1993.

Woodruff, Bob, Roxanna Sherwood & Eric Johnson, "Ask the Experts: What Is a Near-Death Experience?" *ABC News,* Aug 3, 2011, http://abcnews.go.com/Nightline/beyondbelief/experts-death-experience/story?id=14221154.

Wright, J. P., "The Treatise: Reception, Composition, and Response," in Saul Traiger, *The Blackwell Guide to Hume's Treatise*, New YorK: John Wiley, 2008.

Wright, Robert, *The Moral Animal—Why We Are the Way We Are: The New Science of Evolutionary Psychology,* New York: Vintage Books, 1994.

Yancey, Phillip, *Where Is God When It Hurts?* Grand Rapids, Michigan: Zondervan, 1990.

Yule, G. Udny, "On Reading a Scale," *Journal of the Royal Statistical Society*, Vol. 90, No. 3 (1927), 570–587.

Yun, Koo Dong. *Baptism in the Holy Spirit: An Ecumenical Theology of Spirit Baptism,* Lanham, University Press of America, 2003.

Zeyl, Donald and Barbara Sattler, "Plato's Timaeus," *Stanford Encyclopedia of Philosophy*, revision Mon Dec 18, 2017.

Zlatev I., Wang L., and, Steinhardt P.J., "Quintessence, Cosmic Coincidence, and the Cosmological Constant" *Physical Review Letters* (1999) 82, 896.

Zyga, Lisa, "No Big Bang? Quantum equation predicts universe has no beginning," February 9, 2015, https://phys.org/news/2015-02-big-quantum-equation-universe.html.

Zyga, Lisa, "Repulsive gravity as an alternative to dark energy', Part 1: In voids.," January 31, 2012, https://phys.org/news/2012-01-repulsive-gravity-alternative-dark-energy.html.

Zyga, Lisa, "Repulsive gravity as an alternative to dark energy" (Part 2: In the quantum vacuum) February 1, 2012, https://phys.org/news/2012-01-repulsive-gravity-alternative-dark-energy_1.html.

www.ingramcontent.com/pod-product-compliance
Lightning Source LLC
Chambersburg PA
CBHW070249230426
43664CB00014B/2467